ORGANISATIONAL BEHAVIOUR AND ORGANISATIONAL STUDIES IN HEALTH CARE

Also by Lynn Ashburner

THE NEW PUBLIC MANAGEMENT IN ACTION
(*with Ewan Ferlie, Louise FitzGerald and Andrew Pettigrew*)

Organisational Behaviour and Organisational Studies in Health Care

Reflections on the Future

Edited by
Lynn Ashburner

palgrave

Selection, editorial matter and Chapters 15 and 16
© Lynn Ashburner 2001

Individual chapters (in order) © John Øvretveit; Ewan Ferlie, John Gabbay, Louise FitzGerald, Louise Locock and Sue Dopson; Charlotte Dargie and Sandra Dawson; Jill Schofield; Steve Cropper; Annette King, Naomi Fulop, Nigel Edwards and Andrew Street; Ian Brooks and Sandy MacDonald; Diane Berrow and Charlotte Humphrey; Rod Sheaff; Marie L. Thorne; Annabelle Mark; Stephen Timmons; Lynda Jessopp and Sean Boyle; Mansour Jumaa and Jo Alleyne 2001

Published 2001 by
PALGRAVE
Houndmills, Basingstoke, Hampshire RG21 6XS and
175 Fifth Avenue, New York, N.Y. 10010
Companies and representatives throughout the world

PALGRAVE is the new global academic imprint of
St. Martin's Press LLC Scholarly and Reference Division and
Palgrave Publishers Ltd (formerly Macmillan Press Ltd).

ISBN 0–333–94770–3

This book is printed on paper suitable for recycling and made from fully managed and sustained forest sources.

A catalogue record for this book is available from the British Library.

Printed and bound in Great Britain by Antony Rowe Ltd, Chippenham, Wiltshire

Contents

List of Tables, Figures and Boxes

Boxes

Acknowledgements

Thanks are due to the following people who served on the conference advisory panel and were involved in the refereeing process for the contributions now appearing in this book: Sue Dopson (Templeton College, Oxford), Ewan Ferlie (Imperial), Louise FitzGerald (De Montfort University), Annabelle Mark (Middlesex University), Rosemary Stewart (Templeton College, Oxford), David Simms (Brunel University) and Tony White (Bournemouth University). I wish to give special thanks to Katherine Birch, who shouldered the main burden of the conference arrangements, with Steve Cropper, and to Annabelle Mark, whose idea it was to create this conference forum, to nurture debate and development amongst those working in the area of organisational behaviour in health care.

LYNN ASHBURNER

List of Contributors

Jo Alleyne, Health Care and Nursing Management, Middlesex University.

Lynn Ashburner, Consultant in Health Care Management for the World Bank.

Diane Berrow, University College London.

Sean Boyle, Department of Health and Social Care, London School of Economics.

Ian Brooks, University College, Northampton.

Steve Cropper, Centre for Health Planning and Management, Keele University.

Charlotte Dargie, The Judge Institute, Cambridge University.

Sandra Dawson, The Judge Institute, Cambridge University.

Sue Dopson, Templeton College, Oxford University.

Nigel Edwards, NHS Confederation.

Ewan Ferlie, Imperial College Management School.

Louise FitzGerald, De Montfort University.

Naomi Fulop, London School of Hygiene and Tropical Medicine.

John Gabbay, Wessex Institute for Health R&D, Southampton University.

Charlotte Humphrey, University College London.

Lynda Jessopp, Guy's, King's and St Thomas's School of Medicine.

Mansour Jumaa, Health Care and Nursing Management, Middlesex University.

Annette King, London School of Hygiene and Tropical Medicine.

Louise Locock, Templeton College, Oxford University.

Sandy MacDonald, University College, Northampton.

Annabelle Mark, Middlesex University.

John Øvretveit, Bergen University Medical School and the Nordic School of Public Health.

Jill Schofield, Public Services Management Group, Aston University.

Rod Sheaff, National Primary Care Research and Development Centre, Manchester University.

Andrew Street, University of York.

Marie L. Thorne, Bristol Business School, University of the West of England.

Stephen Timmons, Nottingham University.

Introduction
Lynn Ashburner

In looking at what is new in research within the British health sector, this book offers readers an appreciation of the richness and breadth of current research. The contributors are leading academics in the field of organisational behaviour (OB) and organisation studies in health, and the papers were originally presented at the Organisational Behaviour in Health Conference at Keele University in January 2000. The book takes as its theme, what it means to be doing research in this area at this time focusing on new developments within the health sector. Taking the theme of the conference, 'Reflections on the Future', the book explores what it means to be working at different boundaries and this has been interpreted in three ways:

- 'New' ways of seeing/conceptual issues
- 'New' ways of working
- 'New' approaches to understanding/methodology

In many respects the developments are only 'new' in the sense that the different forms of organising that are emerging and the concepts and methodological approaches discussed are relatively new to this particular area. For example, the ongoing debate around 'new' paradigm research is more established within other disciplines and areas, such as psychology and education, whereas in organisation and management studies the current debates are focused more on the area of 'critical' studies.

Management studies and OB have as both their strength and their weakness that they are not a recognised academic 'discipline'. Both are typified by their multidisciplinarity and transdisciplinarity. The 'weakness' of OB, as espoused by Stewart in her preface to this book's predecessor (Mark and Dopson 1999), is that there is no easily defined body of knowledge being accumulated that gives OB the type of 'scholarliness' as defined under a positivist paradigm. This presupposes that this is the only type of knowledge available to academics and practitioners, whereas there are many forms of knowledge. There are also different bases for the accumulation of knowledge, and a full critique of the issues involved can be found in Chapter 15.

The argument presented here is that OB's strength is that it was born of multidisciplinarity and could thrive on transdisciplinarity. I believe the future lies in becoming more varied, responsive and relevant, with the growth of transdisciplinarity. The limitations of traditional research are well-rehearsed and, in several other disciplines, facing up to these limitations has resulted in attempts at questioning the dominant paradigm, as noted above. This does not involve the rejection of the concept of scholarliness but the need to redefine what it might mean, and to question the positivists claim to exclusiveness.

At the close of the first volume, from the earlier conference, Mark and Dopson (1999) identified three main issues in relation to health-sector studies. First, exactly how we can build on the theoretical and empirical knowledge that already exists, and the need for more studies to include a rigorous discussion of the methodologies and research designs used. Second, to understand better the nature of research, and how research can be relevant for both academic and practitioner audiences. And third was the need to recognise the increasing complexity of the issues we seek to study and of the organisations within which we work. It is the applied, as well as the theoretical, nature of much of the research carried on within the health sector that puts the emphasis on to the real-life context. The second point raised is one that we neglect to our cost, which is that we need to make research 'relevant to the practitioner audience'. However, I would add to this '...and co-researchers' as a culture of research is increasingly becoming established within the service. The word 'audience' still suggests a passivity of those being researched and the gulf between the academic with the 'expert' knowledge and the practitioner with their 'practical' or 'situated' knowledge. Research needs to be relevant to what practitioners actually do, and for this there is a need for situation-specific, or socially contextualised, knowledge, which includes both. This, by definition, will differ from the pre-existing knowledge that is normally brought to the identification of the problem, the research design and methodologies used.

In exploring the themes of this book, the aim is to make links between the present and the possible futures for organisational behaviour and organisation studies. It outlines the contribution of each chapter to the themes and encourages the reader to consider the role of methodology as it is explored within each chapter. Evaluation of any research process is only possible with the context of the research design and methodology made explicit. Research is too frequently written up with little or no information given as to how the data was gathered. This is no longer acceptable with the growing sophistication of research funders and users who wish to have a basis on which to evaluate research. A wide range of methodologies are used by the authors of the chapters and this will give the reader an opportunity to assess the strengths and limitations of different approaches in relation to the appropriateness of each for its purpose.

The first chapter, by Øvretveit, was presented as the Keynote Address. It presents an excellent overview of the role of OB in health studies and provides a reflective context for the other chapters. Øvretveit considers what new areas OB should be looking at for the future, some of which are also addressed in later chapters of the book. It usefully links the themes, and links the past with present and future. He stresses the increasing demand and need for relevant research for informing and educating health-service managers and others. OB in health is described as a discipline that has been largely defined by the needs of managers and it is necessary to safeguard against its future development being driven by the move towards evidence-based medicine. He also believes that there needs to be room for the development of 'subjectivist' methodologies, and he suggests how OB can contribute towards practical action and knowledge through a systematic study of how people and organisations behave. He considers the challenges facing OB and the potential for the future, and concludes that to make a greater contribution researchers need to be clear who are the users of the research, provide clear descriptions of methods, relate the research to previous research, ensure that the research is accessible and to work with users to explicate the practical implications of the research.

'NEW' WAYS OF SEEING

'New' ways of seeing the health sector are evident in the use of Futures thinking by Dargie and Dawson. Another new perspective, 'emotional health', is highlighted by Øvretveit and explored in depth by Mark, while the chapter by Timmons shows how even science-based technology is socially constructed. Each of these contributions is intended to challenge existing thinking and to offer new perspectives on the health service. Other chapters focus on organisational or theoretical issues in the context of new perspectives in health care, such as that of evidence-based medicine (Ferlie *et al.*) and clinical governance (Thorne).

Dargie and Dawson take the theme of 'the future' literally. This chapter draws on a research project established to explore future trends and issues in health and health care in the UK forward to 2015, and it describes the objectives, methodology and early results of the study. It reflects a wider concern amongst international bodies such as the World Health Organisation and the Organisation for Economic Cooperation and Development that futures thinking and the analysis of trends can aid policy development and changing practice in health. The overwhelming contribution that a forward look can make is to challenge existing assumptions about the way that health and health care services are organised, planned and delivered. The chapter focuses on one aspect of the project, that of the health workforce, by describing future trends and the policy implications that may derive from them. Future trends identified are: the changing context of recruitment and retention of professional staff; the increasing importance of information and communication technology on NHS work; the changing patterns of skills and the skill mix across the professional boundaries in health care; and societal developments highlighting the interface between staff and patients, users and the public. Many of these themes are taken up by other contributors to this book.

An exploration and mapping of the role of emotion in health care organisation is the focus of the chapter by Mark. The chapter sets out some parameters by which the consideration of emotion should inform the future, in order to establish and maintain the emotional health of the organisation and its workforce and ensure that it can continue to deliver services to the community to meet their needs. It identifies the reasons why this issue is emerging at this time, what current evidence there is for its importance, what definitions are available which can determine the approach and finally to consider what that approach might be. Mark emphasises that the focus on individuals must not obscure the use that the organisation makes of emotion to maintain control of both its providers and increasingly its users.

In areas as diverse as emotion and IT the focus is at the organisational level. Timmons illustrates the need to understand IT developments in the context of professional culture and not as a technological or 'scientific' answer to information and management issues. The implementation of IT systems in health care has not always proved to be straightforward, with large sums of taxpayers money being wasted on systems that do not work and in some cases were never fully implemented. One contributing factor, especially in the field of health services, has been the social environment into which these systems are implemented; sociocultural factors are important determinants of success or failure. The chapter takes a sociological approach to the study of the use of computerised systems for the production of detailed plans for the care of hospital in-patients by nurses in three UK hospitals. It notes the range of indirect means found to resist the new systems, and the failure of sanctions to ensure their use. The systems under study embodied certain ideas about how nursing should be done which, if not shared by the people who use the systems, are resisted.

'NEW' WAYS OF WORKING

The White Paper, *The New NHS Modern and Dependable* (1997), and, more recently, *The NHS Plan* (2000), plus a range of other policy changes have greatly influenced the way the NHS is organised. Overall there has been a very strong push towards a new focus on collaboration and service integration, as well as new ways of involving patients and interacting with them, with the use of IT. As a consequence, there have been considerable changes in the way primary care, in particular, is organised and the relationship of doctors to the NHS. This has been in the context of addressing issues of their accountability, in relation to clinical governance and managerially, with regard to the role of GPs. Some government policies require short-term changes such as the need for more doctors and nurses, but most involve a process of longer-term change working towards what has been spun as the 'modernising' of the NHS. After the competition of the 1990s with its fragmentation of work processes and organisations, there are now new opportunities to rethink how services should be delivered. Some of the key developments are explored here.

In his exploration of how hierarchies and networks are usually contrasted as alternative governance structures, Sheaff suggests that the differences between them should not be exaggerated. All organisations have some attributes of networks, just as all networks have hierarchies 'embedded' in them. Networks can also be a transitional form of organisation and can eventually consolidate into a more traditional organisational form. One such transition can be seen in the formation of primary care groups (PCGs). This raises the question of what conditions promote or retard the transitions between loose networks, more tightly coordinated closed networks and organisation. This analysis generates predictions about which types of PCGs are likely to find the transition easiest, and therefore complete it sooner.

Certain factors which promote organisational formation are beyond policy-makers' reach, for example existing networks' past successes and failures at collaboration; what local network constituents already exist; and, in the short term, what processes of production they use. The chapter concludes by considering the ways that the formation of tighter networks can be promoted.

Central to the new NHS 'partnership' working is collaboration. Cropper examines how collaborative working is regarded as a means of achieving ends which would not so readily be achieved by organisations acting alone or in competition. The chapter views the construction of a multi-organisational venture as one of establishing value in a contested field. There is a general lack of clarity about when partnership, as a mode of organising, becomes or should be established and what makes it work. The chapter considers these issues in relation to the future organisation of acute health services. It reviews the development of institutional theory through to the current preoccupation with the explanation of variety and change in organisational fields, through the idea of institutional entrepreneurs. It then focuses on the institutional pressures shaping the organisation of acute care services, with the specific case looking at the development of collaborative working between providers of paediatric services. The chapter concludes by sketching a development trajectory in which particular elements of organisation form the primary basis and focus for development and legitimation of the collaborative venture.

A further perspective on the issues raised by increased collaboration is presented by King *et al.* They consider the issue of integration of, and cooperation between, services which have become increasingly important for service planning and delivery in health care. As the competitive culture has given way to a more cooperative culture, different agencies and stakeholders in health and social care are being called upon to work in closer proximity and partnership. The development of primary care groups and Trusts will affect health care delivery across primary, acute and community provision. The chapter examines integration and cooperation in service delivery in child health services, using the results of an empirical study of combined and separate acute and community NHS Trusts. It focuses on the organisational conditions and contexts for delivering integrated acute and community child health services, drawing on theories of integration and cooperation. The argument developed is that informal forms of cooperation and collaboration are important determinants of providing integrated services and therefore need to be considered in future partnership working alongside the more formal.

Similar to the concept of a loose network is that of the 'virtual system' of collaboration that is required as the provision of health care increasingly requires integrated contributions from a range of different established organisations. The difference is that these are not transitional organisational forms but ongoing processes of collaboration which require a defined level of integration. Jessopp and Boyle consider specifically how different services are integrated. The provision of effective health care requires contributions from different parts of an overall care system, each operating within its own organisational framework. These are described as a 'virtual care system' involving contributions from different organisations. Rarely is any one organisation focused on a single element of care and there tends to be no-one in control of the whole system as opposed to its parts. They show how the current emphasis on integrated and multidisciplinary collaboration within health care provision has served to highlight the importance of a better understanding of whole- systems issues.

One important part of any 'whole system' in health care is the patient, user or carer. Berrow and Humphrey look at the inclusion of user representatives in committees and groups as one of several forms of user involvement in the health service. Those committees that currently include user representatives come from a variety of sectors within health. For example, research ethics committees, general practice patient groups, research advisory groups and primary care groups. This is in contrast to other parts of the health sector where user input is separate from the forum where decisions are made. The chapter examines the issues and problems which have emerged from the involvement of users in decision-making fora. Issues are raised about the 'representative' nature of the lay people involved and the concern of some professionals about lay members identifying different priorities to themselves. Faith in the process of user involvement might ignore the very real challenges that face those involved in the process.

The chapter by Thorne looks at the responses to the introduction of clinical governance to explore the changing nature of power relationships between the three main groups involved – government, doctors and managers – in the NHS. It focuses on the public discourse generated by the three key groups crucial to its enhancement: the regulators (the government); the implementers (managers); and the regulated (doctors). The first section introduces discourse analysis, and statements from public documents are then presented from government, doctors and management to interpret their discourse of clinical governance; the final section draws these views together to make sense of their meanings and their relationships using the concept of monological and dialogical discourse. Some interesting and perhaps unexpected insights emerge when the three strands of discourse are synthesised and analysed. Each are contested, as the three groups use their positions of power to impose their meaning through implementation.

Continuing a theme of professional power, Brooks and McDonald consider the most recent examples of the use of overseas doctors and nurses. There has been a long tradition of immigration as a source of staffing in the NHS, and both doctors and nursing staff have been targeted. Since the UK joined the EU, migration flows have changed and a mutual recognition of qualifications has provided a framework for the movement of health care professionals between EU member states. However, little research has been carried out on the ways in which the organisation impacts upon these workers, and the differences in experiences between doctors and nurses. The relationship and power differentials across professional boundaries and with other groups in the NHS is not static, and this chapter reports on an empirical study which explores the impact of the presence of immigrant health care workers. It explores issues such as language, contracts, terms and conditions and socialisation. Also explored are the reasons for these workers coming to the UK which has implications both for the staff and for human-resource management.

Influencing all parts of the health sector is the ever-changing role of IT. Schofield examines the late twentieth-century concept of the 'virtual organisation', which has, on the whole, been defined in relation to the use of advanced information technology. The research presented looks at virtuality within health care organisations, which is a consequence of the distance between the 'accountable' body, the clinical professional and the patient. While physical distance between the first two is not new; that between the clinical professional and the patient is. This development is a consequence of advanced telecommunications in the form of 'telemedicine'. The government's IT strategy emphasises the strategic importance of telemedicine, and yet current literature shows a failure to make progress in its adoption and implementation, partly due to organisational and human factors, as noted also by Timmons. The chapter considers how some traditional aspects of health care organisation are altered by distance and virtuality. Empirical data is drawn from four case studies: telemedicine in Ulster; NHS Direct in Wales; medical e- commerce in UK private medical insurance; and from four sites in areas of low population density in rural Canada. The findings suggest that some traditional aspects of health care organising are altered by virtuality, but that the precise effects are a function of the type of 'tele'-medicine in use.

'NEW' APPROACHES TO METHODOLOGY

An appreciation of the complexities of organisational life needs to be reflected in the development of an increasing range of methodologies which each have particular strengths and weaknesses and add to the depth and richness of current research. There needs to be a better understanding of the potential for newly-emerging participatory action-research-based methodologies within all disciplines working within the health sector, and not just within nursing. Research in the health sector plays a critical role in the development of new forms of participative methodologies; its strong history of practitioner research and current policy changes have increased this emphasis. In the real world of research funding, researchers need to remain responsive to the 'problem'-focused nature of funders' calls for bids and the value systems inherent within health care. They also need to be critically self-reflective about the efficacy of their methods to achieve their objectives.

A wide range of methods have been used by contributors, although the case study combined with in-depth interviews and some participant observation remain the mainstays of most of the research. By contrast, however, there is the use by Sheaff of a falsificationist methodology in his study of the emergence of hierarchies and networks within primary care. Insofar as the association is falsified, that is evidence against either the theory of tasks and conditions used, or the underlying elements of Weberian and network theory from which they were derived. Sheaff constructs for each variable a value which allows correlations between predictor scores and signs-of-integration scores to be tested. Such research focuses on the construction and understanding of theory utilising the researcher's constructs, and, as Sheaff notes, any predictions made cannot be tested until a significant amount of time has elapsed. By contrast the study by Thorne takes a very different form of methodology which gives equal weight to three different perspectives and the discourse between them with the objective of ascertaining the extent to which each discourse is dialogical or monological. This focus on developing an in-depth understanding of the processes relating three key areas of influence to the development of clinical governance produces a very different type of data and knowledge. In their own way both types of knowledge can be used to inform both theory and practice.

Ferlie *et al.* explore the outcome of two groups of researchers working in health-service research coming together to reflect on their research activity and to consider the methodological problems of producing overviews of qualitative research in the light of the growth of interest in meta analyses and systematic reviews in quantitative research. Should qualitative researchers seek to produce overviews across different studies? They examine what is meant by good qualitative research, and suggest five possible quality indicators to stimulate debate in the field. It also examines the methodological problems inherent in comparative analyses across case studies. Ferlie *et al.* took seven recently completed studies on the implementation of aspects of 'evidence-based medicine', from three research groups where similar case-study approaches had been used, for a comparative analysis. This produced several common themes which demonstrate that there are low-level patterns emerging from case-study-based research; that of the role of opinion leaders is looked at in more detail. These low-level patterns can be generalised but these generalisations, paradoxically, are about the particularity of each context and the need to be sensitive to an array of local circumstances in understanding how change initiatives are likely to be received. They are not the kind of generalisations which will uncover a set of predictable, reliable levers for change. The problems with the dissemination of research findings raises the question of whether there needs to be a very different style of research in this field, to develop methods which are meaningful and accessible to those whom we are trying to influence; such as action research, formative feedback and the 'reflective practitioner' model.

Combining different methodologies or approaches can strengthen research by providing a range of perspectives and interpretations. Jessopp and Boyle introduce an emerging methodology for the creation of a system learning tool through the combination of three paradigms: health service research and analysis, organisation development and real-time computer simulation modelling. The methodology is illustrated by reference to applications at different levels of the health care system: from hip-fracture care pathways to the whole system of delivering care for people with an urgent need, in a local health economy. Lessons are drawn for the development of the approach as a general tool for dealing with systems of complex organisational structures. Just as the 'real' system must be capable of constant adaptation and renewal, so the methodology will be emergent within any particular context. The methodology is grounded in the belief that by working on practical issues with those involved in delivering and receiving services, it is possible to start to deliver a more conscious and strategic self- organising system. As a way of working and as a way of understanding implicit assumptions, the methodology will challenge prevailing attitudes in a fundamental way.

Jumma and Alleyne reflect on the process of learning, unlearning and relearning through the use of facilitation skills to create 'actionable knowledge' (Argyris, 1993). Forty-six district nurse team leaders took part in the research-intervention case study for a 15-month period using specific software for strategic learning. The study demonstrated that district nurse team leaders could become more effective as clinical leaders through actionable knowledge based on tried and tested concepts, theories and frameworks. That is, by ensuring that clinical goals are specific and agreed; that clinical roles are made explicit; and that clinical processes are clear and clinical relationships are open. The methodology ensured evidence credibility criteria throughout the project, and observed the usability of the ensuing frameworks in everyday clinical leadership activities.

The final chapter by Ashburner explores the rationale for new-paradigm research and its potential to re-energise this area of study by broadening the range of methods used. The chapter sets out the background and development of an alternative paradigm and its philosophical roots. The acceptance of different types of action research lies as much in their establishment of academic rigour based in establishing their validity as in challenging the current dominance of positivism. Dissemination of research findings becomes integral to new forms of participative action research, which are a further development of whole-systems thinking and put a useful spotlight onto issues of 'knowledge' and 'learning'. There is a need to face the challenge from new-paradigm research methods to ensure that future research addresses issues and problems that more traditional methodologies cannot, as well as addressing issues of research dissemination and being responsive to the needs of funders.

In the range of the topics and approaches covered within this volume, the objective is to take forward the need to build on the theoretical and empirical knowledge that already exists, to find ways of doing justice to the complexities of current health-service processes and organisation, as well as ensuring that such research is relevant for both academics and practitioners alike.

References

Argyris, C. (1993) *Knowledge for Action* (San Fransisco: Jossey-Bass).

Department of Health (1997) *The New NHS Modern and Dependable*, Cm 3807, session 1997–9 (London: HM Stationery Office).

Department of Health (2000) *The NHS Plan*, Cm 4818–I (London: HM Stationery Office).

Mark, A. and Dopson, S. (1999) *Organisational Behaviour in Healthcare: The Research Agenda* (Basingstoke: Macmillan – now Palgrave).

Stewart, R. (1999) 'Foreword', in A. Mark and S. Dopson *op. cit.*

1 Organisational Behaviour Research in Health Care: An Overview

John Øvretveit

INTRODUCTION

There is an increasing demand and need for relevant research for informing and educating health managers. This demand is fuelled by the evidence-based medicine movement and the professionalisation of management in health services. Organisational behaviour (OB) is a multidiscipline which has largely been defined by the needs of managers. This chapter describes how organisational behaviour research (OBR) can contribute to practical action and scientific knowledge through a systematic study of how people and organisations behave. It defines OBR (Box 1.1), describes subjects for future research and considers the challenges and the potential for OBR in health care. The chapter also considers whether the model of evidence-based medicine may drive the future development of OB and hinder the use of 'subjectivist' methodologies, as well as whether managerial problems and perspectives will dominate the OB research agenda.

WHAT IS ORGANISATIONAL BEHAVIOUR RESEARCH IN HEALTH CARE?

OB researchers use a variety of methods and perspectives to carry out their systematic studies, drawing on sociology, business studies, psychology, service management and other disciplines. The methods range from traditional positivist experimental and observational methods, to social scientific phenomenological methods and ethnography, and also include action research and consultancy research methods. Examples of organisational behaviour research include studies of the effects of mergers on personnel, gender difference in management styles, conflict in Norwegian health care organisations, the

1

Box 1.1   Definition of organisation behaviour research (OBR) in health care

Organisation behaviour research is the systematic study of the behaviour of individuals, groups and organisations. The aim of OBR in health care is to contribute to the solution of practical problems and to scientific knowledge about people and organisations. OBR does not study health and disease in individuals or populations, but it does consider the effectiveness of different organisational forms for providing health services, as well as the behaviour of patients in relation to health care organisations. Although concentrating on observable behaviour and performance, OBR also investigates perceptions, emotions and cultures which may explain behaviour.

---

role of medical managers, the effectiveness of sequential compared to parallel work organisation in emergency-room teams, patient's experience of coordination of care, a comparative analysis of the structure of hospitals and local health care systems, and the implementation of quality programmes in hospitals.

OB research is not always empirical: some studies use disciplinary perspectives and theories to illuminate and understand organisational behaviour – for example network theory to understand collaboration and interactions between different organisations. Figure 1.1 shows the different types of research encompassed by the category of OB, in terms of level of unit of analysis and range of methods. Organisational behaviour is knowledge from different disciplines which has been organised into a relatively coherent whole for the purposes of educating managers and informing management decisions. It is not a discipline in its own right but a multidiscipline which has so far been defined by the practical needs of managers. This does not mean that the knowledge which falls within this boundary is unscientific or not rigorous. Neither does it mean that OB methods cannot be used to study issues of concern to other stakeholders, or that some OB research is not driven by academic motives to extend or fill gaps in knowledge. This diversity of subjects, methods and theoretical perspectives can be a disadvantage when trying to define or publicise the role of OBR, but it also brings strengths which need to be maintained. OBR

	Positivist experimental or observational	Phenomenological	Action and consultancy research
Interorganisational relations			
Organisational structure, performance and culture			
Group processes, behaviour and interrelations			
Individual characteristics roles, behaviour and feelings			

Figure 1.1   Different levels of analysis and paradigms in organisational behaviour research

is a young and growing multidiscipline in health care. A balance needs to be struck between the need to clearly define the field for the purpose of defining audiences for conferences and journals, to 'market the discipline', and to create databases of OB research, with the need for a flexible and pluralistic approach to methods and subject areas.

Although the field is defined by managers' needs, the future may see more patients and patient associations making use of OBR as well as practising clinicians. Media interest in the findings of OBR may also increase. Managers and policy-makers are likely to be challenged by critics who draw on OB research, for example into stress, or mergers or change implementation: evidence-based opposition will increase.

As well as empirical findings, OBR produces concepts, methods and models which managers and other can use, for example, to analyse situations, plan and manage implementation, and assess options and strategy. This knowledge is applied by practitioners of organisation analysis (OA) and organisation development (OD), such as organisation and management consultants who may be external or internal to the organisation. They too have developed a body of knowledge about how to assist organisation and individual development. Two well-known examples are the strengths, weaknesses, opportunity and threats model (SWOT) and the 7S framework for analysing organisation (Athos and Pascale 1981). These are not the products of OBR but could be evaluated by OBR. Managers and educationalists have, however, accepted these and other methods as useful, without being validated by research or systematic evaluation – there are many useful management methods and concepts which originate from outside of OBR. The systematic methods of OBR are not necessary to establish valid management methods or models, but these could be improved through OBR evaluation.

SOME AREAS AND ISSUES FOR FUTURE OBR

How are subjects for organisational behaviour research in health care identified? One way is 'problem-driven': there is a practical problem or decision to be made and finance is provided to review previous research and conduct studies which will help to resolve the problem. One drawback is that those with power or finance set much of the agenda. Another way is by using academic criteria: there is a gap in knowledge, or conflicting theories or findings and an academically interesting question to be explored. Practical criteria predominate in decisions about which subjects are studied and how they are studied. In part this is because the knowledge base is heterogeneous and not well-defined. This has led to criticisms that OBR in health care is not very rigorous, and does not contribute significantly to building the multi-discipline or to the host disciplines.

The following is a personal view of areas where OBR research can make a contribution to practical decisions, education programmes and scientific knowledge. It is the view of an academic and consultant with an OB action-research background in the UK, but now working in management teaching and research in the Nordic countries and else-where. A UK view is given by Mark and Dopson (1999).

Research Topics

Patients as Part of the Organisation

Traditional organisation behaviour research does not consider consumers as part of the organisation. Yet OBR theories and methods from psychology and sociology has much to contribute to understanding the patient's role and relationship to health care organisations. If OBR is to contribute to management education and action, then we need to apply our methods more to studying patients' and citizens' behaviour and feelings towards professionals and health care organisations. We can also draw on service management research and concepts to understand health consumers' behaviour and attitudes, their demands for convenience, choice, control and their expectations that the service is oriented to their needs. OB, like the health service, needs to view patients and consumers as temporary or permanent parts of health care organisations.

Emotion in Health Care

One gap in OBR concerns theories and empirical knowledge about feelings in health care and how feelings relate to behaviour and decisions. The most sophisticated knowledge about this subject appears to be in British and US television soap dramas, not in OB research journals. Those of us who help health care personnel learn emotional competence at work have few health care research studies to use as examples to draw on. Few definitions of OB refer to feelings, yet feelings profoundly affect management decisions and practice (see Box 1.2). Feelings influence clinical practice, and are important in patients' experiences and behaviour, yet there is little scientific research into or theories about the subject. Management performance could be improved by enabling managers to better understand their own and others' feelings in different situations. OBR could develop models and theories about feelings from empirical research into different health care situations, which would give a relevant research base to compliment other educational methods to develop emotional competence.

There are research and theories from occupational psychology which can stimulate our work in this area. The study of emotion at work has looked at roles which prescribe particular emotional behaviours, such as for hotel receptionists, and the stress and emotional

---

Box 1.2   Feelings at work in health care

- Feelings are facts: practitioners and managers only partially understand a situation if they do not understand their own and others' feelings.
- There is little OB research into feelings or unconscious processes in health care.
- Empirical and theoretical research on the subject in health care settings would improve educational programmes for developing managers' and practitioners' emotional competence at work

labour of such roles. Health organisations put more emotional demands on employees and customers than many other organisations, yet we know little about what those demands are and the strategies which people use to deal with their feelings. Health care demands both the suppression and expression of emotion and skills to know and manage feelings appropriately. Hochschild (1983) refers to this work as emotional labour, 'the management of feeling to create a publicly observable facial and bodily display', and shows how essential it is to many jobs, as well as the exchange value of such labour.

Research in other sectors has looked at strategies for managing emotions and making it possible for people to have greater access to their emotions to enable them better to do their work. This area may become more significant with more litigation for emotional problems caused to employees by their work situation. It has been argued that to understand ways in which work affects people's well-being, it is better to look at specific emotions such as anger, resentment and pride, rather than general notions of stress and satisfaction (Briner, 1997). If one of the discoveries of the last century was of the human unconscious, then this is one discovery which OB research in health care has ignored. Little has been done since Menzies' (1960) ground-breaking study of nurses and the psychological defences they used to cope with mixed feelings of pity, fear, compassion, guilt and hostility. Psychoanalytic concepts and psychotherapeutic models give a starting point for analysing situations and develop practical tools to enable practitioners and patients to be more aware of and incorporate their feelings into action. We know that unconscious factors affect decisions, but little about how unconscious motives and defences operate in groups and in relationships in health care. Interesting recent work has been done on the concept of shame which has obvious relevance to understanding many situations for patients and employees (Walsh, 1999). Many health care employees feel unacknowledged for their efforts even though they have met performance targets and feel criticised for not doing more. Do we know enough about the mechanisms which lead from this to poor morale and less risk-taking and creativity? Do we know enough about how to reverse this spiral?

The deafening silence about feelings and the unconscious in OBR in health care may be because of a positivist predisposition towards observable behaviour and theories which can be tested using conventional methods. Although room has been made for phenomenological perspectives, we will need other perspectives, theories and methods adequately to study feelings in health care.

Ethical Organisation and Management for Health Care

Managers have a responsibility for how work is organised, how work is organised affects the performance of an organisation and the well-being of employees and patients. The money and time spent on designing organisation for well-being and performance – on social 'work-architecture' – is much less than the time and money spent on physical architecture and equipment. Many managers inherit poor organisation but do not have the skills and knowledge to diagnose organisational problems, or to design an organisation which is effective and satisfying to work within. Where they do, they are often not able to implement changes. Another reason is that the OB research in the subject has gaps and is not organised in a way which managers can access and use (see Box 1.3).

The concept of 'ethical organisation' refers to a culture and structure of work roles, tasks and working relations which builds Trust and confidence and enables people to give their best and become the best they can be (Øvretveit, 1996). There was a view that OBR could describe the type of culture and structure which is optimal for an organisation, and give research-based tools for managers to develop such organisation. Research has shown that there is no single best organisational form, but that some organisational forms or features are certain to cause problems. Principles have been developed which can help managers improve organisation, such as principles of role clarity, division and coordination of work, and of communication, but there has been little comparative research to test these principles and relate their presence or absence to performance and well-being in health care.

Box 1.3   Poor management and organisation is a health risk factor

- Management and organisation profoundly affects the health of employees and of patients.
- Poor management and organisation is the cause of avoidable mortality, of inequalities in health and of patient suffering. It may be a larger health risk factor than poor housing, economic disadvantage or pollution.
- Social 'work-architecture' is more important than physical architecture to patients' health, for enabling people to do their work with satisfaction, and in promoting their health and personal growth.

One approach is to describe and analyse dysfunctional and unethical organisations. Do you know or have you worked in such an organisation, characterised by conflict, isolation, mistrust and poor morale? In my organisational development work with teams I found work organisation which was guaranteed to produce not only frustration, but conflict and poor care, and it was only goodwill and exceptional tolerance which kept services going (Øvretveit, 1993). There are many examples from research into multidisciplinary teams, where unclear leadership roles, lack of operational policies and poor communication systems lie at the at the root of poor morale and poor patient care.

The thesis is that there are forms of organisation which are better than others for the type of patients and work to be done, and that creating such a form of work organisation would prevent and resolve many so-called 'personality conflicts'. OB has a part to play in raising consciousness of how the social context of work affects the behaviour of employees and patients, and in giving research-based methods to improve organisation.

Cross-fertilisation with Quality Assurance and Improvement

OBR has already been used to develop strategies for implementing change (Moss *et al.*, 1998), clinical guidelines (Moulding *et al.*, 1999) and quality project team facilitation and team frameworks (Øvretveit, 2000b). In the future OBR can help to develop structures and processes for clinical governance. Future areas for research could include examination of the impact of external regulation and accreditation systems, and comparisons between different quality systems, as well as examining the resources used by such systems compared to the benefits.

OBR can draw on the work done within the quality-improvement movement to understand the links between outcomes and organisational processes and inputs to care, and make use of the well-developed methods for measuring outcome (Batalden *et al.*, 1994). Such models and understanding can help OBR examine the performance of specific services and compare the effectiveness of different organisational forms. Cross-fertilisation between these two disciplines could usefully increase in the future.

Systems Errors

There is a growing recognition that poor quality is as much a result of system errors as it is the result of individual incompetence or negli-

John Øvretveit 9

gence (Leape, 1994). Clinicians are one part of a system of care and it is the system which produces the good or bad outcomes. Organisational behaviour theory and methods are necessary to understand the many factors and causal influences which operate in these systems of care, and OBR in the future can contribute to understanding why medical errors and adverse events occur and to developing systems for preventing errors which take account of human behaviours in different situations and groups. It can help to develop 'simplification engineering' which streamlines and cuts error points to make processes more robust and less affected by the inevitable but chance combinations of events which can disrupt or break the system.

Qualeficiency

There is a convergence of quality improvement, evidence-based health care and cost-performance improvement which is represented in the concept of qualificiency. Qualeficiency is using the fewest resources to achieve a consistent standard of care which meets patients' essential health needs and wants. The concept brings together quality, efficiency and effectiveness; it focuses attention on the most important aspects of performance of health organisations. Organisational behaviour research can contribute to understanding the individual and systems factors which cause waste – waste being a concept linking quality and efficiency. Such research can discover why some teams are successful in cutting costs and improving quality (Øvretveit, 2000b).

Middle and Medical Management

Working with managers teaches us that managers are not special types of people but that each person is a special type of manager. However, only some have the qualities or the potential to be a successful health manager, and this is perhaps most clear when we consider the role of middle and medical managers. The role of middle manager in health care organisations has been identified as a key role in change management and policy implementation (Currie, 1999). Many of these roles are head of department or clinical director roles, often occupied by physicians. The role is the main interface between clinicians and management, and is the locus of conflicts which are likely to increase in the future.

In Swedish hospitals there is a single (medical) head of department and Norwegian hospitals are moving in the direction of single general managers at this level, as are other European countries. In the UK clinical governance will introduce a further challenge to the work of clinical directors and research has shown that this role is not an easy one, or entirely successful (Marnoch 1996). OBR has already made a contribution to understanding the role and the qualities needed for the position (McKee *et al.*, 1999; Ong and Schepers, 1999), and this work needs to be developed, one way being through comparative research. It appears that different qualities are required to be a successful manager in different health care organisations, yet we know little about which organisational and contextual factors are significant and how these relate to the qualities required. The increase in management roles in primary care calls for and allows comparisons, as does the international convergence on a single middle-management role in hospitals and the increase in the number of such managers in private and not-for-profit health care.

Private Organisations, Interorganisational Networks and Collaboration

Most OB health care research in Europe studies publicly-funded and owned health organisations. However, the part played by non-governmental for-profit and not-for-profit organisations is increasing. There is opportunity for comparative studies, such as of working conditions, managerial roles and structures, and for studies of how the different sectors cooperate or compete. Studies are also needed of different forms of collaboration and competitions and of different organisational network forms, such as provider networks of private and public organisations (Robertson and Steiner, 1997; Øvretveit, 1998b).

Power, Politics and Change

OB studies need to make more use of existing theories of power and to develop models of power which are appropriate to health care. Power and politics are important features of health care and not sufficiently considered in OB studies. Health care is political in both senses: health care organisations can be viewed as political systems, and politicians and politics affects what is done and how it is done. This is especially so in the Nordic countries with decentralised and politically controlled public health care. There are few studies of the management – politician interface, of clinician–politician relations, and of unions, pressure groups and other political actors' roles and influence on behaviour in, of and between organisations. OBR studies of change are handicapped by simplistic theories of power and could be improved by drawing on more recent theories from political science, neo-Marxism and women's studies. Power and politics need to be made part of the multidiscipline of OB in health care.

Application of Systems Theory

Systems theory has proved an important resource for conceptualising many subjects within OB, and has made it possible to understand some of the unexpected outcomes of different change processes. However, there are few systems theory tools which can be used easily by managers to understand and analyse different situations. Soft-systems methodology is one technique, as are the models provided by *The Fifth Discipline* field book (Senge, 1992), but OB needs to develop more useable systems models to understand such things as the impact of IT and other changes.

THE POTENTIAL AND CHALLENGES FOR OBR IN HEALTH CARE

The above has showed some areas for future research and the potential of OBR to make an even greater contribution to management education and decisions, as well as to other stakeholders' decisions. There is also a potential to develop action-research action evaluation (Øvretveit, 1998b) and other methods which both promote effective change and contribute to knowledge. Some question whether OBR in health care has established a coherent knowledge base and how much research builds on earlier work (for example Stewart, 1999). Mark and Dopson (1999) refer to a project to identify those studies in health organisation and management which went beyond descriptive research – but few studies were found. There is no lack of concept and model building, but is there a lack of theory building and testing and a failure to link our research to work which has gone before? Certainly more follow-up and replication studies would help to develop the knowledge base by, for example, finding out if similar phenomena occur in different contexts (Øvretveit, 1998c).

The idea of a coherent body of knowledge, which is developed and extended, is central to many conventional disciplines. Is OBR in health care a new discipline that will develop in this direction, and if so what will help and hinder this development? Or is OB nothing more than a convenient way to organise theories and research from different disciplines for the purposes of teaching and informing managers? Do researchers have a greater loyalty to and communication with their discipline of origin? The following notes some issues which need to be addressed for OB in health care to make a greater practical and knowledge contribution.

Who is your Research for – the Main Users?

'So what? What should I or my organisation do differently as a result of this research?' These are questions raised by managers when trying to see the implications of an OBR study and what value would be added to their practice by acting on the research. There may be two reasons why an OB researcher could not give a clear answer to these questions: their research is not designed to inform management decisions, and they do not give sufficient consideration to the practical implications of their findings, for example by working this through with one or more managers.

One way to develop OBR is to take a more user-focused and participatory approach when planning the research (Øvretveit, 2000a); this means paying more attention to who will be the main users of the research and their informational needs. There are six main users of OBR:

- Managers, for making better informed management decisions,
- policy-makers, for making better informed health and health care policies,
- consultants, to help managers to analyse problems and design or carry through changes,
- educationalists, to help managers learn and develop skills,
- other researchers, to see how the research relates to their own, to get ideas, and to help build a knowledge base, and
- the media/the public, to understand what is happening in health care.

If an OB study is to be of maximum use then it is best designed with one or two users and purposes in mind – the more users it tries to serve then the less well it will serve any. At present there is a danger of 'managerialism': of OBR agendas being dominated by management problems such as policy implementation, cost reduction and performance improvement, and of research taking on the perspectives of management. Where are the OB studies of the lowest paid personnel in health care, of the role and influence of minority groups and the practical recommendations to make their lives better?

The Researcher's Value Position

Research is not value-neutral but researchers must strive for objectivity. Researchers need to be aware of their values and where their research stands in relation to three perspectives within OB research:

● The radical perspective, which challenges existing structures and definitions and reveals how some groups achieve and maintain dominance to the disadvantage of others.
● The liberal humanist perspective, which accepts existing structures and definitions but seeks independence in research and to humanise organisations and the services which they provide.
● The conservative perspective which seeks to improve performance and implement policies without questioning their basis or which groups benefit or are disadvantaged by such policies or improved performance.

Most OB research in health care is based on liberal humanist values, but are the funding and other circumstances of OB research reducing the amount of 'radical research' in favour of 'conservative research'? Is there a place for 'critical OB' which considers how power is exercised, and the different economic and ideological systems of domination?

Application and Use of OB

Three of the main users of OB are managers, consultants and educationalists. Some barriers to them making a greater use of OBR are the same as for other stakeholders – because the research is,

● not relevant to their concerns (not 'user-focused'),
● context-specific and not generalisable,
● difficult to find and access (for example few journals and texts for OB in health care, many different disciplines), and
● difficult to assess.

Managers and others have difficulty finding and assessing OBR to help them make their decisions. These problems are connected with the multidisciplinary nature of OBR and also affect the willingness of sponsors to finance OBR. Assessing the quality of OBR evidence to decide whether to act on it is a particular problem. The hierarchy of evidence used in medical research cannot be transposed because OBR studies are made using many different methods. Managers do not have time and cannot be expected to have the expertise to assess the quality of the research, neither do consultants. One option is to produce a series of reviews of studies which are related to particular issues such as mergers, quality assurance, clinical governance, and manager–politician relations.

Methods in OBR – Case-Study and Action-Research Methods

The paradigm wars of the 1970s have passed and a relatively peaceful coexistence prevails between positivist and phenomenological approaches. Two issues for future OBR are how to create more generalisable findings whilst keeping the understanding of context which is so important in health care, and how to develop and incorporate action-research methods within OB.

The case-study method has emerged as a popular approach for OBR in health care (Yin, 1989; Keen and Packwood, 1995). The advantages are that this method provides a framework within which different data-gathering methods can be used, and it gives a way of understanding organisational behaviour in a specific context. Models can be built to explore the relationship between different environmental, structural and cultural factors and different performance variables. A disadvantage of single case studies are that the findings may not be generalisable; this is a problem with many OB studies. Yet understanding of context is not incompatible with generalisability – indeed it helps. By being specific about the context we are better able to test in exactly which settings the same findings apply. Thus to develop the knowledge base we need more replication studies and multiple case studies. Cross-national studies also have a great potential to develop more generalisable knowledge (Øvretveit, 1998c).

Whilst there is a greater understanding and use of qualitative methods, many such studies face difficulties in presenting the qualitative findings economically and in a way in which the link between the conclusions and findings can be understood. Recent texts and writings give guidance for improving such types of research and these could also be used with benefit in action-research studies (Popay *et al.*, 1998). Action research and consultancy research methods have yet to be accepted within OBR. Action research and action evaluation involves collaboration with different parties to diagnose and construct solutions to organisational problems. Some reasons why the knowledge produced by such research has not been recognised are that,

- action researchers often do not build on previous OB theories or studies, or link their findings to this knowledge,
- action researchers often do not publish their studies in journals, often because journals do not accept the methods used, and
- action researchers do not clearly describe their methods and have not developed their methods in response to legitimate criticisms from other researchers.

Action research can make an important contribution to the OB knowledge base, but if it is to do so both action researchers and traditional researchers and journals need to change their approach. The positive influence of the evidence-based medicine movement is to demand a clearer and more precise description of methods in order to allow others to assess validity. Action researchers who respond to this demand will improve their research and the methodology of action research. But it also requires a willingness within OB to accept other methods for constructing and testing knowledge, in the same way that some evaluation researchers have come to accept action-evaluation methods (Øvretveit, 1998a).

CONCLUSION

In health care the purpose of OB research is to contribute to the solution of practical problems in health organisations and to scientific knowledge, although few studies achieve both well. OBR draws on theories and methods from many disciplines, and the variety of methods, subjects and levels of analysis is a problem when trying to access, review and build on previous research. The advantage of the variety is that it provides many perspectives and methods with which to study different issues within health care.

OBR is a multidiscipline which to date has been defined by managers' needs, but has the potential to become a discipline in its own right and one which serves different interests. OBR has an important contribution to make to improving the performance of health care organisations and to humanising organisational life for personnel and for patients. Evidence-based management following the evidence-based medicine model is not likely, but management decisions and education need to be more informed by research. To make a greater contribution, OBR researchers need to be clear who are the users of the research, ensure the research is accessible, and work with users to explicate the practical implications of the research. Action research and action evaluation has still not found a place within OBR, but could make a contribution in the future if a more flexible attitude is taken towards methods, and if action researchers described their methods more clearly and related their work to previous research and theories.

References

Athos, A.G. and Pascale, R.T. (1981) *The Art of Japanese Management* (New York, Simon & Schuster).

Batalden, P., Nelsen, E. and Roberts, J. (1994) 'Linking Outcomes Measurement to Continual Improvement: The Serial "V" Way of Thinking about How to Improve Clinical Care', *Journal of Quality Improvement*, 20(4): 167–80.

Briner, R. (1997) 'Beyond Stress and Satisfaction', Proceedings of the British Occupational Psychology Conference, 1997: 95–100.

Currie, G. (1999) 'The Influence of Middle Management on Emergent Strategy', in A. Mark and S. Dopson (eds), *Organisational Behaviour in Healthcare: The Research Agenda* (London: Macmillan – now Palgrave).

Hochschild, A. (1983) *The Managed Heart: Commercialisation of Human Feeling* (Berkeley: University of California Press).

Keen, J. and Packwood, T. (1995) 'Case Study Evaluation', *British Medical Journal*, 311: 444–6.

Lagasse, R., Steinberg, E., Katz, R. and Saubermann, A. (1995) 'Defining Quality of Perioperative Care by Statistical Process Control of Adverse Outcomes', *Anaesthesiology*, 82(5): 1181–8.

Leape, L. (1994) 'Error in Medicine', *Journal of the American Medical Association*, 272(23): 1851–7.

Mark, A. and Dopson, S. (1999) *Organisational Behaviour in Healthcare: The Research Agenda* (London: Macmillan – now Palgrave).

Marnoch, G. (1996) *Doctors and Management in the National Health Service* (Milton Keynes: Open University Press).

McKee, L., Marnoch, G. and Dinnie, N. (1999) 'Medical Managers: Puppetmasters or Puppets? Sources of Power and Influence in Clinical Directorates', in A. Mark and S. Dopson (eds), *Organisational Behaviour in Healthcare: The Research Agenda* (London: Macmillan – now Palgrave).

Menzies, E.P. (1960) 'A Case Study in the Functioning of Social Systems as a Defence against Anxiety: A Report on a Study of the Nursing Service of a General Hospital', *Human Relations*: 95.

Moss, F., Garside, P. and Dawson, S. (1998) 'Organisational Change: The Key to Quality Improvement', *Quality in Health Care*, 7 (suppl): S1–2.

Moulding, N., Silagy, C. and Weller, D. (1999) 'A Framework for Effective Management of Change in Clinical Practice', *Quality in Healthcare*, 8: 177–83.

Ong, B.N. and Schepers, R. (1999) 'Variations on a Theme: Clinicians in Management in England and the Netherlands', in A. Mark and S. Dopson (eds), *Organisational Behaviour in Healthcare: The Research Agenda* (London: Macmillan – now Palgrave).

Øvretveit, J. (1993) *Co-ordinating Community Care: Multidisciplinary Teams and Care Management in Health and Social Services* (Milton Keynes: Open University Press).

Øvretveit, J. (1996) 'Using Ethics to Make Management Decisions', *Overlakaren, Journal for Doctors in Management*, 6: 22–6.

Øvretveit, J. (1998a) *Evaluating Health Interventions* (Milton Keynes: Open University Press).

Øvretveit, J. (1998b) 'Integrated Care for the Nordic Countries – A Briefing Paper', The Nordic School of Public Health, Goteborg.

Øvretveit, J. (1998c) *Comparative and Cross Cultural Health Research* (Oxford: Radcliffe Medical Press).

Øvretveit, J. (2000a) *Action Research: A User Focused Approach for Evaluating Health Programmes Reforms and Change* (Lund: Studentlitteratur).

Øvretveit, J. (2000b) 'A Team Quality Improvement Sequence for Complex Problems (TQIS)', *Quality in Health Care*, 8: 1–7.

Popay, J., Rogers, A. and Williams, G. (1998) 'Rationale and Standards for the Systematic Review of Qualitative Literature in Health Services Research', *Qualitative Health Research*, 8(3): 341–51.

Robertson, R. and Steiner, A. (1997) *Managed Health Care: US Evidence and Lessons for the NHS* (Milton Keynes: Open University Press).

Senge, P. (1992) *'The Fifth Discipline'* (London: Random House).

Stewart, R. (1999) Forward to A. Mark and S. Dopson (eds), *Organisational Behaviour in Healthcare: The Research Agenda* (London: Macmillan – now Palgrave): ix–xi.

Walsh, S. (1999) 'Shame in the Workplace', *The Psychologist*, 12(1): 20–2.

Yin, R. (1989) *Case Study Research: Design and Methods* (Beverly Hills: Sage).

2 Evidence-Based Medicine and Organisational Change: An Overview of Some Recent Qualitative Research

Ewan Ferlie, John Gabbay, Louise FitzGerald, Louise Locock and Sue Dopson

INTRODUCTION

The health care sector can be rightly proud of its biomedical research base. Its methodological rigour, using elegant research tools such as the Randomised Control Trial (RCT) and more recently systematic reviews and meta-analyses, is enviable (Chalmers, 1998). The RCT is sometimes explicitly seen by those adopting this clinical science paradigm as offering the highest quality of empirical evidence within a hierarchy of evidence model (NHSCRD, 1996), although this position is contested by some social science researchers. Critics argue that the RCT method has limits (see Pawson and Tilley's 1997 critique of the experimental paradigm) as well as strengths (Oakley, 1998) when applied to the investigation of social and organisational phenomena.

Health-services research (HSR) is a more tender plant and is still evolving from its biomedical roots. HSR draws on both clinical sciences and a range of social sciences, including management studies. Organisation and management studies have grown rapidly as a field of both teaching and research over the last 30 years, as evident most obviously in the MBA boom but also in the emergence of a fundamental research base and high-quality journals in which the research is published. Management research uses a range of research methods (Shortell *et al.*'s 1996 American work on health care management, for example, uses a range of methods, including statistical modelling). But those writing from an organisational behaviour (OB) tradition often use case studies or other forms of qualitative analysis, rather

18

than the methods derived from biomedical research. Thus different research traditions coexisting within HSR are competing for influence. Such a situation is not of course unusual in any multidisciplinary field (Becher, 1989). While the debate should be collegial and measured in tone, it should nevertheless address fundamental methodological concerns. The question therefore arises: how should health care management – or service delivery and organisation to quote the formulation used by the NHS R&D (NCCSDO, 2000) – be best researched?

The paradigm of the systematic review is also associated with natural science, but the expanding work of the Cochrane Collaborations has recently been extended into qualitative research (Popay *et al.*, 1998) and now into the professional and subsequently organisational field (Oxman *et al.*, 1995). Most notably, the work of the Cochrane Effective Practice and Organisation of Care (EPOC) group (Bero *et al.*, 1998; Oxman and Flottorp, 1998) and National Health Service Centre for Reviews and Dissemination (NHSCRD) (1999) has shown a special interest in interventions intended to trigger professional behaviour change. EPOC certainly recognises the additional complexities of undertaking work in this area. However, we will argue here that the findings from this stream of work are as yet partial and inconclusive and are likely to remain so, as they are largely limited to reviewing work based only on one strand of the available scientific methods.

Nevertheless, as the OB perspective would predict, such reviews suggest that in order to effect behavioural and organisational change one must use a variety of methods, and that the results of specific interventions may vary according to context. The reviews show that while some interventions such as the use of opinion leaders appear to exert mixed effects, some change strategies (educational outreach in respect of prescribing behaviour in USA settings; reminders as a tool for clinical management) are indeed supported empirically by intervention studies (NHSCR, 1999). Interestingly, NHSCRD (1999) in its search for 'change levers' complements the usual systematic review focus with a broader and more pluralist use of psychological and organisational theory and case studies.

Critics argue that this search for generic levers is unlikely to be fruitful even in the long run, especially in relation to complex processes of organisational change that are even more difficult to control than the clinical decisions of individual physicians. Influential work on innovation increasingly sees it as a non-linear and dynamic process (van de Ven *et al.*, 2000), dependent on context (Kimberly, 1981) and interpersonal networks (Latour, 1987). We will argue here that even if

RCTs and systematic reviews continue to be used over a much longer time period, they are less likely to deliver conclusive results in this field than in their original heartland of assessing the effect of new drugs. This is because the RCT framework assumes a 'black-box' model of the implementation process that pays little attention to such crucial factors as local context, the decision-making process or history. They usually assume a linear, rational implementation process, couched in the terms of achieving planned change. They do not treat organisations as complex systems but attempt to reduce them to their component parts in order to assess the impact of a given intervention. Yet during organisational change the complexities of, say, the interactions between multiple stakeholders may result in a major emergent component which cannot be captured by this reductionist perspective.

So whilst systematic reviews and RCTs do have a role within health care management research, they may be most suited to the more micro-interventions such as individual prescribing decisions. They are less suited to modelling complex or organisational change processes, which constitute the majority of attempts to achieve organisational change. RCTs are not able to uncover complex change processes that involve a range of interacting stakeholders, agencies and occupational groups and that take place in organisational settings that cannot be experimentally controlled. In fact, the basic assumptions of RCTs are violated within such arenas. Even change processes which appear simple can often quickly become complex: for example, the apparently self-contained devolution of a single outpatient clinic from hospital to community (Ferlie *et al.*, 2000) raises the issue of how an evidence-based innovation crosses the interface between secondary and primary care. And the simple change of introducing stroke units, which have been clearly shown by systematic review to save lives, has been shown to contain a multiplicity of local organisational, professional and political dimensions that would render a controlled trial meaningless (CSAG, 1998).

To point out the limitations of the RCT is not to say that everything in the OB garden is flourishing. Far from it. OB has major methodological problems that urgently need addressing. Many OB studies have remained localised, fragmented and unable to influence policy; they have been repeatedly trapped into evaluating ephemeral policy reforms which are abandoned as soon as they are introduced (for instance, who now cares about evaluations of GP fundholding?) and have therefore not contributed to a generic body of knowledge. They have failed to be explicit about their methodological assumptions or about the rules for collecting and analysing data. Stewart (1999) has recently criticised the OB HSR field's preoccupation with producing substantive findings rather than discussing methodology or theory, when these are crucial if the discipline is to advance further as a coherent body of knowledge.

INDICATORS OF QUALITY IN OB RESEARCH IN HEALTH CARE

HSR is an expanding field, but also a disparate one characterised by a wide mix of methods drawn from the natural and the social sciences (as reviewed by Bowling, 1997). There have been calls for the greater use of qualitative methods within HSR (Black, 1994) and there is a noticeable growth in qualitative research techniques which are seen as more likely by policy funders to lead to local development and change. However, HSR is also a field with little consensus, where different academic disciplines, research methods, and basic epistemologies co-exist and sometimes compete for influence.

This chapter provided a rare opportunity for two groups of OB researchers working in HSR to come together to reflect on their findings and to consider the methodological problems of producing overviews of qualitative research in the light of the growth of interest in systematic reviews in quantitative research. Specifically, we ask, 'Should qualitative researchers seek to produce overviews across different studies? If so, how should they do it?'

Features of Good Quality in OB Health Care Research

In any overview one would want to give most weight to high-quality research. One of the advantages of the biomedical paradigm is that there is an explicit hierarchy of evidence that enables a reviewer to weight different sources of quantitative data. But what are the indicators of good qualitative research? Qualitative health service researchers are being encouraged to be more explicit about what those indicators might be (Murphy *et al.*, 1998; Popay *et al.*, 1998), but there remains, however, no consensus among qualitative researchers, where conversations about the validity of collating the results of different studies are only just beginning. We suggest here some early thoughts about five possible quality indicators for OB HSR research, in the hope of stimulating debate within the discipline.

First, good quality OB HSR should get beyond pure empiricism so that there should be a relationship with a body of generic *organisational theory*. The field often appears to be entirely atheoretical or (at best) to lag behind recent intellectual developments in generic organisation theory and hence to be using approaches (for example, planned change models) which have been largely superseded in the OB literature. Theory should be explicitly linked to empirical enquiry and the analysis of data. It can be used deductively (to create propositions) or may emerge inductively as grounded theory. Of course, the field may contain very different and vigorously debated organisational theoretical frameworks (for example, contingency theory; institutionalism; post-structuralist perspectives). These theoretical approaches are not easily reconciled, so that an important decision for some researchers may be to choose between them rather than seek to combine them.

Secondly, there should be an explicit treatment and clear description of *methodology and research design*. What methods have been selected and why? And how, in detail, have they been used? Qualitative analysis has a range of approaches ranging from grounded theory and ethnography on the one hand to purposive selection of cases that demonstrate different outcomes on the other. This latter method shares some features with the logic of quasi-experimental designs, particularly where there is an attempt to 'match' the comparator cases. Other researchers may use narrative techniques, discourse analysis, observation, documentary analysis or focus groups. The chosen method needs to be carefully appraised and justified, and then be carefully operationalised within a well-described research design that governs the appropriate collection of data.

Thirdly, the *empirical data should have strong internal validity* – that is, 'it should tell it as it really is'. OB is rarely in the realm of quantitative data, so questions of statistical power and random sampling are not relevant. Qualitative data should rather generate valid insight into processes that are occurring within the case. Key questions might include the following. Has the range of different stakeholders been fully identified and covered, especially if a form of pluralistic evaluation is being attempted? Is the relation between the interviewer and the respondent such that insightful answers that inform us about the meaning of a situation are more likely to be forthcoming in the interviews than superficial and misleading ones? Have different qualitative methods (observation; documentary analysis and interviews) been used to provide a test through triangulation? Is the data longitudinal in nature or merely cross sectional? Have data on behaviour as well on attitudes been collected? What are the rules for analysis when different stakeholders provide very different accounts of their experience of reality?

Fourthly, it should be a mark of high-quality work that it aims to move beyond purely local studies to *uncover underlying patterns and tendencies across sites*. This patterning may be low-level and partial, but there is an attempt to get beyond the purely local. While not fully generalisable across a population of organisations (some of which may in fact exhibit different contexts and processes), nevertheless cross-case studies provide findings of some scale and importance. So how can qualitative studies be scaled up? One technique would be a multi-site study on a much larger scale than is usual, which would probably employ a number of fieldworkers. The question then is whether the fieldworkers were working in the same way, or whether their perspectives varied by discipline (so that, for example, psychologists might emphasise micro-level processes and sociologists macro-level processes). A second technique would be to take an overview across a related family of studies so as to produce an overview (as this chapter sets out to do). A third would be to commission an overview across all recent published work, although the methodological problems of doing so are complex.

Fifthly, high-quality work should demonstrate *relevance to practice as well as to theory*. There is often within the OB literature a close connection with the concerns of practitioners, especially in action research (Lewin, 1951; Argyris, 1999; Heron, 1996). Research should not only be theoretically sound but also practically useful, seeking to promote local improvements. Technically expert research that failed to promote local ownership of the findings, therefore, would not be seen as fully successful in the OB model.

There are several dilemmas for health services R&D, all of which are heightened in OB research. The first is the tension between research and development. In the NHS R&D programme the research model has prevailed, which assumes that the researcher's primary role is to produce valid knowledge. This neglect of the development function has only sporadically been remedied – even within the R&D programme designed to research into the implementation of research findings (Department of Health, 2000.) However, the advent of the new central programme on Service Delivery and Organisation, and certain NHS regional initiatives such as the South-East Region's Knowledge Management initiative, go some small way to redressing the imbalance between R&D. A second, related, tension is between the model in which participants in the research sites are the passive 'subjects' of research, and that where they become co-producers of knowledge, who may well develop their own research activity in collaboration with specialist researchers. The third dilemma is between locally applicable and (if the emphasis is on development) applied findings, and findings that may be widely generalised. This is of course related to the first two dilemmas, as participant-driven research work is likely to be applied and local in nature, and to be part of local development work. Much OB work is of this nature, and is likely to be concerned to produce 'actionable knowledge' (Argyris, 1999) which leads to local change and development, but on the basis of rigorous data collection and diagnosis. This orientation shapes the nature of the research activity undertaken – for example moving from summative to formative modes of evaluation (another tension particular to evaluative research).

Rather than the usual concern for scientific neutrality and a reluctance to intervene, OB may well entail explicit interventions undertaken within the site. These are aimed at helping managers to ascertain an optimal direction for change, based on early results of data collection, and then iteratively to carry out and evaluate the resulting actions. When the primary focus of analysis and intervention is the single organisation, however, this has the unwanted side effect of diminishing the researchers' ability to draw general conclusions. Yet OB is also engaged in a search for general patterns. How, then, can specific case studies – which are usually developmental, participative, local and formative – be translated into the general, systemic learning more usually associated with the biomedical model of HSR? A first step must surely be to develop better methods for aggregating the findings of case studies carried out by different research teams.

METHODOLOGICAL PROBLEMS IN COMPARATIVE ANALYSIS ACROSS CASE STUDIES

In this section we examine in more detail the methodological problems of comparing and contrasting results from a set of six recent projects based on case studies on the implementation of aspects of EBM into local clinical practice. The studies were recently completed by two groups of OB researchers (one based at Templeton College, Oxford University and at Southampton University, and the other originally based at the Centre for Corporate Strategy and Change, Warwick

Business School).[*] The researchers were active in the same health care system (the NHS) at the same period (the mid-1990s), and were operating from similar theoretical bases. Both groups used similar (though not identical) case-study-based methods and looked at similar questions (see Box 2.1 for an overview of research design and methods). The studies include work in primary and secondary care settings, and include comparisons of cases where changes in the organisation were thought to be strongly 'evidence-based' with others where the clinical research evidence was apparently 'weaker'.

The final reports from these studies, now all published, have formed the basis for this overview. (Wood *et al.*, 1998a,b; FitzGerald *et al.*, 1999; Ferlie *et al.*, 2000; Hawkins *et al.*, 1999; Dopson and Gabbay, 1995; Dawson *et al.*, 1998; Clinical Standards Advisory Group, 1998; Dopson *et al.*, 1999; Dopson *et al.*, 2001; Locock *et al.*, 1999). Even though this overview is not a 'systematic review', still less a 'meta analysis', it goes beyond the usual limited focus on one project. It attempts to create a more comprehensive and non-local body of OB-influenced knowledge, which covers seven studies and 49 cases (involving 1400 interviews) in health care organizations.

There are some methodological problems in comparing the case studies. For example, the extent to which managers' views are reflected in the data varies considerably across the studies, with some focusing almost exclusively on clinical interviewees. Funding constraints may also mean there is pressure to use less resource-intensive research methods. Compare, for example, the reliance on telephone interviewing in the evaluations of Promoting Action on Clinical Effectiveness (PACE) and the Welsh national demonstration projects, with the multiple methods including on-site 'inspections' of the CSAG project, which inevitably affect the depth and quality of data collection. However, despite these differences, we believe that the similarities are so extensive that comparison is possible and that there are common findings that enable us to draw some general conclusions. For example, the two Warwick studies were designed to offer a replication of an earlier acute-sector study within the primary-care setting. The Wales study was conducted explicitly as a continuation and development of the PACE evaluation methods. Our work thus represents a comparative analysis across a grouped family of studies rather than an overview

---

[*] Members of the team are now also based at Imperial College and De Montfort University. Some of the Templeton work draws on a joint project with the Judge Institute of Management at the University of Cambridge (Dawson *et al.*, 1998).

Box 2.1 An overview of research designs and methods

Study	Design	No. of case studies	Face-to-face interviews*	Telephone interviews*	Written questionnaires	Document analysis	Dates
Dopson and Gabbay (1995)	Single stage case studies on four clinical topics	4	58 (RHA and purchasing managers, clinicians and public health)			✓	2 years, 1993–94
Wood et al., (1998a)	Two stages: 1. Overview survey across whole region 2. Case studies, one per clinical topic, selected on evidence of clinical change elicited from first stage	4	71 (mainly front-line clinicians) 48 (mainly clinicians and clinical managers)			✓ ✓	2 years, 1995–97 ,,
Dawson et al., (1998)	Embedded case studies, 2 clinical topics in each of four hospitals	8	256 (clinical staff of various professions and grades)		256 (same group as interviews)	✓	2 years, 1995–97

CSAG (1998) (Gabbay et al.)	Single-stage case-study design, full in 7 sites, telephone and questionnaire (7+6) only in 6	13	250 (front-line clinicians and managers) plus 20 informal interviews with trust and HA managers	321	✓	6 months 1996–97
Hawkins et al. (1999)	Three stages:	38			✓	2 years, 1997–99
	1. Overview across four health authorities on diffusion of innovation		(senior HA managers and GPs)	1317 GPs 256 hospital clinicians		
	2. Overview with same group, concentrated on particular innovations	35				
	3. Case studies on four innovations in primary care	4	40 (GPs and other primary care and physiotherapy staff)		✓	"
Dopson et al. (1999)	Two stages:	16	51		✓	2 years, 1997–98
	Initial round of interviews half-way through project	7 (staff from King's Fund and DoH)	(project team members – managers and clinicians)			

Box 2.1 *cont.*

Box 2.1 *cont.*

Study	Design	No. of case studies	Face-to-face interviews[*]	Telephone interviews[*]	Written questionnaires	Document analysis	Dates
	1. Second round at end of project, using themes elicited during first stage			122 (project team members, other senior managers and clinicians)	150 (front-line clinicians)	✓	"
Locock *et al.* (1999)	Single-stage case studies, after project completion	6	18 (front-line clinicians)	65 (project team members, other senior managers and clinicians, Welsh Office reps)	238 (front-line clinicians)	✓	6 months, 1998–99

* All interviews were in-depth and semi-structured.

across the whole field, and therefore represents only a first step in the process of analytic aggregation. To illustrate the process of aggregation, we use the role of opinion leaders in facilitating a more evidence-based approach to clinical practice as an exemplar.

Theoretical Assumptions and Methodological Issues

Problems encountered in undertaking comparative analysis include the following. Researchers always come with theoretical frameworks, implicit and explicit; this includes positivist, clinical researchers as well as those from more sociological or political perspectives. It is important to stress this, given the tendency to see the clinical research paradigm as value-free and therefore offering a more objective standard of proof. For example, as Wing has noted there is nothing politically neutral, pure and objective about studying, for example, the relationship of race to disease without ever studying racism, or the role of radiation exposure in causing cancer without ever studying the processes of the military-industrial complex that produce the radiation (Wing, 1994).

In the reflexive world of qualitative ethnographic research, the subjectivity of researchers has become a truism – but perhaps precisely because it has become such an undisputed tenet, it may not receive much explicit attention before embarking on each study. There is a temptation to assume that we are all sensitive to the need to be self-aware, so we do not need to discuss it formally as a team. Our two teams include researchers whose backgrounds are in organisational analysis, medical sociology, social policy and public health. None of us would subscribe to a rationalist model of organisational behaviour and generally adopt a political perspective, but would place varying emphasis on the importance of, for example, culture, power and structure in explaining what we find. Indeed, we would probably all use all of those factors at different times, depending on the context we are researching. However, we have not always been very explicit in stating these different theoretical perspectives at the outset, either to each other within each team, or when publishing our results.

It may be important at this stage to note the constraints involved in doing short-term, policy-relevant research commissioned by institutional funders who seek a clear pragmatic message from the results. This may lead to a downplaying – conscious or unconscious – of the complex ambiguities of theory, even though we try to reflect those ambiguities in the research narrative. At a more micro level, individual researchers may attach subtly different meanings to the questions and terms used in interview schedules, even though we are superficially using the same questions. The way we conduct interviews and how far we pursue particular aspects of the interview schedule will also vary. Each of our six overall studies encompassed several separate case studies, which may have been carried out by different researchers. We thus have to cope with intra-study issues of comparability and consistency between the different case studies – although the benefits of having a team of researchers who can provide internal challenge and validation should not be underestimated (see final section).

At an inter-study level, there is also the question of how far we mean the same thing when we use the same terms in our analyses. When both teams describe scientific evidence as 'socially constructed', we needed to be sure that we shared the same underlying interpretation. Even when we attempted to clarify our definitions more explicitly, we used yet more subjective language to explain the definition. In preparing this chapter we have used each other's final reports and published articles as the basis for comparison. Alternatively, we could have gone further back, using each other's individual case-study accounts, or even individual interview data. But, pragmatically, this was not realistic. Even if we had had the time to use each other's interview transcripts, we would still have been left with the problem of different researchers asking the same questions yet possibly probing in terms of a particular preferred theoretical interest or perhaps personal interest, and thereby evoking different responses.

Three other factors affecting comparison are worth mentioning here. The first is the issue of time. A number of questions emerge: were the different case studies longitudinal or not? Even in the case of snapshot studies, was the data collected in one short burst or over weeks or even months? Were the case studies done at the same time, and if not how far had the political and organisational context changed? Were they real-time or retrospective?

The second factor, of profound importance, is the context of each case study, encompassing matters of geography, local organisational arrangements, the pattern of power relationships, local history and tradition, and so on. As we all stress in our own research reports, the importance of context and its interaction with other variables makes it impossible to draw hard and fast general conclusions.

The third factor is also concerned with context, as the Templeton/ Southampton team discovered when it undertook a mutual validation exercise with another research team. The two teams exchanged summarised interview reports and assessed each other's reports while blind to the originating team's interpretations. While gratified to find a good deal of concordance in their reciprocal assessments of the data, there were concerned by several points of substantial difference. Further and more detailed discussion and comparison, however, inevitably led to the agreed conclusion that the original team had 'more correctly' interpreted the data, as they had a great deal more tacit, implicit knowledge about the context and relevant local information gleaned from the study.

Emerging Themes

Our comparison of the seven studies has drawn out several common themes, which we argue demonstrate that low-level patterns emerge from this set of wide-ranging case-study-based research in health care. We do not have space here to do more than list them, and then look at one of them – the role of opinion leaders – in more detail.

- Despite growing acceptance of the principle of evidence-based practice, there is still a weak relationship between the evidence base and clinical behaviour change. Although change is more likely where the evidence is seen as 'strong', it is not in itself sufficient.
- The production of evidence is a social as well as a scientific process. There is no single 'body of evidence' but rather competing bodies of evidence to support many positions. Acceptance of evidence follows a sometimes lengthy process of local challenge, negotiation and adaptation.
- 'Evidence' takes different forms, differentially accepted by individuals, local groups and professional communities. Professions take different views about whether the RCT should be seen as a privileged form of knowledge. Within the perceived hierarchy of knowledge, the relative position relates to the credibility of the source as well as the 'hardness' of the data.
- Although the medical profession generally regards the RCT as the 'gold standard' of evidence, in practice medical behaviour is shaped as much by experience and peer comparison as by scientific evidence from RCTs or other high-quality studies. And as doctors still retain a high degree of professional autonomy and authority over work practices, this attitude translates into organisational clinical policy.
- Specific organisational and social factors shape the flow of knowledge into the field, including: the many professional boundaries

that we found; the role of local clinical groups, together with their learning and change capability; the presence of a local clinical change champion, the support given by senior managers, and the presence of a coherent implementation strategy.

- The role of clinical opinion leaders is complex; expert opinion leaders may be important in the early stages of negotiating the evidence, whilst peer opinion leaders may be more influential during implementation. A crucial factor is the presence of hostile opinion leaders who may undermine the views of the change champions, or may dilute the influence through internecine tensions. The position of the expert in the social and organisational hierarchy could also be an important factor.

- Matters specific to primary care include the non-hierarchical, individualised nature of practice; informational complexity, partly because of the wide range of conditions treated; the part played by social, family, environmental and psychological influences when making clinical decisions; and low levels of multidisciplinary diffusion of changes in practice.

- Evidence in primary care is often scarce, and GPs are sceptical of the transferability of acute-sector RCT findings to primary-care settings. Scientific evidence appears to be only one of a range of critical influences on clinical decision-making. Most GPs seem to feel it could/should have a greater role to play, but do not believe it will ever be the only or dominant influence; indeed they do not want it to be.

- Evidence is also relatively scarce for the practices of nurses and professions allied to medicine, and this has important implications both for the evidence base of a large proportion of clinical work, and for the perception of EBM by the majority of health care professionals.

An Exemplar: The Role of Opinion Leaders

There is ample theoretical reason to suppose opinion leaders are influential in promoting or opposing change, but randomised controlled studies have so far found it hard to demonstrate a significant effect (see the Cochrane review on local opinion leaders, Thomson O'Brien *et al.*, 1999). The evidence from our qualitative studies suggests that there is an effect, but that it is part of a wider process and cannot be seen in isolation from other contextual variables with which it may interact. It should also be noted that the effect is not always 'positive', in the sense of supporting the desired change – the influence of hostile or ambivalent opinion leaders is an important and neglected area, and one that both teams explore.

Our two research teams adopted different terms, with the Warwick team preferring 'champions' or 'product champions', and the Templeton/Southampton team preferring 'opinion leaders'. This gives rise to a number of observations: firstly, it implies that we started with somewhat different theoretical perspectives. The term 'product champion' is rooted more firmly in management studies, especially diffusion of innovation studies, whilst the term 'opinion leader' reflects a more mixed approach stemming from both innovation studies and social influence theory. However, these different perspectives were implicit, and we had probably not been aware of this difference between the two teams until we started to examine the topic in detail across the studies.

Both research teams had in practice explored the issue of hostile reactions among key players; however, the Templeton/Southampton team had explicitly encompassed these within their definition of 'opinion leader', whereas the Warwick team had preferred the term 'product champion' and dealt with hostile stakeholders as a separate issue. It required a trawl through each report or article to pick up possibly relevant material. This perhaps raises a question about how far one can 'systematically' review material when such different terms and definitions are in use, and the reviewer is in part acting as a translator. Different subjective understandings of these terms on the part of each research team (let alone each individual researcher) will have affected the way that questions about opinion leaders were constructed and asked, and the way in which responses were interpreted and categorised.

Furthermore, respondents will also have brought their own subjective understandings to bear. At a broader level, a review of the literature on opinion leaders undertaken by the Templeton/Southampton team has revealed that the problem of inconsistent definitions is widespread and is not confined to health care research (Locock, 2001). It is unlikely that the goal of a single replicable description is realistically achievable; the best we can strive for is to make our definitions more explicit both in designing and reporting our research. And of course the task was made easier in the present overview as the teams were able to discuss and explore their differing assumptions – which could only be tentatively inferred if one were simply reviewing the written data. An important implication here is that reports of such studies should aim to be more explicit about their theoretical basis than they usually are at present.

Despite these differences between the teams, in practice there were strong common findings. Indeed, the issue of different definitions was empirically, as well as methodologically, very important. Subjective understandings amongst respondents of what an opinion leader is or does can differ substantially in each local setting. Both our teams found a spread of very different types and categories of opinion leaders: some were experts, some peers; some were hostile, some very positive; and some had enthusiasm that occasionally went too far. Some had an ambivalent or hidden agenda; some were cynical about what they were doing but did it successfully nonetheless; some were part of the managerial drive towards change, and some acted independently of it:

> Opinion leaders with their own agenda can be damaging. They come forward for a reason – it may be partly out of the goodness of their hearts or an evangelical mission, but they all have vested interests, which may work for you or they may work against you.
>
> (Dopson *et al.*, 1999)

Perceived inconsistencies between what the opinion leader says and what he or she does may have a profound effect on their influence. For example opinion leaders in secondary care sometimes did not follow the same guidelines they were recommending to GPs, signalling that they preferred to rely on their own clinical judgement as a higher form of knowledge. This illustrates the problem of getting a single replicable description to be used in testing opinion leaders as an intervention to achieve change. It also underlines the need to be alert to the fact that the opinion leader whose impact is being tested may not be the only local opinion leader influencing the practitioners concerned. The influence of negative or hostile opinion leaders not formally part of the project may be cancelling out any effect. Ferlie *et al.* (2000) caution against 'the unwritten assumption that innovation is a positive thing'; opinion leaders' opposition to an innovation may in fact be beneficial resistance to an organisationally inappropriate change.

The presence of hostile opinion leaders is one example of the wider problem of isolating other local contextual influences on the change process. The Templeton/ Southampton team (Locock *et al.,* 2001) suggest:

> although the support of opinion leaders is helpful, desirable, and even necessary, it is not itself a sufficient condition for change. It is one piece of a locally unique jigsaw, where evidence, peer comparison,

clinical experience, interpersonal relationships, concerns about the quality of care, managerial action and funding – to name but a few – also need to fit together.

It is important to bear in mind that opinion leadership is a relationship, exercised within that local set of circumstances. As well as the structural or other contextual factors which moderate the relationship, the skills and style of different opinion leaders may affect their ability to persuade others and the dynamic between two individuals (or more) is vital. An opinion leader who works well with one practitioner may fail to make progress with another. Wood *et al.* (1998a) noted that

> where good interpersonal relationships exist there is greater opportunity for modalities of practice to be discussed and a common way forward found. Where this was the case, our evidence suggests practitioners would be better able to respond to information and decide to change practice or not on the basis of it. Surgeons were far more likely to listen to the views of others whom they thought were important and who in turn thought their point of view was important. (p.43)

Locock *et al.* (1999) explore the potential to distinguish between two main categories of supportive opinion leader, which could be described as experts and peers. Inevitably these categories oversimplify, as it is possible to be both a peer and an expert, but one role may be more evident than the other in particular situations. The expert opinion leader is seen as a higher authority (often an academic or consultant) able to explain the evidence and respond convincingly to challenges and debate, or alternatively whose support for the initiative is itself sufficient endorsement. Their role appears particularly important in the initial stages of sowing an idea, endorsing the evidence and translating it into a form acceptable to practitioners, and takes account of their local experience. However, they may be less suited to following through to implementation and may even provoke hostility. Both suites of studies have noted particular ambivalence towards academic experts, who may be felt to be too remote from the concerns of practitioners to persuade them effectively. Ferlie *et al.* (2000) suggest that

> the development of hybrid researcher-practitioner roles (rather than reliance on external scientists) may help. The construction of alliances between researchers and clinicians, where there is feedback

in exchange for the enlisting of patients in trials, may also build up 'ownership' of research findings.

The peer opinion leader, particularly in primary care, is seen as someone who has applied the innovation within their own practice and can give colleagues confidence that they could do it too. They thus have a stronger role in the later stages of practical implementation.

It makes people think 'the ordinary GP can do it. If he can do it perhaps I can'. It's not just the super-efficient, well-known people.

(Dopson *et al.*, 1999)

There is evidence from several of the studies that new peer opinion leaders, who would not previously have been recognised by their colleagues as educationally influential, can be created or identified – provided that they are genuinely credible to their colleagues. The danger of innovators who step too far beyond the current norm to retain their credibility is however a recurring theme. FitzGerald *et al.* (1999) suggest that, especially in primary care, 'to retain their credibility, individual professionals need to continue to practice. One could therefore envisage the development of part-time roles within local contexts.'

There is support from all the studies for the idea that innovation is achieved through a repeated process of social negotiation, adaptation and construction; if this is the case, the role of the opinion leader may be important but deeply embedded within and contingent upon this process. They may act as a catalyst or a mediator, but ultimately the group needs to move forward as a body for professional norms to be reconstructed and real changes in practice to become established. The impact of opinion leaders is therefore shaped both by their intrinsic features (for example, whether they are experts or peers) and by extrinsic factors – for example, how the opinion leaders interact with the set of emerging themes such as local professional boundaries as discussed above.

The complex roles of different kinds of opinion leaders at different stages in the innovation process must be borne in mind in planning future research, and in trying to understand the results from available research. Greater attention also needs to be paid to describing the impact of other extrinsic contextual variables in each case. Only then can we begin to understand how far opinion leaders themselves are exercising an influence as opposed to other factors, and to what extent their influence has been moderated by particular local circumstances.

CONCLUDING DISCUSSION AND STRATEGIC IMPLICATIONS

Moving towards Comparative Analysis

One of the indicators of quality advanced earlier was the production of a body of knowledge of some scale and coherence which could produce more general forms of knowledge than single case studies. We suggested that one way forward was to conduct a comparative analysis over a family cluster of existing studies, particularly when the teams involved had been working to a similar agenda and in a similar way. This chapter has attempted to undertake such an analysis across a set of seven studies, taking the opinion leader theme as a particular example. It is interesting that the conclusions of this overview are more supportive of the role played by the clinical opinion leader than the Cochrane review of RCT-based studies. This raises the intriguing possibility – if confirmed in other case studies – that findings may in part be dependent on methods. It will be interesting to see whether other teams of OB researchers also find it useful to band together to produce other such overviews.

Why has OB Work Not Maximised its Impact?

Finally, we return to some more strategic issues about HSR research. Stewart (1999) argues that the results of some 15 years or so of work in OB HSR have so far been disappointing; the discipline has failed to generate a coherent knowledge base or a sophisticated body of theory. It has failed to influence policy to any substantial degree, and implementation strategies continue to be devised without reflecting the available lessons from the considerable body of research into change management. While much UK health services OB work was produced in the late 1980s (in the wake of the introduction of general management), this momentum has not been sustained in the 1990s and the field has, if anything, slipped back.

Why this disappointing outcome? Perhaps some of the causes are external to the discipline but there are also some internal reasons for this disappointment. Certainly OB fits badly with the dominant research paradigm within HSR, although opportunities may now be emerging as earlier rationalistic approaches to R&D have largely failed to produce convincing findings or solutions in the field of organisational change. But there is also a need for substantial internal disciplinary development. There has been an over-reliance on localised, under-theorised and over-applied work. The methods have often been opaque and often poorly described. The core constituency of NHS general and clinical managers who should have been advocating the need for OB research has not been engaged, and has not lobbied for a long term R&D agenda.

A Shift to Overviews?

While we have not adopted the full paradigm of systematic reviews, we have undertaken a preliminary overview of a related cluster of case studies of the implementation of EBM. We would argue that comparison of findings across the studies enable us to detect low-level patterns, which can be generalised to some extent. Yet the generalisations we can make are often, paradoxically, about the particularity of each context, and the need to be sensitive to an array of local circumstances in understanding how change initiatives are likely to be received. They are not the kind of generalisations that will uncover a set of predictable, reliable levers for change.

If OB researchers in health care can make one contribution to the current debate surrounding change management in the NHS, it would be precisely to challenge the dominant thinking that if only we can design the right studies, and look hard enough and long enough, we will come up with the 'right' formula for achieving change. Even though the Cochrane Effective Practice and Organisation of Care Group acknowledge the complexity of the variables affecting change, they are still ultimately seeking a mechanism or set of mechanisms to solve the complexity, to cut through it and provide a well-ordered answer. The contribution of OB is to re-state the inevitability of complexity, to encourage managers and clinicians to accept it and be sensitive to it, and to change the NHS's thinking away from technical/rational solutions. But above all it is to try and help us to understand the nature of that complexity, not only as an academic endeavour in its own right, but as a means to better management of health services.

It would be wrong to conclude on a negative note as there are also strategic opportunities for OB research within HSR. Service Delivery and Organisation research is now a field of growing policy-level import-ance nationally in the UK, where all these studies were based. The question of how research-based evidence diffuses within complex health care organisations is now high up the national agenda, and there is increasing recognition that the linear models of technology transfer originally adopted are misleading. The question of behaviour within complex organisations is re-emerging once rationalistic and linear interventions have been tried and once again found wanting. The world of HSR has recently discovered that the implementation phase can indeed be problematic (and this a mere 25 years after classic studies within social science!) (Pressman and Wiladavsky, 1973; Alford, 1975).

Do we need to be undertaking a very different style of research in this field? The lack of emphasis on the development in NHS R&D may well lead to disengagement from practitioners in the field, and a failure to secure research impact or payback (except when measured in narrow academic terms such as number of refereed papers produced). This could eventually lead to erosion of political and then financial support for NHS R&D. To avoid this outcome, we need to find ways of conducting Research that lead to a much greater concern with Development and which establish much stronger links between the two sets of activities.

In particular, we need to develop methods that are meaningful and accessible to those that we are trying to influence, rather than construct a highly technical and inaccessible discourse. And yet we have argued that such work should be more self-conscious of its theoretical base. This suggests the need to consider a wider range of experiments with such methods as action research, formative feedback and the 'reflective practitioner' model. We need to find ways of broadening the inter-actions between researchers and practitioners, perhaps by establishing hybrid roles or mixed careers, by making the theoretical frameworks understandable to practitioners, and by persuading managers to sup-port OB research. For example, a clinician who has become a PCG Clinical Governance Lead may be trying to develop that organisation. He or she may well find that this becomes a topic for an action research style PhD and hence go on to develop – or encourage among others – a secondary research role. This would be particularly germane if he/she recognises the relevance of the current debates on the role of, say, opinion leaders or linear diffusion of evidence-based practice.

It is by getting practice into research that we may succeed in getting research into practice. Perhaps the most strategic contribution of the

OB tradition – reflecting its own history and orientation – is that it can provide models and tools that can facilitate this wider shift within HSR in alliance with like-minded colleagues. It is not enough to produce high quality knowledge: it should (in Argyris' terms) also be 'actionable knowledge' of meaning and relevance to the wider world of practice.

References

Alford, R. (1975) *Health Care Politics* (London: University of Chicago Press).
Argyris, C. (1999) 'Some Unintended Consequences of Rigorous Research', in *On Organisational Learning* (Oxford: Basil Blackwell).
Becher, A. (1989) *Academic Tribes and Territories* (Milton Keynes: Open University Press).
Bero, L., Grilli, R., Grimshaw, J., Harvey, E., Oxman, A. and Thomson, M.A. (1998) 'Closing the Gap between Research and Practice – an Overview of Systematic Reviews of Interventions to Promote Implementation of Research Findings by Health Professionals', in A. Haines and A. Donald (eds), *Getting Research Findings into Practice* (London: BMJ Books): 27–35.
Black, N. (1994) 'Why We Need Qualitative Research', *Journal of Epidemiology and Community Health*, 48: 425–6.
Bowling, A. (1997) *Research Methods in Health* (Buckingham: Open University Press).
Campbell, D.T. and Stanley, J.C. (1963) *Experimental and Quasi-experimental Designs for Research* (Boston: Houghton Mifflin).
Chalmers, I. (1998) 'Unbiased, Relevant, and Reliable Assessments in Health Care', *British Medical Journal*, 317: 1167–8.
Clinical Standards Advisory Group (1998) *Clinical Effectiveness* (London: Clinical Standards Advisory Group.
Dawson, S., Sutherland, K., Dopson, S. and Miller, R. in association with Law, S. (1998) *The Relationship between R&D and Clinical Practice in Primary and Secondary Care: Cases of Adult Asthma and Glue Ear in Children*, final report (Judge Institute of Management Studies, University of Cambridge, and Said Business School, University of Oxford).
Department of Health (2000) The evaluation of methods to promote the implementation of research findings: http://www.doh.gov.uk/ntrd/rd/implem/index.htm
Dopson, S. and Gabbay, J. (1995) *Getting Research into Practice and Purchasing (GRiPP)* (Oxford Region, NHS Executive).
Dopson, S., Gabbay, J. and Locock, L. with Chambers, D. (1999) *Evaluation of the PACE Programme: final report* (Templeton College, University of Oxford and Wessex Institute for Health Research and Development, University of Southampton).
Dopson, S., Chambers, D., Locock, L. and Gabbay, J. (forthcoming) 'Implementation of Eevidence-based Medicine – Evaluation of the PACE

Programme (Promoting Action on Clinical Effectiveness)', *Journal of Health Service and Policy Research.*

Ferlie, E., FitzGerald, L. and Wood, M. (2000) 'Getting Evidence into Clinical Practice? An Organisational Behaviour Perspective', in *Journal of Health Services Research and Policy* 5(2): 96–102.

FitzGerald, L., Ferlie, E., Wood, M. and Hawkins, C. (1999) 'Evidence into Practice? An Exploratory Analysis of the Interpretation of Evidence', in A. Mark and S. Dopson (eds), *Organisational Behaviour in Health Care* (London: Macmillan – now Palgrave).

Hawkins, C., FitzGerald, L. and Ferlie, E. (1999) *Achieving Change Within Primary Care: Final Project Report* (University of Warwick: CCSC, 1999).

Heron, J. (1996) *Co-operative Inquiry: Research into the Human Condition* (Thousand Oaks: Sage).

Kimberly, J. (1981) 'Managerial Innovation' in P. Nystrom and W.H. Starbuck (eds), *Handbook of Organisational Design* (Oxford: Oxford University Press).

Latour, B. (1987) *Science in Action* (Cambridge, Mass: Harvard University Press).

Lewin, K. (1951) *Field Theory in Social Science* (New York: Harper & Row).

Locock, L., Chambers, D., Surender, R., Dopson, S. and Gabbay, J. (1999) *Evaluation of the Welsh Clinical Effectiveness Initiative National Demonstration Projects: Final Report* (Templeton College, University of Oxford and Wessex Institute for Health Research and Development, University of Southampton).

Locock, L., Dopson, S., Chambers, D. and Gabbay, J. (forthcoming) 'Understanding the role of opinion Leaders in getting Clinical Effectiveness Evidence into practice', *Social Science in Medicine.*

Mark, A. and Dopson S. (eds) (1999) *Organisational Behaviour in Health Care* (London: Macmillan – now Palgrove).

Murphy, E., Dingwall, R., Greatbatch, D., Parker, S. and Watson, P. (1998) 'Qualitative Research Methods in Health Technology Assessment: A Review of the Literature', *Health Technology Assessment*, 2: 16.

NCCSDO (National Co-ordinating Centre for Service Delivery and Organisation R&D) http://www.lshtm.ac.uk/php/hsru/sdo/

NHS CRD (National Health Service Centre for Reviews and Dissemination) (1996) *Undertaking Systematic Reviews of Research on Effectiveness* (University of York: NHSCRD).

NHS CRD (National Health Service Centre for Reviews and Dissemination) (1999) *Effective Health Care – Getting Evidence into Practice*, 5(1) (University of York: NHSCRD).

Oakley, A. (1998) 'Experimentation and Social Interventions: A Forgotten but Important History', *British Medical Journal*, 317: 1239–42.

Oxman, A.D., Thomson, M. and Davis, D.A. *et al.* (1995) 'No Magic Bullets – A Systematic Review of 102 Trials of Interventions to Improve Professional Practice', *Canadian Medical Association Journal*, 153: 1423–31.

Oxman, A. and Flottorp, S. (1998) 'An Overview of Strategies to Promote Implementation of Evidence Based Health Care', in C. Silagy and A. Haines (eds), *Evidence Based Practice in Primary Care* (London: BMJ Books): 91–109.

42   *Evidence-Based Medicine and Organisational Change*

Pawson, R. and Tilley, N. (1997) *Realistic Evaluation* (London: Sage).
Popay, J., Rogers, A. and Williams, G. (1998) 'Rationale and Standards for the Systematic Review of Qualitative Literature in Health Services Research', *Qualitative Health Research*, 8(3): 341–51.
Pressman, J. and Wildavsky, A. (1973) *Implementation* (Berkeley: University of California Press) Shortell, S., Gillies, R., Anderson, D., Morgan Erickson, K. and Mitchell, J. (1996) *Remaking Health Care in America* (San Francisco: Jossey Bass).
Stewart, R. 'Foreword' in Mark, A. and Dopson, S. (1999) *Organisational Behaviour in Health Care* (London: Macmillan).
Thomson O'Brien, M.A., Oxman, A. D., Haynes, R.B., Davis, D.A. Freemantle, N. and Harvey, E. L. (1999) *Local Opinion Leaders: effects on Professional Practice and Health Care Outcomes (Cochrane Review)* in The Cochrane Library, Issue 3 (Oxford: Update Software).
Van de Ven, A., Polley, D., Garud, R. and Venkataraman, S. (2000) *The Innovation Journey* (Oxford: Oxford University Press).
Wing, S. (1994) 'Limits of epidemiology', *Medicine and Global Survival*, 1: 74–86.
Wood, M., Ferlie, E. and FitzGerald, L. (1998a) *Achieving Change in Clinical Practice: Scientific, Organisational and Behavioural Processes* (University of Warwick: CCSC).
Wood, M., Ferlie, E. and FitzGerald, L. (1998b) 'Achieving Clinical Behaviour Change: A Case of Becoming Indeterminate', *Social Science and Medicine*, 47(11): 1729–38.

3 Policy Futures for UK Health: Examining the Future Health Workforce

Charlotte Dargie and Sandra Dawson

INTRODUCTION

This chapter takes the title of the symposium, 'Reflections on the Future' literally. It draws on a research project established to explore future trends and issues in population health and health care in the United Kingdom forward to 2015. It explores how futures thinking can aid policy development in the health sector and illustrates through a discussion on workforce issues how this might be done.

A considerable body of work now explores health futures. Consultations held by the World Health Organisation (WHO) have raised the level of debate and stimulated both methodological discussions and the policy relevance of forward thinking (for useful reviews of the health futures field see the special issue of *World Health Statistics Quarterly*, 1994, and Garrett and Bezold, 1995). In the health sector the Canadian and Australian governments have both carried out futures exercises. In Wales in the 1980s 'Health and Social Care 2010' was established by the Welsh Health Planning Forum to link national strategy with local health care strategies.

Many of the various UK policy institutes and think tanks have carried out recent futures exercises of one form or another including the Institute for Public Policy Research (IPPR), the King's Fund and the Public Management Foundation. The NHS Confederation conducted a futures exercise for the 50th anniversary celebrations of the NHS in 1998. The resulting 'Madingley Scenarios' produced two alternative futures for the NHS entitled 'Find My Way' (a system focused around individual choice) and 'Trust Their Guidance' (a professional-led system) (Ling, 1999). There is a national, government-wide futures programme entitled 'Foresight', from which the health care panel recently published a consultation document on future health care (Foresight Healthcare Panel, 2000).

The aim of this chapter is to propose futures thinking as a useful tool for policy-makers and commentators in challenging existing assumptions about the way population health and health care services are organised, planned and delivered. The chapter introduces futures thinking and describes the design and method of a policy futures project. It then presents some summary findings on the health workforce and draws on the recent NHS Plan to illustrate the relevance of futures thinking and policy analysis. Finally, we suggest how work might be used and developed.

APPLYING FUTURES THINKING TO HEALTH POLICY

It is also worth restating the social, economic and political importance of health. Health is defined as a social 'good', which enables individuals to function in society. It is also defined subjectively by individuals. Health embraces treatment and care, and the prevention of the causes of ill-health in society. The director of the World Health Organisation (WHO), Dr Gro Harlem Brundtland, recently highlighted the importance of health in securing economic growth and the elimination of poverty. Health can be viewed both as a determinant and an outcome of societies. Developments in demography, society, technology and genetic research are forcing pertinent questions to be asked about opportunities for health and providing adequate future health care systems for all.

Health policy is an important political issue in the UK, particularly in terms of the state of the National Health Service (NHS). It is a subject that provokes huge public interest. Politicians know the political significance of their 'stewardship' of the NHS and the national media reinforce these concepts by bringing issues to national attention. The government is also responsible when it makes electoral pledges such as cutting hospital waiting lists that drive resource allocation and operational matters within the service. It is significant that the recent NHS Plan launched by the UK government on investment and reform of the health service was presented to parliament by the Prime Minister, Tony Blair, rather than the Health Secretary, Alan Milburn. The Prime Minister has described daily meetings in his own schedule on health in the period running up to the launch of the plan.

The international community regards the NHS as a strong model for health care organisation; the UK was recently ranked 18th in the world on health-system performance by WHO (WHO, 2000). Whilst the

NHS has remained a centralised organisation to date, the full impact of devolution, where health policy as well as organisation of health services is part of the devolved responsibilities, has yet to be felt.

Futures thinking and futures studies cover a wide range of subjects, approaches and objectives (see Coyle, 1997, for a review of futures studies). Techniques include economic forecasting, the aggregation of opinion, analysing trend data, and scenario planning. Organisations are increasingly interested in using futures thinking, particularly the use of scenario planning in helping them anticipate the future (Ringland *et al.*, 1999). Taken at face value the idea of forward thinking or prediction does not sit easily with the world of academia whose primary function is about explaining the world we live in today using theoretical approaches that can be tested with evidence. How can the future be explored when it has not yet happened, and how can it be tested? It is beneficial to view futures thinking as a set of techniques with which to explore commonly-held assumptions, debates and practices. It is also beneficial to view futures studies as having a range of purposes. In a review of national futures studies in the health sector, Garrett (1994) identifies views that are held about the future and about the purpose of futures studies.

First, it is assumed that futures studies are carried out in order to predict. Policy-makers may then be sceptical about the ability to foresee developments in health, other than demographic and epidemiological trends that might be reasonably discerned from projections, or 'conditional statements of what might be expected if certain assumptions hold' (Joshi, 1996: 222). Second, it is assumed that futures studies are carried out for planning purposes. The activity of 'planning' within the context of UK government and particularly in the health sector went distinctly off the agenda during the 1980s and early 1990s. Planning might be said to be making a return to the UK health sector with the election of the Labour government in 1997 and its modernisation agenda for public services; but attempts to plan for a single future is unlikely to succeed in health.

Garrett points out that futures studies are likely to be carried out for a number of purposes, which may relate to the assumptions people hold about the future. For some the future is predictable and largely determined by current forces. In this context in health we can learn much from studying long-term trends in disease patterns. For others the future is unpredictable and something that cannot be foreseen. In health, we might focus on the promises of human genetics research, which may fundamentally alter how we understand and treat disease in the future. The future is likely to be made up of both these 'probabilities' and 'possibilities'. So, futures studies can aid policy development by both highlighting the 'big picture' in health and also by prompting debate about what factors might change the status quo.

THE POLICY FUTURES FOR UK HEALTH PROJECT

The *Policy Futures for UK Health* project was set up by The Nuffield Trust and the Judge Institute of Management Studies to examine UK health futures. Its purpose was both to produce reports on future trends and issues for UK health, and to prompt policy debate about the issues. An 'environmental scan' was conducted in order to examine the wide range of factors that impact on population health and health care services in the UK. Ten subject areas or 'scan categories' were identified as likely to have an impact on health and health care in the future. The ten categories were the global context, the physical environment, demography, science and technology, economy and finance, social trends, organisation and management, workforce, public expectations and ethics.

The time horizon chosen was 2015, which reflected two concerns; first, that the issues be longer-term than current policy thinking, which is dominated by five-year electoral cycles, and second that the period in question was both imaginable and confinable. Looking back fifteen years shows what can change in that period. Those who are engaged in developing population projections agree that longer-term analysis becomes unstable, and less meaningful due to the range of possibilities (Shaw, 1994 and 1998: 43–9; Armitage and Scott, 1998: 281–97).

Reports covering each of the scan categories were commissioned and the results of the scan were debated and discussed by the research team, the reports' authors, members of the Nuffield Trust and an appointed advisory group. From here a draft policy report, which focused on the policy implications of the scan, was produced in 1999 for public consultation and launched at a policy workshop attended by more than 70 senior health policy-makers who debated future issues using the project findings. In 2000 a revised policy report, which summarised the work to date, was published (Dargie, Dawson and Garside, 2000).

EXAMINING THE HEALTH WORKFORCE

To illustrate our approach, we now focus on examining the health workforce, one aspect of the policy futures exercise. Approximately one million people work in the NHS, which accounts for roughly one in 20 of the United Kingdom's (UK) working population. They account for approximately 70 per cent of the NHS budget. The health workforce includes medical and dental staff, nursing and midwifery staff, professional and technical staff, management staff, administrative staff, ambulance staff, ancillary and maintenance staff, general medical practitioners, practice staff and private-sector nurses. Nurses account for almost half of the NHS salary bill. The health workforce is undergoing significant change in the work that is undertaken, how that work is organised, and who is doing it.

The Changing World of Work

Before discussing more specific health workforce issues, it is relevant for a futures perspective to outline the main drivers and the key issues within the world of work more generally. In terms of the context in which the health workforce operates, technological change, demographics and political and economic developments will influence the health workforce. Information and communication technology is changing the work we do and how we do it. Technological change may influence where we work with increasing possibilities for working at home and also developments in travel and work possibilities whilst travelling. Some futures thinkers suggest that we will be working fewer hours each day because of improved communication (The Henley Centre, 1998) (although similar projections in the past have so far been proved wrong).

Two established macroeconomic trends that affect the UK workforce and look set to continue are the shift from manufacturing to services, and the growing flexibility of organisations and of the workforce. These trends may seem peripheral to the considerations of the NHS workforce; however, there are some possible implications. In the future the health professions will have to compete for recruits with an increasing range of interesting and well-paid professions in other sectors. Some of the literature on future workforce issues highlights the rigidity of health service careers that might make medicine or nursing less attractive than other career paths in the future. One converse trend is that, as the insecurity of work becomes an issue across the service and manufacturing sectors, health careers – such as the medical profession – that continue to have relatively secure tenure, might be considered more attractive than other, less secure careers. The issue of flexible working is particularly relevant in primary care where an increasing proportion of GPs are women who are more likely to require career breaks or part-time work during their careers.

Looking across, a summary of future labour-market trends in Great Britain includes the following (statistical trends are calculated for great Britain, not the whole UK):

- The labour force (those aged 16 or over in employment or unemployed) is projected to increase slowly in the future, reaching 29.8 million by spring 2011 (there are no official projections beyond 2011 because of uncertainty).
- Of the expected rise of 1.7 million, women account for 1.3 million. As a result, women are projected to make up 46.1 per cent of the total labour force in 2011, compared with 44.2 per cent in 1997.
- The labour force will be a little older on average in 2011 than in 1997. The overall activity rate (the percentage of the population of different age/sex groups in the labour force) for those of working age is projected to increase slightly in the future.
- Economic activity rates for women are projected to increase at all ages above 20 between 1997 and 2011. Slight falls are projected over the same period in activity rates for men at ages over 25. Activity rates projected for men remain higher than those for women at all working ages.   (Armitage and Scott, 1998)

Women are taking a rising share of jobs, the share of jobs occupied by full-time employees is falling, the self-employed and part-timers in the workforce are increasing, there is increasing flexibility of workers and work, and there is greater importance of the informal economy – caring, home and the community. These features characterise the UK labour market.

The nature of work is also changing. There are no jobs for life, there is increasing diversity of work and work roles, workers are becoming less inclined to have a secure 'place' within the workforce because jobs are changing, and there is more flexibility in work with tele-working and working from home. There are positive and negative effects of change. Overall, increasing hours spent at work and reduced job security across the workforce are causes for anxiety, insecurity and stress. Linked to these changes is the increasing reliance on workers to plan and manage their own careers. Employers are no longer to be relied upon for planning and managing an individual's career and developing workers' skills. Whilst skills and education are becoming more important to the workforce, responsibility for acquiring these skills and attributes lies with the worker.

A significant factor for the future of work are inequalities between those who are able to keep up with the pace of change, the skills required and the demands of work, and those who are left behind (Booth and Arulampalam, 1997). A *Time* magazine article in 1995 entitled 'A New Divide between Haves and Have Nots?' looked at the pay differentials between the computer literate and those not computer literate (Ratan, 1995). There are disadvantages predicted for those who do not have the IT and communication skills required in future work (Handy, 1984). In a study of today's managers, conducted jointly by the Institute of Management and the University of Manchester Institute of Science and Technology (UMIST) it was found that amongst the issues that managers were concerned about for the future was employability (Worrall and Cooper, 1998). The downside of the fast pace of change and development in the world of organisations and work is that, for those people who are excluded, they become relatively disadvantaged the longer they are out of work and privy to the changes and the skills and training that organisations offer. Education, benefits, pensions and taxation are ways in which government can prevent the spread of inequalities between the technology 'haves' and the technology 'have nots' (Bayliss, 1998).

An important related social issue is the body of work that is looking at the health effects of work, through, for example, addressing the effect of unemployment on health (West and Sweeting, 1996), the effect of future work life on health (Theorell, 1997), and the health and social effects of reduced job security for particular groups of workers (Ferrie *et al.*, 1998; Robinson, 1998). Finally, a relevant future question is what will 'work' mean to us in the future, both as workers and employers? On the one hand work appears to be consuming more of our lives with the increased participation of women and shorter career breaks for women with families, and also the growth of convenience food, nursing homes, and childcare. Conversely, work is becoming less important for people, and will become less so in the future, as we are defined by factors outside the paid work that we do (Handy, 1984). An illustrative example of the latter comes from British Medical Association (BMA) studies, which have found that young doctors are far less likely to see medicine as a vocation than their elder counterparts, and wish to combine their career with family and leisure time (BMA, 1995a, b).

A Europe-wide assessment of changes in work and their consequences corroborates many of the issues outlined here. The main changes in work are identified as: changes in economies (the pace of change at economic, political and social level), changes in enterprise structures (new forms of employment, with particular developments in 'flexibility' – flexibility in organisation, flexible working hours, flexible working practices and flexibility in competence and skill of personnel), new job content (increasing mental and social content rather than muscular and manual), competence demands (increasing psychosocial competence required), and changes in the work environment and conditions of work (ageing and segregation of the workforce, time pressures at work such as longer working hours and increasing unconventional working hours, information technology with its positive and negative effects, and hazards such as stress) (Rantanen, 1999).

POLICY ISSUES FOR THE FUTURE HEALTH WORKFORCE

These broad developments in the changing world of work have relevance for the health workforce. Technological change which leads to increased home working, shorter working hours and the expectation of literacy in information technology might affect recruitment in the health sector as the skilled workforce has stronger alternative career opportunities. Other developments in science and technology such as human genetic research and advances in medical technology have the potential to change our understanding of health and medicine, and consequently how to monitor and treat patients.

In 1997 the editor of the *British Medical Journal* (*BMJ*), Richard Smith suggested that information technology and consumerism would transform health care worldwide (Smith, 1997). In 1999 the *BMJ* published a special issue on the impact of new technologies in medicine. There are developments in surgical techniques; in tele-medicine or tele-health, which allow consultation and procedures to be carried out remotely from the patient; the impact of information technology on how patient information is recorded and utilised; evidence-based medicine; managing data across the different components of the health system; and the development of entirely new services such as on-line and telephone services as part of NHS Direct.

Changing technology is probably the main force driving the substitution of health care resources. This is because new treatments, procedures and diagnostic techniques allow conditions to be managed in different settings by different staff.

(Hensher *et al.*, 1999: 1127)

Medical technologies push treatment out of the district general hospital and into primary-care settings and more dispersed, specialist hospitals (Wilson, 1999).

The increased participation of women in the labour market also raises questions about the continuing validity of traditional career structures and recruitment planning. Part-time working, flexible working hours and career breaks for parents may conflict with traditional models such as the independent contractor in general practice and the intensive training period for full-time house doctors. Continuing skill acquisition in the wider labour market is increasingly becoming the responsibility of the worker rather than the employer, and this may not sit easily with the way institutions and professional bodies presently control up-front recruitment and training for health professionals.

Social change is resulting in a diversity of household and family structures, which may be relevant to the health workforce. Demographic trends are showing an increasing proportion of divorce, step-families and also of single-person households. With more women working there is a changing balance of household income. For those in work, and particularly for those in professional occupations, more time is being spent at work, which has its own material rewards and also strains. For those who are unemployed there is the opposite problem of having time but no income to be able to participate in material rewards or to engage in skill acquisition in order to regain employment (Pahl, 1999).

The ageing population and its effect on the demand for health and social care services is probably the most significant demographic trend in the UK population forward to 2015. The government recently responded to the Royal Commission on Long-Term Care stating that nursing care wherever it was provided would be funded as part of the NHS but personal care in nursing homes would be separate and subject to means-testing. For the workforce there is an additional issue here, which is that as the population is ageing, so too are sections of the health workforce that might not be replaced. Attention has been focused on the ageing nursing population (Buchan *et al.*, 1998) and, in general practice, the projected retirement of a significant cohort of Asian doctors over the next twenty years that is not being replaced by later generations (*Health Service Journal*, 3 December 1998).

Looking further afield, globalisation is changing people's expectations of work. The expansion of multinational corporations with mobile capital and improved communications means labour is also expected to be mobile. Where there is competition, there is likely to be less security of employment for those economies that have higher labour costs. For health, globalisation is having a significant effect, including the push towards a global perspective on health and global policy-making on health whilst at the same time a focus on solving local health issues from within the local community.

Finally, political changes have implications for the future of the health workforce. With devolution, there is increasing responsibility for local decision making in the health sector, with implications for national workforce planning where it still exists. At the same time, despite Wales, Scotland and Northern Ireland having responsibility for their own health services, the NHS has traditionally been a centralised organisation with tensions arising between decision-making at the national level and local and regional management. Devolution presents the opportunity for policy learning across the devolved systems. At the same time the European Union single market and working-time directive may mean the convergence of health systems in Europe, including staffing and regulation of staffing. Already the working-time directive is having a direct impact on the health workforce: doctors' working hours have to be reduced from the current 56 to a 48–hour week by 2012; and a European directive on the mutual recognition of specialist qualifications was accepted in 1993.

In the following section some of these developments are brought together to consider some key policy issues for the future health workforce. Of necessity, the examples are illustrative rather than comprehensive and examples commonly relate, where specific, to the two largest groups within the health workforce, medical and nursing staff. However, the trends are pertinent to the whole health workforce. To illustrate how future trends and issues relate to current policy, evidence is taken from with the government's recently published 10–year plan for the NHS (Department of Health, 2000).

HOW SUSTAINABLE IS CENTRAL WORKFORCE PLANNING IN THE HEALTH SECTOR?

The sustainability of workforce planning for doctors and nurses is questioned by the rapidly changing work context and changing patterns of participation in the labour market. Questions are raised about the future recruitment of professional and non-professional staff in the health sector because of developments in flexible working and favourable terms and conditions in other parts of the service sector. For the future, an important public policy question is what are the comparative attractions for skilled people to work in the NHS as opposed to other occupations? Workforce planning currently takes place at the aggregate level for individual professional groups with committees estimating likely future demand for staff numbers within the NHS and controlling supply through training places at medical schools and nursing colleges, which are publicly funded. The UK currently operates with a shortage of doctors, with overseas-trained staff meeting demand. The Medical Workforce Standing Advisory Committee (1997) recommended that the annual medical student intake be increased by 1000 by the year 2005, a 20 per cent increase on present levels of 5000 students. Future demand for doctors is estimated to continue along the same path.

There has been debate about how much the UK relies on overseas-trained doctors, with some commentators suggesting that we should look outside the UK for our extra doctors. In their recent review of the physician workforce, Maynard and Walker (1998) propose both the substitution of physicians by other staff and migration as policy options to deal with physician shortage. Strong ethical arguments state that it is wrong to draw on overseas-trained doctors from developing countries to meet demand in the UK (*The Independent*, 26 October 1998). About 76 per cent of doctors in the NHS are from the UK, according to the Medical Workforce Standing Advisory Committee (MWSAC).

Nursing shortages have been in evidence since before the establishment of the NHS (Buchan *et al.*, 1998). Since 1996, workforce planning for non-medical professions has been the responsibility of local educational consortia covering groups of health authorities and Trusts, with an overview by the NHS Executive (Dowie and Langman, 1999). With current problems of nursing shortages in certain areas of the country and certain specialisms, a return to centralised planning has been proposed (Buchan, 1998). Fewer nurses are registering and the nursing workforce is becoming older. By the millennium it was projected that almost half the nursing workforce in the UK would be aged over 40 (Buchan *et al.*, 1998; Smith and Seccombe, 1998). The overall impression is that there is not much slack in the nursing system, and that nursing is becoming an increasingly unattractive career for young women. For ethnic minority nurses, racial discrimination and equal opportunities for senior nursing grades was recognised as a cause for concern in the early 1990s. The future participation of ethnic minority nurses in a system without equal opportunities has been questioned (Cortis and Rinomhota, 1996). A report from the Institute for Employment Studies suggests that family-friendly policies are the solution to recruitment and retention problems in nursing, but points out that few nurses are benefiting from them now.

One of the most significant trends in the GP labour market is the growing proportion of women GPs, which has had the effect of reducing average hours of work both through the likelihood that women will take career breaks and that they work part-time. One of the consequences is that traditional GP employment arrangements are unsuitable, such as the commitment to partnership in a practice and the poorer opportunities for those not securing a partnership. These factors are particularly significant since over half of medical graduates are now women (Young and Leese, 1999). The number of women doctors in hospitals is also increasing, reaching a third of medical staff in hospitals in 1998 (Dowie and Langman, 1999). A review from the National Primary Care Research and Development Centre at the University of Manchester advocates better retention and deployment of existing labour in response to current trends, which contrasts with the recommendations of the Medical Workforce Standing Advisory Committee on increasing medical student intake (Young and Leese, 1999).

The NHS Plan states that there will be 7500 more consultants and 2000 more GPs, 20000 extra nurses and 6500 extra therapists and 1000 more medical school places by 2004. These increases will come from extra training and medical school places, and in the interim international recruitment will be used to fill current supply shortages. In April 2000 the government published its review of workforce planning, which proposed that in place of the various committees representing different specialties, a unified system of local boards led by local management would determine workforce requirements for all staff, medical and non-medical, with a regional and a national tier – a 'National Workforce Development Board' chaired by the NHS Chief Executive. These developments seem to reflect growing service-led pressure on the traditional boundaries between the various professional and non-professional groupings that comprise the health workforce and these are considered next.

CHANGING ROLES FOR THE HEALTH WORKFORCE

An important policy issue for the future health workforce is the issue of roles – who does what to whom, how and where within the health sector. Health-service reform as well as technological innovation is changing what health professionals do, and in what setting. There are important issues here about professional demarcation, regulation and education and training. Relating back to our earlier discussion of 'probabilities' and 'possibilities' in terms of futures analysis, the potential of human genetics research may be to alter fundamentally organisational structures and roles in health. For example, primary care could be the main site for routine genetic testing carried out by nurse practitioners rather than the traditional practice of diagnosis and treatment by the general practitioner along with referral to the local hospital. On the other hand, one could argue that it is the preservation of professional roles in health that has been the more important trend since the establishment of the NHS and one that is likely to continue for the next ten to fifteen years.

Organisational restructuring is sometimes proposed as the driver of change with changing work roles the consequence. However, policy shifts, technology change and cost might themselves be driving organisational change more than the autonomous shift in health care delivery and organisational design. Like many trends and developments in health, these factors are interrelated. Technology and cost would seem to be clear first-order drivers, but they too are the outcome and consequence of organisational and societal developments. An editorial in the *British Journal of General Practice* (Baker, 1997) contemplated the unlikely survival of the GP as a personal doctor, citing the current organisational development of general practice as a movement against the small-scale, personal care offered in the traditional model. One recent example of a shift in service delivery is NHS Direct where over 15000 qualified nurses are now operating as direct respondents to calls from the general public.

Broader societal changes are affecting what health workers do, and what issues they have to deal with. There is growing acceptance and understanding of the social, economic and environmental determinants of population health. Consequently, health services need to be redesigned to tackle these factors. There are calls for primary-care practitioners to take a population view of health, rather than an individual patient view (Dixon, 1998), which fits with the current policy shift towards tackling broad health indicators at the local level and reducing national population health inequalities. Health Action Zones tackle health issues with a range of local organisations. Today's GPs have to deal with a range of health problems, calling for specialist training in certain areas, for example drugs (Albery *et al.*, 1996), alcohol (Albery *et al.*, 1997) and mental health (Kerwick *et al.*, 1997; Sainsbury's Centre, 1997; Stanley and Manthorpe, 1997; Goldberg, 1998). One of the consequences is shifting professional roles. To date, the most significant change has been the expansion of nursing roles. Easing pressure on doctor workloads is cited as a key factor behind this change but nurses are also carrying out new roles in reorganised nurse-led care. Policy shifts also lead to changing roles such as with the Department of Health report on changing childbirth (1993) (Read and Shewan, 1998).

There have been significant policy developments in this area in the last year. The first report from the Future Healthcare Workforce Project in 1996 was met with some controversy in proposing generic training elements and new work roles (University of Manchester, 1996). More recently, the president of the Royal College of Physicians has called for a new medical assistant role, in response to the pressures of doctor workload. However, the most far-reaching changes appear to be those set out in the NHS Plan. The plan sets out an ambitious redesigned health system whereby protocols specify treatment and the appropriate staffing to carry them out. There are to be common elements to training so those nurses who wish to become doctors do not have to begin their training again from scratch. The report also announces new positions such as the 'nurse consultant' and the 'modern matron'. New roles for appropriately qualified nurse midwives and therapists include: the right to make and receive referrals, admit and discharge patients, order investigations and diagnostic tests, run clinics and prescribe drugs. By 2004 the plan states that a majority of nurses should be able to prescribe.

HUMAN-RESOURCE STRATEGIES FOR THE HEALTH WORKFORCE

A third major policy issue is the development of human resources, staff development and education and training for the health workforce to match those in other sectors, and to match future demands.

The most basic element of a human-resource strategy would seem to be the protection of staff. This may seem a fundamental point that would not need re-iterating. However, trends in litigation, assaults on health care staff, and general levels of health including mental health of the workforce are causes for concern. In 1996 the NHS set up a litigation authority and a clinical negligence scheme for Trusts. In 1999 the *British Medical Journal* reported on the increasing litigation faced by GPs (*BMJ*, 1999). Most recently, a report from the Public Accounts Committee drew attention to 15 000 currently unpaid clinical negligence claims that could cost the NHS £2.8 billion (Public Accounts Committee, 1999). Increasing demand is being placed on health professionals including the expectations of patients who come to surgeries with extensive information on their conditions from the Internet. Poor performance and negligence amongst health professionals has been highlighted with significant failures such as Bristol heart surgeons and the gynaecologist Rodney Ledward, along with Harold Shipman, a GP who murdered a number of his elderly patients.

Recent research undertaken by the Nuffield Trust found that there is a considerably higher incidence of ill-health in the NHS workforce than in other occupations. Whilst the industry average is 3.7 per cent sickness absence, the rate in the NHS is 5 per cent, which costs the NHS more than £700 million per annum. Twenty-seven per cent of health care staff reported high levels of psychological disturbance, compared with 18 per cent of working people generally (Williams *et al.*, 1998). Recent research that examined stress amongst recent medical graduates found that the demand that work places on personal life, excessive workload and long hours were primary causes (BMA, 1998: ii; Hardy *et al.*, 1997; Baldwin *et al.*, 1997; Prosser *et al.*, 1997). Measures to avoid stress were focused on changing the working environment – for example, by adhering to appropriate guidelines regarding staffing levels and locum cover.

Violence against the health workforce is increasing, is underreported, is most likely (outside psychiatric wards) to occur in accident and emergency departments, and is most likely to be perpetrated against nurses (*Nursing Standard*, 1996; 1997a, b; 1998; Jenkins *et al.*, 1998; *Nursing Times*, 1997a,b; Rose, 1997; Scott, 1997; O'Connell and Bury, 1997). At the end of October 1998, Health Secretary Frank Dobson launched a joint RCN/NHS campaign on violence against staff, which included guidelines and collaboration with the Home Office to ensure prosecution of offenders.

The second element of a human-resource strategy might be that of
incentives – how to attract and motivate the health workforce. The
preceding discussion might suggest that there is much work to be done
here! In terms of recruitment, the nursing profession has faced falling
applications whilst there is increasing pressure for medical places. On
retention, the drop-out rates for nurses is being addressed by a current
recruitment drive by the NHS. As was discussed earlier in the wider
context of the world of work, careers and employment are becoming
more flexible and the health workforce will have to adapt to these
changes, which means action on the part of employers and the representative bodies.

The third element of a human-resource strategy might be education
and training of the health workforce. In addition to professional
training and skills mentioned above, external trends are also having
an impact on changing work. For example, does education and training for health professionals deal with information technology and
information management (for example, IT skills, searching databases,
dealing with electronic records), communication skills, ethics (for
example, training and guidance in the areas of genetic counselling
and end-of-life decisions), working with other professionals, and the
integration between health and social care, which are all factors that
might characterise some of the current and future demands on health
care professionals?

Once again, the NHS Plan outlines a vision of health care according
to the government's latest thinking and provides a useful current
response to these future challenges. Under the NHS Plan there will
be individual learning accounts of £150 per annum or dedicated training to NVQ level two and three for staff without professional qualifications. There will be new joint-training across professions in
communication skills and in NHS principles and organisation. The
NHS Plan identifies a new 'Performance Framework for Human
Resources' that is incorporated into the Performance Assessment
Framework for NHS organisations. NHS employers will be assessed
against performance targets and a new 'improving working lives'
(IWL) standard. The IWL standard will cover elements such as investment in training and development, tackling discrimination and harass-
ment, violence against staff, reducing sick absences, providing better
occupational health and counselling services and more flexible working conditions.

The National Institute for Clinical Excellence, The Commission for
Health Improvement and the system of clinical governance are likely

to be important instruments for achieving quality and performance improvements under the NHS Plan. Developments in information technology will allow the systems required for performance and quality improvements. However, cultural, institutional and managerial change is required to develop these systems across the health workforce and here supportive strategies will be needed in order to encourage beneficial change amongst professional groups within health.

CONCLUSION

We have identified some of the trends and issues that will impact on the health workforce forward to 2015 and policy issues that follow. The benefit of a futures perspective and 'environmental scanning' is that it allows a wider perspective to be taken and this can lead to the questioning of commonly-held assumptions. Some of those assumptions that may or may not hold in the future (or may even be tested now) might be: that the doctor is in face-to-face contact with the patient during consultation; that most GPs and hospital doctors are male, in full-time careers; that most training takes place at the beginning of the health professional's career; that the NHS workforce is sustainable; that patient records are held on paper in the general practice or hospital setting; that the health workforce, particularly junior doctors, work long hours to train; that NHS services are provided and funded only within the UK; and that health professionals all go through clearly demarcated training programmes. Drawing evidence from the recently launched NHS Plan shows how significant policy shifts can occur. However, implementation of the plan is only just underway, and change in a politically-led service is likely to be full of unexpected consequences.

Implementation of preferred futures is perhaps an appropriate point to end the discussion. The next stage in planning that lies beyond the scope of this chapter is to think about the strategic decisions, actions and likely time-scales that are required for implementation of preferred futures – this is putting futures thinking into practice. If identifying the likely direction of change is difficult, then assessing the pace of change and making required implementation decisions is more so. To illustrate, of the many developments taking place in the health sector those in information and communication technology and its associated features could have the biggest impact, simply because they underpin so many other changes. It is worrying that IT and technology more generally are largely absent from the NHS Plan despite the fact that many of the ambitious system changes and service redesign rely on sophisticated IT systems and technology. This may be one of the areas where planned change underestimates what is required in practice.

References

Albery, I.P., Durand, M.A., Heuston, J., Groves, P., Gossop, M. and Strang, J. (1997) 'Training Primary Health Care Staff about Alcohol: A Study of Alcohol Trainers in the UK', *Drugs Education and Prevention Policy*, 4(2): 173–86.
Albery, I.P., Heuston, J., Durand, M.A., Groves, P., Gossop, M. and Strang, J. (1996) 'Training Primary Health Care Workers about Drugs: A National Survey of UK Trainers' Perceptions towards Training', *Drug and Alcohol Review*, 15(4): 343–55.
Armitage, B. and Scott, M. (1998) 'British Labour Force Projections: 1998–2011', *Labour Market Trends*, 106(6): 281–97.
Baker, R. (1997) 'Will the Future GP Remain a Personal Doctor?', *British Journal of General Practice*, 47(425): 831–3.
Baldwin, P.J., Dodd, M. and Wrate, W.R. (1998) 'Young Doctors' Health: 1. How do Working Conditions affect Attitudes, Health and Performance?', *Social Science and Medicine*, 45(1): 35–40.
Bayliss, V. (1998) *Redefining Work* (London: RSA).
Bezold, C. (1994) 'Scenarios for 21st-century Health Care in the United States of America: Perspectives on Time and Change', *World Health Statistics Quarterly*, 47: 126–39.
British Medical Association (Health Policy and Economic Research Unit) (1995a) *Professional Values: First Report (Part II)* (London, BMA).
British Medical Association (Health Policy and Economic Research Unit) (1995b) *Core Values for the Medical Profession in the 21st Century: Survey Report* (London: BMA).
British Medical Association (Health Policy and Economic Research Unit) (1998) *Work-Related Stress among Junior Doctors: A Report from the BMA Cohort Study of 1995 Medical Graduates* (London: BMA).
British Medical Journal (1999) 'GPs Face Escalating Litigation', *British-Medical Journal*: 318, 830.
Booth, A.L. and Arulampalam, W. (1997) 'Labour Market Flexibility and Skills Acquisition: Is There a Trade-off?' Institute for Labour Research Discussion Paper.
Buchan, J. (1998) 'Your Country Needs You' *Health Service Journal*, 16 July, 22–5.
Buchan, J., Seccombe, I. and Smith, G. (1998)' *Nurses' Work: An Analysis of the UK Nursing Labour Market* (Aldershot: Ashgate).
Cortis, J.D. and Rinomhota, A.S. (1996) 'The Future of Ethnic Minority Nurses in the NHS', *Journal of Nursing Management*, 4(6): 359–66.

Coyle, G. (1997) 'The Nature and Value of Futures Studies or do Futures have a Future?', *Futures*, 29(1): 77–93.

Dargie, C., Dawson, S.J.N., Garside, P. (2000) *Policy Futures for UK Health: 2000 Report* (London, The Nuffield Trust and the Stationery Office). Also accessible at www.nuffieldtrust.org.uk.

Department of Health (1993) *Changing Childbirth: Report of the Expert Maternity Group* (London: HMSO).

Department of Health (2000) *The NHS Plan: A Plan for Investment, a Plan for Reform* (Cmd 4818-I London: HM Stationery Office).

Dixon, D.L. (1998) 'Will Future Physicians Learn to Treat the Individual or the Population?' *Journal of the American Medical Association*, 280(4): 327.

Dowie, R. and Langman, M. (1999) 'Staffing of Hospitals: Future Needs, Future Provision', *British Medical Journal*, 319: 1193–5.

Farrell, G.A. (1997) 'Aggression in Clinical Settings: Nurses' Views', *Journal of Advanced Nursing*, 25(3): 501–8.

Ferrie, J.E., Shipley, M.J., Marmot, M.G., Stansfeld, S.A. and Smith, G.D. (1998) 'An Uncertain Future: The Health Effects of Threats to Employment Security in White-collar Men and Women', *American Journal of Public Health*, 88(7): 1030–6.

Foresight Healthcare Panel, *Healthcare in 2020* (London: Office of Science and Technology, 2000).

Garrett, M.J. (1994) 'An Introduction to National Futures Studies for Policy-makers in the Health Sector', *World Health Statistics Quarterly* 47, (3/4): 101–117.

Garrett, M.J. and Bezold, C. (1995) (eds) 'Special Issue: Our Health, Our Future', *Futures*, 27: (9/10).

Goldberg, D. (1998) 'Training General Practitioners in Mental Health Skills' *International Review of Psychiatry*, 10(2): 102–5.

Handy, C. (1984) *The Future of Work* (Oxford: Blackwell).

Hardy, G.E., Shapiro, D.A. and Borrill, C.S. (1997) 'Fatigue in the Workforce of National Health Service Trusts: Levels of Symptomatology and Links with Minor Psychiatric Disorder, Demographic, Occupational and Work Role Factors', *Journal of Psychosomatic Research*, 43(1): 83–92.

Health and Safety Commission 1997 *Violence and Aggression to Staff in Health Services* (Sudbury: HSE Books).

Health Service Journal (1998) 'Asian Few', 3 December.

Hensher, M., Fulop, N., Coast, J. and Jeffreys, E. (1999) 'Better Out than In? Alternatives to Acute Hospital Care', *British Medical Journal*, 319: 1127–30.

Jenkins, M.G., Pocke, L.G., McNicholl, B.P. and Hughes, D.M. (1998) 'Violence and Verbal Abuse Against Staff in Accident and Emergency Departments: A Survey of Consultants in the UK and the Republic of Ireland', *Journal of Accident and Emergency Medicine*, 15(4): 262–5.

Joshi, H. (1996) 'Projections of European Population Decline: Serious Demography or False Alarm?' in D. Coleman (ed.) *Europe's Population in the 1990s* (Oxford: Oxford University Press).

Kerwick, S., Jones, R., Mann, A. and Goldberg, D. (1997) 'Mental Health Care Training Priorities in General Practice', *British Journal of General Practice*, 47(417): 225–7.

Ling, T. (1999) 'Which way to a Healthy Future? Reflections on the Madingley Scenarios', *Foresight*, 1999, 1(1): 17–34.

Lyne, P.A. (1997) *Taskforce for Continuing Education and Practice: The Future of Nurses, Midwives and Health Visitors* (Cardiff, Nursing Research Centre, School of Nursing Studies).

Maynard, A. and Walker, A. (1998) *The Physician Workforce in the United Kingdom* (London: The Nuffield Trust).

Medical Workforce Standing Advisory Committee, (1997) *Planning the Medical workforce: Third Report* (London: Department of Health).

Nursing Standard (1997a) 'Violence at Work' *Nursing Standard*, 12(5): 22–4.

Nursing Standard (1997b) 'Fear Factor' *Nursing Standard*, 11(39): 18.

Nursing Standard Editorial (1998) 'On Violence and Aggression in A&E', *Nursing Standard*, 12(34): 1.

Nursing Times (1997a) 'In the Line of Fire', *Nursing Times*, 93(43): 30–2.

Nursing Times Editorial (1997b) 'Violence in A&E Departments', *Nursing Times*, 93(20): 3.

O'Connell, P. and Bury, G. (1997) 'Assaults against General Practitioners in Ireland', *Family Medicine*, 29(5): 340–3.

Pahl, R. (1999) *The Social Context of Healthy Living* (London: The Nuffield Trust).

Prosser, D., Johnson, S., Kuipers, E., Szmukler, G., Bebbington, P. and Thornicroft, G. (1997) 'Perceived Sources of Work Stress and Satisfaction among Hospital and Community Mental Health Staff, and their Relation to Mental Health, Burnout and Job Satisfaction', *Journal of Psychosomatic Research*, 43(1): 51–9.

Public Accounts Committee Fifth Report, (HC 128) (1999) *NHS (England) Summarised Accounts 1997–98 – Report together with the Proceedings of the Committee relating to the Report, Minutes of Evidence and an Appendix* (London, The Stationery Office).

Purves, I.N. (1996) 'Facing Future Challenges in General Practice: A Clinical Method with Computer Support' *Family Practitioner*, 13(6): 536–43.

Rantanen, J. (1999) 'Future Work and Health in Europe', draft paper for 4th European Consultation on Future Trends, held jointly by World Health Organisation Regional Office for Europe and The Nuffield Trust, London, 13–14 December.

Ratan, S. (1995) 'A new Divide Between Haves and Have-Nots?', *Time*, spring, 145(12): 25–6.

Read, S. and Shewan, J. (1998) *A Review Of The Recent Literature On Role Developments For Nursing Staff At All Levels In The NHS* (Sheffield: University of Sheffield).

Rees, C. and Lehane, M. (1996) 'Witnessing Violence to Staff: A Study of Nurses Experiences', *Nursing Standard*, 11(13–15): 45–7.

Ringland, G., Edwards, M., Hammond, L., Heinzen, B., Rendell, A., Sparrow, O. and White, E. (1999) 'Shocks and Paradigm Busters (why do we get surprised?)', *Long Range Planning*, 32(4): 403–13.

Robinson, P. (1998) 'Beyond Workfare: Active Labour-Market Policies', *Institute of Development Studies Bulletin*, 29(1): 86.

Rose, M. (1997) 'A Survey of Violence Toward Nursing Staff in One Large Irish Accident and Emergency Department', *Journal of Emergency Nursing*, 23(3): 214–9.

Scott, H. (1997) 'Why do Nurses Face Violent Assault in A&E?', *British Journal of Nursing*, 6(10): 540.

Shaw, C. (1994) 'Accuracy and Uncertainty of National Population Projections for the United Kingdom', *Population Trends*, 77.

Shaw, C. (1998) '1996-based National Population Projections for the United Kingdom and Constituent Countries', *Population Trends*, 91(1): 43–9.

Smith, G. and Seccombe, I. (1998) *Changing Times: A Survey Of Registered Nurses In 1998* (Brighton: Institute for Employment Studies).

Smith, R. (1997) 'The Future of Healthcare Systems: Information Technology and Consumerism will Transform Health Care Worldwide', *British Medical Journal*, 314: 1495–6.

Stanley, M. and Manthorpe, J. (1997) 'Risk Assessment: Developing Training for Professionals in Mental Health Work', *Social Work and Social Sciences Review*, 7(1): 26–38.

Sylvester, R. (1998) 'Most new NHS Doctors are Foreign', *The Independent*, 26 October.

The Guardian (1998) 'Sick and Tired', *The Guardian*, 28 October

The Henley Centre (1998) *2020 Vision* (London: Barclays Life).

The Sainsbury Centre for Mental Health Launches new Training Strategy for all Mental Health staff (1997) *Journal of Advanced Nursing*, 26(6): 1061.

Theorell, T. (1997) 'How Will Future Work Life Influence Health?', *Scandinavian Journal of Work, Environment and Health*, 23(S4): 16–22.

University of Manchester and Conrane Consulting (1996) *The Future Healthcare Workforce* (Manchester: University of Manchester).

Warner, M., Longley, M., Gould, E. and Picek, A. (1998) *Healthcare Futures 2010* (University of Glamorgan, Welsh Institute for Health and Social Care) (Commissioned by the UKCC Education Commission).

West, P. and Sweeting, H. (1996) 'Nae job, nae future: Young People and Health in a context of Unemployment', *Health and Social Care in the Community*, 4(1): 50–62.

Williams, S., Michie, S. and Pattani, S. (1998) *Improving the Health of the NHS Workforce* (London: The Nuffield Trust).

Wilson, C.B. (1999) 'The Impact of Medical Technologies on the Future of Hospitals', *BMJ*, 319: 1287–1291.

World Health Organisation, (2000) *The World Health Report 2000, Health Systems: Improving Performance* (Geneva: World Health Organisation).

World Health Statistics Quarterly (1994) 'Health Futures Research', *World Health Statistics Quarterly*, 47: (3/4).

Worrall, L. and Cooper, C.L. (1998) *The Quality of Working Life* (Manchester: Institute of Management).

Young, R. and Leese, B. (1999) 'Recruitment and Retention of General Practitioners in the UK: what are the problems and solutions?, *British Journal of General Practice*, 49: 829–833.

4 Virtually Caring: Organisational Consequences of Distance-Mediated Care*

Jill Schofield

INTRODUCTION

The late twentieth-century concept of the 'virtual organisation' has, on the whole, been defined in relation to the use of advanced information technology (Jones, 1995). From this assumption there has developed a structural definition of such organisations as being without physical form or boundary and unbound by rules and regulations. Some authors like Quinn and Jackson (1996) have studied control in the IT-dominated virtual organisation emphasising the importance of trust as a controlling mechanism amongst teleworkers. Others, like Davidow and Malone (1997) have considered virtuality without the role of technology.

The research presented in this chapter seeks to look at virtuality within health care organisations as a consequence of distance between the tripartite relationship of the accountable body, the clinical professional and the patient. Whilst physical distance between the accountable body and the clinical professional is not novel, the idea of a lack of physical proximity between the clinical professional and the patient is new. The argument is made that virtuality is being introduced into this tripartite relationship as a consequence of advanced telecommunications, referred to collectively as telemedicine.

The root base of the word *tele* derived from the Greek *telos*, meaning distance, is important in understanding the concept of virtual. Wootton (1998) has pointed out that telemedicine had been practised years

* The Canadian research described in this chapter was made possible by finding from the Canadian High Commission 1999 under the Canadian Studies Faculty Research Programme.

before the advent of telecommunications; the single consultation of a doctor by post as far back as the eighteenth century can be counted as telemedicine. The development of telemedicine has reached such a stage that it is now possible for researchers to address the broader consequences of the technological changes and this has been effectively done by Roberts, Rigby and Birch (1999) and Rigby, (1999). However, within much of the contributing literature which addresses the organisational and managerially consequences of telemedicine, there is a belief that it has never quite got off the ground.

The British government's IT strategy document *Information for Health* (DoH,1998) emphasises the strategic importance of telemedicine and the consequent allocation of development funds. Other recent endorsements have come from the joint Institute of Health Services Management/ Department of Trade and Industry report, *Telemedicine and Health* (1998), which provides a concise summary of the benefits of the technology. A further example of the gathering pace of renewed interest in telemedicine can be found in the European shared information initiatives, *Accelerating Electronic Commerce in Europe* (www.ispo.cec.be/ecommerce). The summary report from the collected initiatives suggests that healthcare will be a significant part of electronic commerce:

> with its 10% share of GDP and in line with the future growth of home care, but it is to be expected that its integration will be a slow process.

The EU initiatives and the portfolio of projects presented, suggest that this integration will be slow because of the tripartite structure of the third-party player; patient (buyer) and professional (seller).

Indeed, the general feeling from the contributing literature on the adoption of telemedicine is one of malaise and failure to make progress in its adoption and implementation (McLaren and Ball, 1995; McClelland *et al.*, 1995; Wootton, 1998). Apart from technical difficulties some of the reasons proffered for this apparent slow diffusion of telemedicine are organisational and human factors (Mair and Whitten, 1997). What is interesting from an organisational behaviour perspective is that almost no reference is made to the social construction of technology literature (Bijker, Hughes and Pinch, 1990), nor to the implementation of information technology literature as a guide to what exactly these human and organisational factors might be. Furthermore, it is possible that any future discussion about telemedicine is subtly converted into a discourse of 'e-health'. The concept and pressure of the 'net imperative' (Symonds, 1999) is so strong that future discussions about the very real technical and work-practice challenges of telehealth may get subsumed under the rhetoric of e-commerce.

The discussion presented in this chapter does not purport to explore the organisational reasons for the slow adoption of telemedicine. Rather, it explores how some of the traditionally acknowledged aspects of health care organising, are altered by distance and virtuality. The empirical data has been gathered from four different cases of distance mediated care, namely telemedicine in Ulster; NHS Direct in Wales; medical e-commerce in the UK private medical insurance sector (PMI); and from four sub-field sites in areas of low population density in rural Canada. These sub-field sites were, The Yukon, Labrador, British Columbia and New Brunswick. The methodologies involved at the different sites were non-participant observation, semi-structured interviewing and a piece of action research. The latter part of the chapter explores some of the associated methodological issues involved in conducting such research 'from a distance'.

The organisational axes which have been used to analyse the impact of virtuality are (i) Power, (ii) Structure, (iii) Work Routines, (iv) Time and (v) Learning. The chapter is structured according to this analysis and concludes with a discussion of some of the reasons for the contradictory findings which are presented, the important role of the intermediary in the relationship between doctor and patient and the dominance of control factors regardless of distance.

VIRTUALITY AND POWER

The results from the field sites have highlighted different aspects of the alteration in the power relationship between the tripartite of actors. The use of teleradiology in New Brunswick demonstrated a subtle downgrading of the role of the radiographer vis-à-vis the consultant radiologist at the associated regional hospital, which is where the images were sent to be read. However, in Labrador, this issue of power and status were reversed. The 'bush' nurses who were physically situated in the remote coastal communities of N.E. Labrador experienced an increase in their status to that of nurse practitioner as a result of teleconsultations between the nursing stations and the main hospital at Goose Bay.

The Labrador data also demonstrated a very interesting example of telemedicine and equal opportunities. The two aboriginal groupings (aboriginal is the preferred user term for the Innu and Inuit peoples) of Innu and Inuit peoples had differential power relations with the predominantly white clinical staff. This behaviour seemed to be a function of how easily eye contact was made with the clinical staff: the white, non-aboriginal staff preferring eye contact, whilst the Innu culture regard this as ill-mannered. The Innuit patient behaviour on the other hand was much more immediate, open and demonstrative. However, at the coastal nursing stations this imbalance did not exist mainly because of the small number of white clinical staff, and because the local Innu were still able to access clinical opinions from the secondary care centre via the teleconferencing link without the actual face-to-face experience.

The telemedicine literature which has addressed human factors tends to concentrate upon the communication and relational issues between healthcare professional and patient. Normally the effects of telemedicine are compared to an idealised experience of the face-to-face clinical encounter. Park (1974, 1975) has given an early but enduring explanation of why telemedicine varies from this ideal; some of the reasons are mainly related to the attenuation of spatial relationships and dimensionality which occurs when tele-technology is used. It has long been known that the micro aspects of para-verbal and non-verbal behaviour within the clinical encounter have a direct effect on the patient experience, and Park (1974) points to the existence of 'frame tension' (discomfiture about what lies outside the camera field of view) as one of the spatial alterations which occurs. Other non-verbal behaviour which can occur with telemetry is 'gaze dysfunction' (the apparent failure to meet a gaze). Both these effects within the Labradorian experience were in fact *preferable* rather than a diminishment of the idealised face-to-face consultation.

A further aspect of power relations within a virtual environment is that of the intermediary. Two types of intermediary are suggested here, firstly the amanuensis, and secondly the credentialer – or in wider terms, the 'informediary'. Teleconsultation and teleradiology depend upon an amanuensis, and a relationship rapport tends to develop between the patient and the amanuensis. This again is a subtle but important departure from the traditional power relationship that is predominantly based on trust, between the doctor and the patient. One of the aspects which contributes to how this fleeting but important trust is constructed is because of the physicality, intimacy and tactile nature of the doctor/patient encounter: an encounter which becomes displaced with the advent of an amanuensis. Thus we have an example of where the use of medical technology introduces a dichotomy between its possibilities and its potential dehumanising effect. Rosch and Kearney (1985) have extended the discussion about this dilemma in their debate about allopathic and holistic medicine.

The role of the amanuensis raises a number of questions about power. Does the power relationship exist between patient and distant doctor, or does it exist between patient and amanuensis? The data derived from the Ulster example goes some way towards explaining this. The Ards peninsular is geographically remote from the district general hospitals of Belfast, and telemedicine has been used in post-natal care and the teaching of breast-feeding techniques. The Edinburgh Healthcare Telematics Centre has already pioneered remote ultrasound scanning and video conferencing (Lamb, Eydmann and Boddy, 1997) for remote maternity clinics. The findings from this centre have been disseminated and consequently there is a fair degree of experience with the technology. In the Ulster example there seemed to be more of a relationship of equals between the teacher (in Belfast) and the new mother (in the Ards peninsular). Whether this was because of the relationship being cast as a *learning and teaching* role, or because of the mediating influence of technology, it is difficult to say.

However, the analysis of the role of the credentialer is very different. The major PMI companies are seeking to minimise their benefit to premium-paid ratios and one of the ways by which they seek to control demand is by 'credentialising' the patient's benefit entitlement with their medical condition. This process occurs *after* the patient has had a consultation with their GP and received a referral to a specialist. The encounter always takes place via the telephone usually to a 'customer care centre' which is staffed by clinically qualified personnel. The telephone encounter between patient and the PMI organisation can take a number of forms varying from the endorsement of the original referral and a commitment to meet the future expenses incurred, or the patient will be directed to a preferred provider which is part of a price-controlled participating scheme with the PMI organisation.

The whole technique of pre-verification of entitlement introduces a new power factor into the tripartite relationship, that of the gate-keeping role of the credentialer (Kenny and Wilson, 1984; Pettigrew, 1973). Moreover, the credentialer's power is greater than that of the doctor in the traditional doctor–patient relationship. Interestingly, it is via the stance of professional licensure that this form of 'inter-ference' in the doctor–patient relationship is being challenged in the USA.

ORGANISATIONAL STRUCTURE

The argument presented in this chapter is that distance-mediated care is made possible by the technologies of telemedicine. Consequently, one of the most obvious organisational effects is that of the impact not only of distance, but also the effect of the technology itself on organisa-tional structure. The whole socio-technical school of thought in organ-isational behaviour attests to the direct relationship between the technology in use and how organisations communicate and control both internally and externally (Trist and Bamforth, 1951; Woodward, 1965)

The complexity and power of modern information and telecommuni-cations is analysed by Roberts and Grabowski (1996) when they explain technology's dual nature not only as a product and a process, but also one which has become *the* structuration process by which organisations coordinate themselves. Thus, the very nature of organising at a distance, or virtually organising, is made possible because of the structuring effect of advanced telecommunications. It would also be possible to apply a postmodern analysis to such technologically-induced structuring, as Deetz (1994) and Alvesson and Deetz (1996) refer to when considering the possibility of hyperreality wherein the image is more than the reality. Intellectually attractive as such ideas are, they are in fact anathema to what telemedicine is trying to achieve technically in terms of image accuracy, or true representational reality. In addition, a postmodern perspective poses significant methodological problems because of the degree of fragmentation and the difficulty of checking or comparing real-world references with perceived images in the medical field.

The empirical data from the sites has, however, suggested two organisational themes for further discussion. Namely the issue of intra-organisational workplace cohesion, and how far telemedicine has influenced the internal coordination of the organisation, and, secondly, the inter-organisational perspective. in particular the devel-opment of new external relationships within a network structure.

The literature on remote or teleworking suggests that there is a fair degree of collectivism developed from a shared occupational culture, and, in turn, this collectivism helps create workplace cohesion (Bahrami and Evans, 1997; Fortin *et al.*, 1997; Eby and Dobbins, 1997; Lococo and Yen, 1998; Civin, 1999). It is tempting to apply this literature to telemedicine, however I would suggest that the fit is a poor one because those workers involved in telemedicine are not necessarily (in fact very rarely) home workers.

There was evidence of workplace cohesion within the PMI organisation but this was because it was structured as a call centre. Within the Belfast and Canadian examples only certain departments were using telemedicine and it was as an adjunct technique to the dominant real-time face-to-face medicine. Consequently, the workplace cohesion which was apparent was due in the main more to a shared, professional and departmental socialisation coupled with locally-shared organisational rationalities.

It is possible that the comprehensive adoption of the Electronic Patient Record (EPR) and networked telemonitoring within a hospital/health care setting will impact on internal work structures in a more obvious way (Dodd, 1997; Bishop, 1998). There is also some suggestion that integrated clinical workstations (ICWSs) will become the new network centres of such organisations. There was, though, no evidence of EPRs nor ICWs at any of the field sites. The PMI company had, however, structured itself both corporately and geographically according to the private patients' 'account progress'. Thus the stages of policy sales – pre-verification and benefit reimbursement – were mirrored in the functional and geographical arrangement of the various departments. Overall corporate integration and control was exercised in this differentialised structure by the networked electronic *account* and list of episodes of the policy holder rather than their clinical records.

The evidence relating to the impact of telemedicine and virtuality on the interorganisational structures at the field sites was much stronger. Two main findings were revealed, firstly that being in a virtual relationship forced the organisations to look beyond their immediate networks and to develop new relationships beyond their own organisation. Secondly, there was evidence of new patterns of interdependency and external coordination as a result of 'hub-and-spoke' relationships between a specialist centre and an outlying hospital/clinic.

The development of new networked relationships in the British Columbian example was very marked. The province has a high proportion of First Nation Peoples and some of the community hospitals in the very rural areas have developed holistic healing centres to reflect native health preferences. The federal health agencies have been made more aware of the possibilities of these types of centres because of video links and associated web pages. Traditionally, the federal agencies in Vancouver rarely made the physical trip to Northern communities such as the Skeena River area and as such did not realise the impact and cost of isolation on local health care.

The important role of teleradiology in New Brunswick has meant that the community hospital on Grand Manen Island has developed a hub-and-spoke relationship with the regional hospital at St John. The 'hub' hospital specifies the clinical protocols used in the 'spoke' hospital for radiological investigations. For the hospital physicians in both the Yukon and Labrador, the availability of video conferencing has meant that the feeling of professional isolation is reduced and this helps in the recruitment of doctors to the area.

From a theoretical perspective, network analysis provides the ideal framework by which to study the interorganisational relationship between the concrete and virtual organisation which is created by telemedicine (Nohria and Eccles, 1992). Network analysis also provides a succinct framework by which to analyse power and dependency, information and knowledge flows and structural responses to the environment. In many ways the physical patterns of the tele-links can help such an organisational analysis because technically a link has to be designed between the remote site(s) and the real-time site (Epley, 1998), but to date little advantage seems to have been taken of this predefined network.

WORK ROUTINES

The more technically-oriented literature purports that distance medicine technology enables greater continuity of care (Balas *et al.*, 1997). However, upon closer inspection of the data used in such studies it is apparent that they tend to refer to telephone follow-up and reminders, a technique where an improved continuity should be expected. In order to understand how virtuality impacts upon work processes it helps to understand some of the data-transfer techniques. These can be interactive or pre-recorded; video or still images; audio or written data. Added to these categories are passive and active systems. For example, a passive telepathology system means that a digitised image from a microscope is relayed to a remote location but there is no control over the image by the recipient. Active or real-time telepathology means that the recipient can manipulate and scrutinise the image to their own requirements (Leete, 1999).

The findings from the field sites suggest two, almost paradoxical findings, first that telemedicine has supported the development of work/ clincial protocols for the clinical work routines. Secondly, the technology itself has meant that established work routines have been altered in favour of more craft-based technical skills. The latter finding may be because of the novelty of the technology, therefore this could be a transitional phase until the newly-acquired skills are themselves routinised.

Both the NHS Direct site and the PMI site use clinical protocols, but for different reasons. Within NHS Direct the protocols are used for decision support; within the PMI organisation the protocols form part of the pre-verification and credentialing process. In those cases where the policy holder has a policy which is part of a preferred provider scheme, the clinical protocol is also checked against the clinical notes and length of stay, for cost-control purposes.

It is however the literature on call-centre organisational behaviour which provides more insights into the effect of working with protocols and in turn how these impact upon individual work practices, individual discretion and personal work routines (Richardson and Marshall, 1999; Westin, 1992). The literature on telemedicine which does attempt to address organisational issues appears to adopt a fairly simplistic view of the role of protocols and would suggest that such control is a positive measure; hence

> it is important to impose structure on the fluid situation that develops to reduce error and increase efficiency and satisfaction ... to develop effective telemedicine protocols. (Moore *et al.*, 1998: 130)

There is a definite tension created in terms of work practises for users of telemedicine. Over time, clinical staff will have developed their own *modus operandi* for face-to-face consultations. They are then faced with pressure to develop explicit protocols which address their investigative routines when using telemedicine. Such *telecompetent* work routines become further confused when telemedicine procedures are grafted onto existing routines. This presents real problems of time scheduling, especially if the clinician works in more than one site not all of which have telemedicine facilities.

Whilst the aforementioned has focused upon the technological impact of work practices, there are also behavioural issues for the clinicians to take account of. A good example of this, and a particular worry of those interviewed, concerns physical appearance and feeling self-conscious when appearing on camera. Whilst specific training is available for improving manual dexterity for remote procedures, few of the people interviewed received any training at all about personal presentation. Furthermore, with some of the future technologies, particularly with the use of virtual reality headsets, there is likely to be more emphasis on the craft, rather than the routine nature of work practices. This rediscovery of the craft basis of medicine may come as a surprise to those who envisage telemedicine as a route to improved efficiency and patient throughput.

TIME

Analysing the temporal elements of the organisational consequences of virtuality were the most difficult aspects of the study. Different types of time were suggested from the data: time *delay* and the associated anxieties and frustrations from both the NHS direct and PMI call centres; time *pause*, which occured at the Canadian teleradiology unit where, rather than report immediately upon the image as it was received, the consultant radiologist stored the image to allow time to reflect and consider. Time could also be analysed as an aspect of *control*, this was suggested from the PMI centre. Delays in patients submitting their claims could affect their benefit entitlement. In addition, the whole of the corporate accounting system was organised centrally and remotely and any delays from local operating units in reporting their daily activity was monitored. Finally, and much more difficult to define was the role which time played in respect of *patience* or lack of immediacy. This was demonstrated in New Brunswick and Labrador with remote teleconsulting. At these sites, although the consultation was interactive, after disconnection the patient was in a form of limbo awaiting a conclusion to the interaction, whilst the clinician sought to gain time for reflection and to plan a treatment regime.

Sparse as the literature is on the organisational aspects of telemedicine, any discussion about the impact of time is hardly mentioned at all. Wooton (1998) refers to the logistical problems of having all partners for a teleconsultation present at the same time, and Berliner (1998) refers to the use of telephone triage to deny care whilst mentioning the delays experienced by patients trying to access the service. On the other hand, the literature on organisational behaviour which does address time provides a helpful theoretical framework, and Hassard

(1996, 1990) provides one of the most comprehensive summaries of the time structures which occur in organisations. It would have helped if the activities observed at the field sites could have been classified as conforming to a project structure, since the literature in this area has attempted to analyse time both in terms of the temporary nature of projects (Schofield and Wilson, 1996), and in terms of using group theories (Gersick, 1988; McGrath and O'Connor, 1996). However, there was little evidence that either project structures or project norms were in use during the period of the fieldwork.

There does appear, however, to be two broad analytical categories by which to try and understand the impact of time in a virtual relationship, namely the functional analysis of time in the linear quantitative tradition (Hassard, 1990), and the phenomenological analysis of time better suited to a cyclic-qualitative time analysis. Lundin, Soderholm and Wilson (1998) provide a good example of where both approaches can be used in studying time events in organisations. Such an analytical division means that a functional analysis of the virtual relationship could deal with the logistical and power issues of time, whilst a phenomenological analysis could deal with the personal time-ordered feelings and experiences of clinicians and patients. However, it would seem that there is a 'special' aspect of virtuality which neither approach really deals with, and this is the issue of 'asynchronisty'; that is, activity moving through time at different paces. It may well be that it is this aspect of telemedicine which makes it feel different to the time ordering of real-time medicine.

LEARNING

There is a substantial body of literature which links learning with information processing and knowledge diffusion (Stinchcombe, 1990). Similarly, the relationship between knowledge transfer and complex technologies is acknowledged within the literature and Attewell (1992) places technological diffusion within the broader context of organisational learning. The examples from the field sites support many of the ideas in the literature. Thus, the hub-and-spoke models in Ulster and Canada were a good example of knowledge transfer being helped by telemedicine. The ability to capture and store the interactions between patient and doctor on video also adds to the learning potential of telemedicine. Furthermore, this facilitates more accurate agreement about diagnoses and interventions between the GP and specialist.

Other examples of learning are also linked to points previously made about control and power. The networking of patient-accessed knowledge bases at NHS Direct heralds the promise of developing a more health-literate population. Kretschmer and Nerlich (1999) point to the fact that the half-life of medical knowledge is two and a half years in some specialities, therefore demonstrating the benefits of artificial computer-based intelligence. Such intelligence is also available to practitioners as part of their education. In fact, data from 1996 demonstrated that 35 per cent of telemedicine applications studied under European Union Directive DG XIII were for research and development purposes, whilst 42 per cent were pilot studies and only 17 per cent were established installations, serving to further emphasise the important role which telemedicine can play in learning. All the field sites also demonstrated the role of learning in terms of their ability to access expertise from remote areas, which in turn has meant improved equality of access for the remote populations.

METHODOLOGICAL ISSUES IN REMOTE RESEARCH

The data presented here has been derived from research in the field – the remote field. This obviously results in number of issues, one of which is the resource-intensive nature of such research, particularly in terms of the cost of travelling to geographically remote areas. In terms of data verification, it could be argued that the researcher needs to experience both loci of activity, namely the host health care institution and the remote location, but this is not always practicable.

Indeed, those research techniques normally associated with non-remote research such as interviewing, questionnaires and surveys are widely used in the study of telemedicine. In their study of remote collaboration technology in the high-technology film industry, Palmer *et al.* (2001) used interviews rather than observation of the nature of remote collaboration between film studios and their collaborators. Similarly, in their study of the Labrador telemedicine project, Jong *et al.* (1999) used patient and clinician satisfaction questionnaires together with action research to assess the effectiveness of telemedicine.

It would appear that in the literature the technological advances which are possible with telemedicine have not been replicated with research techniques which also rely on virtuality or even hyperreality. The obvious development here is in terms of real-time action research which itself depends upon electronic networks; the use of e-mail for the compilation of actors' diaries is one methodology which could be facilitated by electronic communication.

The calibration of findings from remote field sites is also an issue. Given the variation in clinical experiences between the host and the remote site this is not surprising, but needs to be addressed in the analysis and interpretation of primary data. Perhaps, above all, the work on telemedicine needs to move away from an assessment of the technological capabilities towards an assessment of the organisational and cultural impact of such technologies on the institutions and the users of health care.

DISCUSSION AND CONCLUSION

To summarise the research findings, firstly five axes were used to analyse the potential and the real effects of virtuality on the organisational behaviour of distance-mediated health care organisations. These axes were power, structure, work processes, time and learning. Within each of these categories particular explanatory categories emerged, namely, *power* – the role of the amanuensis and the credentialer; *structure* – the potential for structuring by networks and the structuring influence of the technology itself; *work processes* – the alteration to established work routines and the recognition of the importance of craft-based techniques; *time* – the alteration in time-ordering approaches and the impact of asynchronisity; and finally *learning* – the potential for wider involvement and knowledge dissemination.

The findings would suggest that some traditionally acknowledged aspects of health care organising are altered by virtuality, and a particularly strong example of this is the subtle alteration in the relationship between patient and clinician. This alteration seems to occur because of the introduction of an intermediary between the clinician and patient. Another example of the impact of virtuality is the potential for control and a surveillance role furnished by the technology itself. The control potential and the exercise of power by the third-party is particularly strong and in this respect the third-party behaviour is more akin to that of a concrete organisation. However, it is suggested that the organisational effects of virtuality are a function of the type of 'tele' medicine in use. The use of the electronic patient record or expert system does not impact upon the patient–clinician relationship in the same way as teleconsultation or teletriage. In turn, the differential effects of the types of telemedicine have a differential impact on the component members of the tripartite relationship.

Lehoux *et al.* (1999) acknowledge the enabling and constraining effects of telemedicine. They try to use structuration theory to explain how users gradually modify their practises and behaviours in the face of a new structure (technology) in order that practise can be embedded and in time extend the technology itself. There are data limitations in the cases reported here, not least that the telemedicine (except for the PMI example) is relatively new and it could be argued that much of what was observed could be interpreted as an adaptation to change. Other authors deal with the possible theoretical explanation of the impact of telemedicine in terms of transaction-cost economics (Pelletier-Fleury, 1997), or via the dialectic of medical technology verses holistic medicine (Rosch and Kearney, 1985). One certainty does seem to exist and that is the fact that the whole of the field concerning the organisational consequences of virtuality is wide open for further research.

The potential for further research could be helped by reference to some of the theories which are used to understand the social construction of technology. In turn, there would also appear to be a need to gather more ethnographic data, preferably from sites which are using different types of telemedicine. Finally, there is also the potential to conduct more longitudinal studies which address the adaptive changes within organisations as a consequence of virtuality.

References

Alvesson, M. and Deetz, S. (1996) 'Critical Theory and Post Modernism Approaches to Organizational Studies', in S.R. Clegg, C. Hardy and W.R. Nord (eds), *Handbook of Organization Studies* (London: Sage).

Armstrong, I. and Haston, W. (1997) 'Costs and Benefits of a Telemedicine Link for a Remote Community Hospital', *British Journal of Healthcare Computing and Information Management*, 14 (16 July).

Ashley, L. and Kelly, J. (1997) 'Telecomplications', *Health Service Journal*, 107 (5583) (11 December, suppl.): 4–6.

Attewell, P. (1992) 'Technology Diffusion and Organisational Learning', in M.D. Cohen and Sproull, L.S. (eds), *Organisational Learning* (Thousand Oaks, Cal.: Sage).

Bahrami, H. and Evans, S. (1997) 'Human Resource Leadership in Knowledge-Based Entities: Shaping the Context of Work', *Human Resource Management*, 36: 23–8.

Balas, E. (1997) 'Electronic Communication with Patients: Evaluation of Distance Medicine Technology', *Journal of the American Medical Association*, 278(2): 152–9.

Barnes, D. (1998) 'MOSS and the First Operational Telemedicine Link via Satellite for the Defence Medical Services', *British Journal of Healthcare Computing and Information Management*, 15(4) (May): 34–5.

Berliner, H. (1998) 'America on Line', *Health Service Journal*, 108(5589) (January): 28–9.

Bijker, W.E., Hughes, T.P. and Pinch, T. (1990) *The Social Construction of Technological Systems* (Cambridge, Press.: MIT Press).

Bishop, P. (1998) 'Integration with I.C.W.S', *British Journal of Healthcare Computing and Information Management*, 15(2) (March): 32–5

Cashdan, E. (1998) 'Smiles, Speech, and Body Posture: How Women and Men Display Sociometric Status and Power', *Journal of Non-verbal Behaviour*, 22: 209–27.

Civin, M.A. (1999) 'On the Vicissitudes of Cyberspace as Potential-Space', *Human Relations*, 52: 485–506.

Clegg, S.R., Hardy, C. and Nord, W.R. (1996) *Hand book of Organisational Studies*. (Thousand Oaks, Ca: Sage.)

Cochrane, P. (1997) 'A Virtual Revolution', *Health Management*, 1(4) (June): 18–19.

Deetz, S. (1994) 'Representative Practices and the Political Analysis of Corporations', in Kovacic, B. (ed) *Organisational Communications New Perspectives* (State University of New York, Albany.: New York).

Darkins, A. (1996) 'Telemedicine: Remote Medicine and Remote Risk?'.: *Health Care Risk Report*, 2(9) (September): 15–18.

Davidow, W.H. and Malone, M.S. (1992) *The Virtual Corporation* (London: Harper Business).

Dodd, N. (1997) 'Enhanced Alarm Detection for Telemonitoring using the Neural Network Alarm Monitor', *British Journal of Healthcare Computing and Information Management*, 14(6) (July): 20–2.

Eby, L.T. and Dobbins, F.H. (1997) 'Collectivistic Orientation in Teams: An Individual and Group-Level Analysis', *Journal of Organizational Behavior*, 18: 275–95.

Epley, T.K. (1998) 'Network Design for Telemedicine Programs', in Viegas and *Dunn Telemedicine: Practicing in the Information Age* (Philadelphia: Lippincott-Rowen).

Forster, R. (1999) 'Exploiting the Scope for Enhanced Screening', *British Journal of Health Care Management*, 5(11) (November, suppl.): 10–14.

Fortin, D.R., Westin, S. & Mundorf, N. (1997) 'On the Predispositions Toward Information Technology: A Three-Way Cross-Cultural Study', *Telematics and Informatics*, 14(145).

Gergen, K. (1992) 'Organizations Theory in the Post Modern Era', in Reed, M. and Hughes, M. (eds) *Rethinking Organisation* (London: Sage).

Gersick, C.J.G. (1988) 'Time and Transition in Work Teams: Towards a New Model of Group Development', *Academy of Management Journal*, 32: 9–41.

Halvorsen, P.A. and Kristiansen I.S. (1996) 'Radiology Services for Remote Communities: Cost Minimisation Study of Telemedicine', *British Medical Journal*, 312(7042) (25 May): 1333–6.

Harrison, R. Clayton, W. Wallace, P. (1996) 'Can Telemedicine be Used to Improve Communication Between Primary and Secondary Care?', *British Medical Journal*, 313(7068) (30 November): 1377–80.

Hassard, J. (1996) 'Images of Time in Work and Organisation', in Clegg, Hardy and Nord *op cit*.

Hassard, J. (ed.) (1990) *The Sociology of Time* (London: Macmillan – now Palgrave).

Jardine, K. and Clough K. (1998) 'Technically the Winner', *Health Management*, 2(5) (June): 8–10.

Jones, S.G. (ed) (1995) *Cybersociety: Computer-Mediated Communications and Community* (London: Sage).

Jong. M.K.K., Horwood, K. and Robbins, C.W. (1999) *Labrador Telemedicine Project-A cost Effective Store and Forward Technology for Remote Communities* unpublished working paper. Rural Health Academic Centre. Memorial University of Newfoundland.

Kenny, G.K. and Wilson, D.C. (1984) 'The Interdepartmental Influence of Managers: Individual and Sub-Unit Perspectives', *Journal of Management Studies*, 21(4): 404–27.

Kretschmer, R and Nerlich, M. (1999) 'Assessing the Impact of Telemedicine on Health Care Management', in Nerlich, M. and Kretschmer, R. (eds), *The Impact of Telemedicine on Health Care Management* (Amsterdam: IOS Press).

Lamb, A. Eydmann, M. Boddy, K. (1997) 'Remote Maternity Clinics', *British Journal of Healthcare Computing and Information Management*, 14(7) (September): 22–4.

Leete, B. (1999) '21st Century Toy? Real-Time Telepathology: Another Novel Concept of Cost-Effective Investment?', *British Journal of Health Care Management*, 5(6) (June suppl.): 6–7.

Lehoux, P., Sicotte, C. and Lacroix, L. (1999) 'Theory of Use Behind Telehealth Applications', in M. Nerlich, and R. Kretschmer (eds) *The Impact of Telemedicine on Health Care Management* (Amsterdam: IOS Press).

Lococo, A. and Yen, D.C. (1998) 'Groupware: Computer Supported Collaboration' *Telematics and Informatics*, 15: 85–101.

Lundin, R. Soderholm, A. and Wilson, T. (1998) 'Notions of Time in Projects and Organisations', Paper presented at IRNOP III (International Research Network on Organising by Project) Conference, The Nature and Role of Projects in the Next 20 Years, University of Calgary, Alberta, Canada, July 6–8.

Mair, F. Whitten, P. and Allen, A. (1997) 'Interpersonal and Organizational Issues in Telemedicine', *Health and Social Care in the Community*, 5(1): (January): 55–59.

McClelland, I. Adamson, K. and Black, N.D. (1995) 'Information Issues in Telemedicine Systems', *Journal of Telemedicine and Telecare*, 1: 7–11.

McGrath, J.E. and O'Conner, K.M. (1998) 'Temporal Issues in Work Groups', in M.W. West (ed.) *Handbook of Workgroup Psychology* (Chichester: Wiley).

McLaren, P. and Ball, C.J. (1995) 'Telemedicine: Lessons Remain Unheeded', *British Medical Journal*, 310 (6991): 1390–1.

Meara, R. (1997) 'Marriage of Convenience', *Health Management* (April 14–15).

80 *Virtual Caring*

Moore, M.B (1998) 'Organization for Telemedicine Services ; Developing Administrative, Clinical and Technical Protocols', in S.F. Viegas and K. Dunn (eds) *Telemedicine Practising in the Information Age* (Philadelphia: Lippincon-Raven Publishers).

Nohria, N. and Eccles, R. (1992) (eds) Networks and Organisations: Structure, Form and Action (Boston: Harvard Business School Press).

Palmer, I., Dunford, G., Rura-Plloey, T. and Baher, E. (2001) 'New Forms of Organising Film Production: The Existence of Dualities in the Use of Technology for Remote Collaboration', *Journal of Organisational Change Management* (forthcoming).

Park, B. (1975) 'Communication Aspects of Telemedicine', in R.L. Bashshur, P.A. Armstrong and Z.I. Youssef (eds), *Telemedicine–Explorations in the Use of Telecommunications in Health Care* (Springfield: Charles C. Thomas).

Park, B. (1974) 'Human Communication in the Interactive Television Medium'. In An Introduction to Telemedicine Interactive Television for Delivery of Health Service (Alternate Media Center, School of the Arts: New York University).

Pelletier-Fleury, N. *et al.* (1997) 'Transaction Costs Economics as a Conceptual Framework for the Analysis of Barriers to the Diffusion of Telemedicine' *Health Policy*, 42(1) (October: 1–14).

Pettigrew, A. (1973) *The Politics of Organisational Decision Making*, (London: Tavistock).

Quinn, J.J. and Jackson, P. (1996) *Control In The Virtual Organisation*. Paper presented at the British Academy of Management Conference, (Aston University: Birmingham) September 10–16.

Richardson, R. and Marshall, J.N. (1996) 'Teleservices, Call Centres and Urban and Regional Development', *Service Industries Journal*, 19(1): 96–116.

Rigby, M. (1999) 'The Management and Policy Challenges of the Globalisation Effect of Informatics and Telemedicine', *Health Policy*, 46(2) (January): 97–103.

Roberts, K.H. and Grabowski, M. (1996) 'Organisations, Technology and Structures', in S.R. Clegg, C. Hardy and W.R. Nord, *op. cit.*

Robinson, N. (1999) 'NHS Direct: "Gateway to the NHS"?', *British Journal of Healthcare Computing and Information Management*, 16(5) (June): 25–26.

Rosch, P.J. and Kearney, H.M. (1985) 'Holistic Medicine and Technology : A Modern Dialectic', *Social Science and Medicine*, 21(12) 1405–1409.

Schofield, J. and Wilson, D.C. (1996) 'The Role of Capital Investment Project Teams in Organisational Learning', *Scandinavian Journal Of Management*, 11(4): 423–436.

Symonds, M. (1999) 'The Net Imperative', *The Economist*, 26 (June): 84.

Thick, M. (ed.) (1996) *Telemedicine: Risks and Opportunities* (London: Royal Society of Medicine Press).

Trist, E. and Bamforth, K.W. (1951) 'Some Social and Psychological Consequences of the Longwall Method of Coal Getting', *Human Relations*, 4(1): 3–38.

Viegas, S.F. and Dunn, K. (1998) (eds) *Telemedicine: Practising in the Information Age* (Philadelphia: Lippincott-Raven Publishers): 383.

Turner, J. and Peterson, C.D. (1998) 'Organizational Telecompetence: Creating the Virtual Organization', in S.F. Viegas and K. Dunn (eds) *Telemedicine Practising in the Information Age* (Philadelphia: Lippincon-Raven Publishers).

Westin, A.F. (1992) 'Key Factors that Belong in a Macroergonomic Analysis of Electronic Monitoring – Employee Perceptions of Fairness and the Climate of Organizational Trust or Distrust', *Applied Ergonomics*, 23(1): 35–42.

Woodward, J. (1965) *Industrial Organisations: Theory and Practice* (London: Oxford University Press).

Wooton, R. (1998) 'Telemedicine in the National Health Service', *Journal of the Royal Society of Medicine*, 91(12) (December): 614–621.

Wootton, R. (1996) 'Telemedicine: A Cautious Welcome', *British Medical Journal*, 313(7069) (30 November): 1375–7.

5 Changing Institutional Frameworks: Formalisation as a Means of Institutionalising Collaborative Activity among Health Care Providers

Steve Cropper

INTRODUCTION

'Perhaps the most outstanding achievement of the NHS at the end of the 1980s . . . was that it had established itself as Britain's only immaculate institution' (Klein, 1995: 229). As if to this script, the NHS Plan (Department of Health, 2000: 2) opens with an affirmation of the value placed on the NHS, whilst casting a warning shadow:

> The NHS is the public service most valued by British people. Ever since its creation in 1948, the NHS has been available when we've needed it . . . Its founding principles . . . remain as important today as in 1948. In an age when our lives and jobs are undergoing constant change, it is reassuring to know that the NHS is there and will take care of us in times of need . . . Yet, despite its many achievements, the NHS has failed to keep pace with changes in our society.

This chapter concerns continuity and change in the NHS. In particular, it concerns the ways in which ambiguous or conflicting institutional pressures can be understood and managed as the search for effective organisational arrangements in health care proceeds. It draws on institutional theory to explore, generally, how organisational and institutional processes interrelate, and specifically how new organisational forms might emerge and become more or less accepted and valued elements of the institutional framework. It illustrates, or rather starts to build, the arguments using a case study of a wide area (sub-regional) partnership of acute and community NHS Trusts established to promote quality of childrens' health services.

Klein's conclusion to *The New Politics of the NHS* is that 'The NHS is likely to remain a self-inventing institution, responding incrementally both to the evolving and unpredictable pattern of health care delivery and to the ideological biases of whichever party happens to be in power' (1995: 253). Five headings cover the challenges posed by New Labour in *The NHS Plan* (Department of Health, 2000): partnership; performance; professions and the wider NHS workforce; patient care; and prevention. Through attention to these devices, the Plan signals change both in the organisational system supporting health care delivery, and in the complex system of institutional relations which shape that system. How institutional pressures interact with, limit and shape the search for effective organisational arrangements is, however, poorly understood: this chapter explores some of the issues involved.

It starts with a review of the development of institutional theory. The review draws a line from Selznick's seminal observation of institutional pressures on the form and behaviour of specific organisations (Selznick, 1957), through a concern with the institutional patterning of organisational types, to a current preoccupation with emergence and change in organisational fields. Different institutional mechanisms, or pillars, suggested by Scott (1995) are linked to a framework for understanding elements of organisation in which institutions might be embodied, and through which organisational challenge to prevailing institutions might also be expressed.

A brief characterisation of the institutional field of health focuses on certain institutional pressures shaping the organisation of acute care services. In response to calls for longitudinal field studies which capture the creation and evolution of institutions (Scott, 1995), a case study of collaborative working between providers of paediatric services is presented. The story tells of movement from *ad hoc* linkages through an informal planning network to a more formalised partnership arrangement, and exposes the interplay between institutions and organisations, and between continuity and change, in the health field. The chapter concludes by tentatively sketching a development trajectory in which particular elements of organisation form the primary basis and focus for development and legitimisation of a collaborative venture.

This raises questions in institutional theory, and for the management of health service organisations.

INSTITUTIONS AND ORGANISATIONS: THEORETICAL ISSUES AND PROGRESSIONS

In exploring the effects of institutions on organisational life, institutional inquiry has tended to emphasise one or other of two (composite) levels of analysis: the organisation in its context; or the organisational field and its constituent organisational populations.

Early studies of institutional effects on organisations highlighted the way in which the structure, functions and missions of organisations could be corrupted as organisations sought to adjust and represent their behaviour as receptive to powerful interests; that is, as they sought to establish and maintain legitimacy. In a classic study, Selznick (1957: 20) argued that: 'Organizations do not so much create values as embody them. As this occurs, the organization becomes increasingly institutionalized.' Selznick emphasised the unique history of institutionalisation that would characterise any particular organisation, but also suggested that the operation of institutional processes was contingent on characteristics of the organisation, of which some might be shared with other organisations. Thus:

> Institutionalization is a process. It is something that happens to an organization over time, reflecting the organization's own distinctive history, the people who have been in it, the groups it embodies and the vested interests they have created, and the way it has adapted to its environment... The more precise an organization's goals, and the more specialized and technical its operations, the less opportunity there will be for social forces to affect its development.
> (Selznick, 1957: 16)

In this way, Selznick indicated a route, subsequently taken by institutional theory, into the study of types or groups of organisations which might be subjected to common institutional pressures. Thus, the new institutionalists argue: 'Organizational forms, structural components, and rules, not specific organizations, are institutionalised' (Di Maggio and Powell, 1991: 14). The study of institutional effects on organisations has shifted, then, to explore effects within groups of organisations which together constitute an organisational field – 'those organizations that in the aggregate constitute a recognised area of institutional life ... the totality of relevant actors' (DiMaggio and Powell, 1983: 148).

Institutional Processes: The Relationships between Organisations and Institutions

Extending Selznick's (1957) analysis, institutional theory draws attention primarily to the processes by which organisation might become patterned and stable. Selznick noted the importance of commitment and attachment as the defining quality of an institution. Thus:

> to institutionalize is to infuse with value beyond the technical requirements of the task at hand ... From the standpoint of the committed person, the organization is changed from an expendable tool into valued source of personal satisfaction. (1957: 17)

Selznick also noted the need for clarity about which groups did see such value in the organisation:

> All this is a relative matter and one of degree ... For the group that participates directly in it, an organization may acquire much institutional value, yet in the eyes of the larger community the organization may be readily expendable. (*Ibid.*: 19–20)

As the search for or maintenance of value became a dominant concern, the representation of the organisation as a unique contributor to its organisational field would become a preoccupation. Thus, in a classic development from Selznick's work, Meyer and Rowan (1977) argue:

> By designing a formal structure that adheres to the prescriptions of myths in the institutional environment, an organization demonstrates that it is acting on collectively valued purposes in a proper and adequate manner ... The incorporation of institutional elements provides an account of its activities that protects the organization from having its conduct questioned. The organization becomes, in a word, legitimate. (Meyer and Rowan, 1977: 349)

The argument rests on a distinction between 'production organisations' which are structured to manage (coordinate and control) relations within and across their boundaries, and 'institutionalised organisations' the survival of which is dependent on observing the 'ceremonial demands of highly institutionalised environments' (Meyer and Rowan, 1977: 353). As Scott (1995: 134) notes:

> Rather than focus on rational or strategic choice, or on a search for organizational distinctiveness, the theory has sought, rather, to explain how organizations can, through institutional processes, replicate and mimic what is legitimate, and so converge in their forms and behaviours.

Reflecting, later, on the supposed correspondence between infusion with value and institutionalisation, Selznick (1996: 271) recognises other routes to the formation of 'social entanglements or commitments'. Where later versions of institutionalisation emphasise the adoption of the 'trappings' of successful organisations, Selznick's sense of institutionalisation rests on the processes which take an organisation beyond a technical arrangement of resources to a committed polity. In either version, the issue is to understand whether, how and with what consequences organisations embed and represent valued behaviours.

Institutional Mechanisms

Scott (1995) has traced the development of three 'pillars of institutions' – cognitive, normative and regulative, which build on but slightly crosscut DiMaggio and Powell's (1981) distinction between mimetic, normative and coercive mechanisms. The three pillars suggest the mechanisms by which legitimacy is instilled into organisational form, legitimacy being, in Scott's terms, 'a condition reflecting cultural alignment, normative support, or consonance with relevant rules or laws' (Scott, 1995: 45). For each, the basis of compliance, the underlying logic, indicators and basis of legitimacy (Scott, 1995: 35) (see Table 5.1).

DiMaggio and Powell (1983) suggest that the tendency towards bureaucratic forms of organisation is 'effected largely by the state and the professions, which have become the great rationalisers of the second half of the twentieth century' (1983: 147). These coincide with the regulative and normative pillars respectively. First, regulative systems solidify and cohere, most commonly in the form of legal requirements or policies which range from sheer imperatives to softer, permissive mandates. Second, normative pressure is equated, essentially, with the professions and professionalisation through which

Table 5.1   Three pillars of institutions

	Regulative	Normative	Cognitive
Basis of compliance	Expedience	Social obligation	Taken for granted
Mechanisms	Coercive	Normative	Mimetic
Logic	Instrumentality	Appropriateness	Orthodoxy
Indicators	Rules, laws, sanctions	Certification, accreditation	Prevalence, isomorphism
Basis of legitimacy	Legally sanctioned	Morally governed	Culturally supported, conceptually correct

Source: Scott (1995: 35).

belief and value systems, distinctive ideology and normative commitments become widely shared and reproduced. Professional education is one carrier; another is the elaboration of professional networks, which link organisations. Finally, and perhaps most diffuse, the cognitive pillar includes taken-for-granted beliefs, cultural rules and frameworks that guide behaviour in organisational worlds.

Organisational Behaviour and Institutional Change

In tracing the effect of institutions in organisational fields, the distinctive contribution of institutional theory has been in the explanation of conformity and inertia (Greenwood and Hinings, 1996; Scott, 1995). 'What makes organisations so similar?' is the question posed by DiMaggio and Powell (1983), yet, interpretations of the theory have been confounded by observations of variety and change (DiMaggio, 1988; Greenwood and Hinings, 1996). Two points are important here. First, the arguments about institutional processes so far have not fully captured the complexity and equivocality of signals and cues (Greenwood and Hinings, 1996: 1029): there is more room for variety, difference and active choice than the 'over-determining' theory would suggest:

Much of the important work by institutional theories over the past two decades has been in documenting the impact of social and symbolic forces on organizational structure and behaviour.... Organizations are affected, even penetrated, by their environments, but they are also capable of responding to these influence attempts creatively and strategically. By acting in concert with other organizations facing similar pressures, organizations can sometimes counter, curb, circumvent, or redefine these demands.

(Scott 1995: 132)

This objection is echoed in general arguments about strategic responses to institutional pressures (Oliver, 1991). Second, the focus on stability and conformance leaves the question of institutional origins unexplained, and DiMaggio (1988: 14) suggests this is an opportunity to bring agency (actors intentionally pursuing interests) back into institutional analysis. 'New institutions arise when organised actors with sufficient resources (institutional entrepreneurs) see in them an opportunity to realise interests that they value highly.'

Collaborative Working and Institutional Analysis

The importance of collaboration to institutional analysis lies in its distinctive character as a mode of organising (Human and Provan, 2000), and in its lack of a strong institutional base: in general, collaboration as a mode of governance is less well-established than hierarchy or market. What, then, are the components of organisational action which might be created or carried by collaborative ventures to effect change in institutional pressures?

Two recent studies are of interest here. Human and Provan (2000) report a study of legitimacy-building in the evolution of organisational networks, from formation or emergence to stable presence in the field (or demise). Their longitudinal analysis suggests two basic strategies for legitimacy-building for collaborative network ventures – work predominantly with members of the collaborative network, and work starting with stakeholders outside the collaborative network. They also identify three dimensions of judgement about the legitimacy of collaborative ventures: the network as form; the network as entity; and the network as interaction. All may be seen as problematic by powerful organisations. A focus on collaborative action may require, then, attention to three matters: first, what, in general, it takes for collaboration to be a valued mode of organising; second, the processes by which specific organisations renew and maintain legitimacy, in particular; and, third, how organisations, establishing legitimacy can balance response to institutional pressures with pressure to change institutions.

Lawrence *et al.* (1999) take Scott's observation and explore how collaborative organising, newly-valued as a general mode of organising within the specific organisational field of interest, might act as a means of altering, extending and challenging existing institutions. Their starting point, then, is with the network as form: but they confirm that collaborative ventures arising also require legitimisation as entities; and they point to two bandwidths of interaction – that more intensive form of interaction pattern likely to hold within the network; and the pattern of relationships which embed the network into the wider field. Lawrence *et al* (1999) also point to the materials or media of institutional work, distinguishing between (i) practices (patterns of action which are repeated, held in place by sets of rewards and sanctions); (ii) technologies (more or less commonly understood methods for solving problems – the toolkit that makes practices possible) and (iii) rules (normalised understandings of legitimate behaviour). (*ibid.*: 10–11). Collaborative ventures, they suggest, are sites in which the rules of the game may be (re)negotiated. Thus, Lawrence *et al.* suggest that

> The negotiations associated with collaborations often require intense interactions that lead to new understandings, norms and practices which, in turn, may be transmitted throughout the field ... Sometimes collaboration reproduces existing institutionalised practices, technologies and rules, and further entrenches inter-organizational networks ... In other circumstances, collaboration can change institutionalised practices, rules and technologies ... Indeed, one of the most common arguments for entering into inter-organizational collaboration is its potential for innovative solutions to complex problems. (1999: 7–8)

A crucial issue is the basis for initial formation and stabilisation of new organisational arrangements (Human and Provan, 2000; Ritti and Silver, 1986; Singh, Tucker and House, 1986). Institutional theory emphasises the way in which organisations construct value through the ordering of various materials, including importantly symbolic resources, and so establish legitimacy (Cropper, 1996, 1999). In particular, it suggests that collaborative ventures will draw from the three institutional pillars in order to represent themselves as a legitimate *form* of organisation; and in particular:

- as an *entity* (i) providing needed capacities, (ii) appropriately set within the institutional framework and (iii) directed towards valued purposes; and

- as a framework for appropriate, valued conduct, both formal and informal arrangements for *interaction*.

Each of these elements of organisation is a basis on which to claim legitimacy and value (Table 5.2) as specific organisational arrangements seek to establish themselves and to achieve longevity. Thus, analysis of collaborative arrangements might explore in what terms:

- A meaningful and legitimate *purpose* is expressed in the collaborative arrangements or activity.
- The set of resources (potentially) at its disposal suggests that collaborative working would represent an improved *capacity* to deliver activity against that purpose?
- The arrangements are deemed to represent appropriate *conduct*?
- The collaboration would make a distinctive contribution to, and within, the existing institutional framework?

Form: Institutional Factors and Health as an Organisational Field

Health, certainly no less than other industries or sectors, is heavy with institutional pressures. These form more or less stable points of reference and identity, even as the NHS's constituent organisations are reordered (or modernised). Without exploring, generally, the institutions which sustain and moderate the NHS, we can note that each of Scott's (1995) 'three institutional pillars' are powerfully evident: the NHS is constituted and governed by laws, rules and policies (regulative); it is subject to the values, norms and other effects of professional socialisation and social expectation (normative); and there are strong beliefs, expressed and embodied in arguments about technologies of health and health care (cognitive). The strict separation of these pillars, as analytical categories, blurs in practice. Also, because the elements in the institutional system have plenty of 'give' and are not strictly

Table 5.2   Institutional pillars and expression within any organisational entity

	Regulative	Normative	Cognitive
Purpose			
Capacity			
Fit			
Conduct			

aligned, the NHS often appears more as a place of ambiguity or contest: institutional factors compete to influence how organisations are arranged and behave.

Configurations of Acute Hospital Services

The acute sector of the NHS is one place in which the contingent relation between policy and practice is most evident. Since the last national hospital plan in 1962, the basic and strongest frame of reference for health services planning has been the population of the District Health Authority, with the District General Hospital as the basic infrastructure. Provision and development of specialist services locally has been limited: tertiary services have been largely developed within specialist regional centres. A hierarchical model of service organisation with specialist/high technology hospital centres serving catchment populations from 300 000 to 2 million, supported by district, town or community hospitals has been taken for granted. This convention is now under challenge (for example, Harrison and Prentice, 1996; Mistry, 1997; Joint Working Party, 1998; West, 1998). Various changes in the organisational form of acute health care provision have been witnessed: scaling up through whole-hospital Trust mergers, but also more selective, relational arrangements between provider organisations. Some, as in the case of cancer networks, are centrally mandated and regulated: others are voluntary agreements.

The Organisation of Clinical Services

One powerful driver for change has been the movement towards sub-specialisation in medicine. Bennett (1996) suggests that this is a highly political process, in which high-status professionals within medicine champion and draw interest to emerging issues or niches, like care for HIV/AIDS. A consequence of sub-specialisation is that the scale at which it becomes appropriate to provide services changes, varying service by service. The possibility of coherence of services planned and provided at a uniform scale from a single organisational unit such as the DGH is no longer tenable. As Smith (1999) reports:

it doesn't make sense for hospitals serving 150,000 to try to provide all acute services ... The surgeons are keen on hospitals that serve 500,000 ... But such hospitals cannot make sense everywhere.

For this and other reasons, the organisation of services is currently in transition. One strategy for repair lies in collaborative working. In Scotland, a review of acute services (Scottish Office, 1998) recognised that there would necessarily be differences in the way different acute services should be organised, but provided a strong vision and specific mandate to promote the development of what it termed 'managed clinical networks':

> The Review sees the development of managed clinical networks as the most important strategic issue for acute services in the NHS in Scotland. Such distributed networks offers the best basis for equitable, rational and sustainable acute services, are flexible and capable of evolution, and allow greater emphasis to be placed on service performance and effectiveness. The concept is ... presented here as an extension of a process of organisational change which has already begun.   (para 48)

Restructuring of services is made less sure by a lack of relevant evidence (Edwards and Harrison, 1999) and by inconclusive evidence (Posnett, 1999). More fundamentally, however, it is recognised that the factors influencing future configuration of services produce tensions or dilemmas which are unresolvable by any (singular) body of evidence. Smith (1999: 797) suggests that:

> Although there are no solutions, there are principles that can be agreed. Firstly, the whole exercise is about trading access, quality and cost. Each will have its own geography, existing services, problems, trade offs and values, making a universal solution impossible. Local decision makers must be free to create their own solutions, ... and the sixth principle must be to think differently.

There is now great interest in certain forms of response: managed clinical networks are seen as a means of adding value to service provision without the costs, and lack of benefits, of merger, especially forced merger. It has not always been the case. And, even where there is the strongest, most specific form of mandate for the development, those involved in the development of such networks make clear 'Developing the network is proving challenging' (Baker and Lorimer, 2000: 1153).

The case-study account that follows tells of a multilateral partnership between trusts providing childrens' health services and the ways in which, in its process of formation, it has incorporated certain elements of the institutional environment in order to create the conditions in which it can test and challenge the possibility of change in others.

CASE STUDY: PARTNERS IN PAEDIATRICS

The Initiation and Development of Collaborative Activity

Initiated in November 1997, shortly before the White Paper, *The New NHS: Modern, Dependable* (Department of Health, 1997) was published, Partners in Paediatrics (PiP) started as a series of informal discussions between clinicians and managers from nine NHS Trusts providing acute paediatric services between Birmingham and Manchester. All services are based in District General Hospitals rather than specialist service centres. Links between two Trusts provided the catalyst. Clinical collaboration, including referral and shared care arrangements had been recently supplemented by joint appointment of a consultant paediatrician. A senior manager in the smaller Trust, also recently appointed, had been involved in development of a collaborative arrangement between the paediatric services offered by three hospitals in an adjacent sub-region of England and was highly supportive of the idea. Although that previous arrangement was not seen as a model to be replicated locally, it provided a precedent and was a potential source of learning.

A letter was circulated to consultant paediatricians with management responsibility for paediatric services in the nine Trusts, inviting them to attend a meeting, independently facilitated, to

> discuss the opportunities for developing greater collaborative links between providers of paediatrics in this geographical area. It is apparent from work [elsewhere] that this can prove very beneficial for units involved ... The purpose of the meeting would be to discuss whether we, as a group, are interested in developing something along similar lines ... There are already signs that collaborations are developing in an informal way. (Letter 6 October 1997)

The invitation suggested that each centre might send one or two consultants plus a business manager. Twenty people attended and, after a presentation by the consultant paediatrician who had led the earlier collaboration in which issues of process and conduct were to the fore – for example, 'You have to play the health management "game"'

– the meeting considered what the proposal to 'strengthen collaborative links' might mean. The meeting concluded with a sense that there was a rationale for collaborative action to help in addressing some of the issues felt to be facing paediatric services.

The issues related to perceived discrepancies between health care need, professional standards and the current arrangements for provision of care, including the pattern of provision of specialist services. The bulk of paediatric medicine is carried out by general paediatricians, many of whom will take a special interest in particular diseases or patient groups – diabetes, cystic fibrosis and so on – without being a 'card carrying' specialist, trained and accredited in that particular subspeciality. There are implications for quality of paediatric health care service, here, which were given added salience (on publication of *The New NHS: Modern Dependable*, DoH, 1997) by the importance attached to access to local health care services and by the equally strong emphasis on other facets of quality of service.

The meeting also reached some agreement about the rules of engagement. A first decision of principle was that this would be a partnership of equals. Any collaborative arrangement should not be modelled on the 'hub and spoke': and no single Trust should consider itself a dominant 'hub'. The meeting concluded with an agreement that this group would consult clinical colleagues, and that a paper setting out 'a shared statement of the purpose and rationale for collaboration between providers' would be circulated widely. A small group was mandated to take responsibility for reporting, liaison between meetings, and arrangement of the next meeting.

At the next meeting, representatives indicated there was support for the idea, albeit with some caveats; for example there could be no immediate defection from existing strong service links with tertiary centres. Some suggested names of paediatricians located in community health service Trusts who they felt should be invited to attend. There was, again, much discussion about the nature of the venture: different from commissioning, yet seeking to influence commissioning of services through a collective voice; not actually providing service (the task of the Trusts) but rather clinicians exploring how quality care could be delivered to a (big) population. One of the Trusts had arranged a summit meeting with its health authority to discuss problems with a number of paediatric services: the meeting agreed the Trust should explore the potential contribution of a provider network with the commissioning authority. Spurred by this, the statement of purpose was sharpened and elaborated in three objectives (Box 5.1).

Box 5.1   Partners in paediatrics: objectives

- BALANCING SERVICES MEETING LOCAL NEEDS
  AND PROVISION OF HIGH QUALITY SPECIALIST
  SERVICES

  The partnership takes as a first and basic objective to comple-
  ment and support primary care and community paediatric services by maintaining local access to both general paediatric
  services and high-quality specialist medical and surgical services.
  The aim is to avoid the need for children and families to travel
  long distances to access specialist services and to realise the full
  potential of investment in local resources.

- MANAGING MANPOWER, TRAINING AND RESEARCH

  The partnership takes as a second objective to recruit high-
  calibre medical and nursing staff by offering attractive posts
  encompassing relevant areas of specialisation and to maximise
  their contribution by developing effective teaching/training programmes and building on the use of evidence-based medicine.

- ADVISING COMMISSIONING AGENCIES AND GROUPS

  To develop a strategic and coordinated approach to purchasing,
  moving away from volume-based contracting to a system of
  commissioning which better reflects the needs of children, better
  addresses aspects of service quality and outcome, and better
  supports local hospitals in delivering local services.

The rationale for development of provider collaboration lies in the
necessity to secure a catchment population sufficiently large to
justify and sustain specialist services. Such specialisation is a pre-
requisite to appoint and train high-calibre clinicians, especially in
the light of initiatives such as the junior doctors hour legislation and
the Calman training scheme. The local availability of specialist
clinicians will, in turn, promote and sustain high-quality general
paediatric services.

Box 5.1   *cont.*

Box 5.1   *cont.*

The catchment population of the participating providers is approximately 2 million which is large enough to sustain the provision of most specialist paediatric medical and surgical services. There is already significant clinical collaboration across the participating providers, in recognition of the current distribution of specialist services. In promoting a clearer basis for the provision/accessibility and development of paediatric services, a more coordinated approach would maximise the value of investment in those services and secure the best deal for local children.

Variously termed paediatric provider 'collaboration', 'consortium', 'network' and 'group', the initiative gathered a head of steam with a series of facilitated open meetings and a growing distribution list, as clinicians from services not initially represented joined the group. Over a period of ten months, the group established an open, participatory organisation and means of developing the shared purpose into actionable projects. Working groups, with members drawn from across the Trusts, were formed to take forward work on the future agenda and language of the New NHS and a 'broad mapping' of the range of paediatric services in the area.

A move from four to eleven working groups either in place or proposed, caused concern about support, coordination and control: rules started to become defined – for example 'Documents and analyses to be circulated at least one week before the meeting'.

The message coming back was that a number of Trusts, corporately, were now interested to know more about the partnership and its vision. Six months after the first event, an Open Meeting agreed 'to invite Chief Executives of all Trusts involved in the Group to a presentation of its work'. Trust 'lead contacts' were asked to brief their Chief Executives about this impending invitation. Terms of reference were issued to the working groups, each led by a named individual with particular knowledge of or commitment to the working group's defined service area: the groups were asked to prepare a case for continued work where there might be advantage in pursuing collaborative action.

The conference was well-attended, and the case for a programme of collaborative work was given and debated. Advice on priorities was incorporated into a partnership business plan (Box 5.2) and circulated back to Trust Chief Executives, inviting subscription to membership. Discussion of organisational arrangements for the Partnership had also been encouraged, couched in terms of the degree of formalisation of the partnership as an organisation. The existing, informal arrangements seemed insufficient to sustain the level of activity which, it had been agreed, would provide a reasonable test of the validity of the idea of partnership. But a leap to the degree of formalisation represented by a 'consortium' model was seen as undesirable, the arguments fuelled by Trusts' experiences of other 'consortia'. A middle way was agreed, with an appropriately constituted Steering Group acting as the governance system and with administrative support, financial control and, most important, some continuing central focus agreed in principle. A signature to the Partnership and a modest financial subscription were the conditions for a seat on the Steering Group, which oversees the conduct and work of the Partnership. Eleven Trusts subscribed to a second year (Partners in Paediatrics, 1999) and membership now runs at 13 trusts (Partners in Paediatrics, 2000).

The Case for Formalisation

The preparations for and the agreements reached at this first conference reinforced the gradual assimilation of more formal practices, technologies and rules that had occurred during the first year. Summing these for the conference, it became clear that the partnership could not maintain involvement and make progress without the formal stamp of approval from the participating organisations to underpin the informal agreements, and without resources to support management of the collaborative organisation. Underlying the debate about organisational form were questions about the conditions in which Trusts would see the partnership as an entity to which they could commit. The design for partnership had to assure:

- a clear mandate (and resources) to undertake such work – a shift from individual commitment to corporate commitment;
- clarity and equality of representation of Trusts;
- agreed mechanisms for Partnership guidance and decision-making;
- clarification of scope for action for mutual gain; and

Box 5.2   The partnership activity portfolio and plan

Seven key service areas	*Partnership objectives*
Child and adolescent mental health	Response to West Midlands Regional Review of Specialist CAMHS
Paediatric surgery and anaesthetics	Service Options Discussion Paper
Paediatric gastroenterology	Business case for service development
Paediatric Neurology	Business case for service development
Child protection	No specific action Year 2
Neonatal intensive care	No specific action Year 2
Paediatric diabetes	Detailed mapping of care packages Liaison with National Diabetes Information System Developments

Four cross-cutting areas	*Partnership objectives*
Workforce planning	Partnership workforce strategy
Medical education and training	Develop materials and methods for formal web-based/ distance-learning courses
Non-medical education and training	No specific action Year 2: service groups to consider as part of reviews
Clinical governance	Web site development, co-location of guidelines from partner Trusts & development of one new guideline
Engaging stakeholders	Communication with stake-holders Partnership conferences

• a stronger sense of mutual accountability – Partnership to Trust, Trust to Partnership and thus Trust to Trust.

The process of creating arrangements for representation and reporting with each provider organisation had already taken place (lead contacts in each Trust) at the group's agreement and prompting, but in practice this had been patchy. The move to incorporate the collaborative venture raised the question: who should be invited to participate?

Boundary Issues

A proposal had been put to an open meeting that invitations should be sent only to the Chief Executives of provider organisations which had been represented, even if informally, at previous open meetings. A counter-proposal was to invite Chief Executives of other providers of services within the partnership area, even if no-one from their organisation had yet been involved. These organisations were needed to complete the picture and to make for an appropriate capacity. The debate turned rather on the conduct of the collaboration to that point. Not all the people attending had been formal representatives; nor had they, then, fully briefed colleagues on the development of the collaboration; nor had they necessarily made clear to colleagues from other organisations that they continued to be welcome to attend the conference: and lastly, no final invitation had been issued to ensure procedural justice. In the end, the criterion of 'demonstrated commitment' rather than 'geography' prevailed, with a clear proviso that the policy of inclusiveness would remain through mechanisms other than the Steering Group itself. For example, the Partnership has used its working groups to broaden and sustain wider involvement. The clinical network that was strengthened in the first year of informal working has remained a critical resource for the Partnership.

From Interaction to Embeddedness

Formalisation has also now moved the partnership from a process of intense interaction *within* the partnership to more extensive work across its boundaries, as it has sought to represent itself to external constituencies. This has served to increase its embeddedness in the local institutional framework that most immediately related to the issues of concern. A case for development of an accredited specialist service centre for paediatric gastroenterology has been a lead activity; a service and workforce planning workshop and a conference focusing on anticipated problems in the future provision of general surgery for children have all taken the partnership far outside its own boundaries.

FORMALISATION

Formalisation is commonly discussed as the tendency towards the use of explicit rules and procedures as a means of coordinating and controlling work activity, so as to ensure reliability and consistency in the operational/administrative working of organisations. This emphasis on standardisation and routinisation of work activity returns to Weber's conception of bureaucracy as independent of particularistic influence. Meyer (1983) has suggested that formal organisations will emerge from a cultural context in which definable purposes, technologies (or means–ends relationships) will, when embedded in appropriate organisation, help to insure reliable performance and accountability.

Here, in addition to this standard use, I take formalisation to be both a movement towards and a point of stabilisation in the process of construction, appropriation and ordering of material and symbolic resources for the partnership as a distinct organisational entity:

First, formalisation provides a means of summarising 'what PiP already had become' – an attempt to articulate or invoke 'a collective identity as a means of imputing or maintaining the sense of organisational coherence or co-operativeness' (Gioia, in Whetten and Godfrey, 1998: 17–31).

Second, formalisation provides a basis and source of legitimacy – for the effort that had been invested in the development of the partnership and to capture commitment to investment (and reward) in the future. In this sense, formalisation was, as Meyer and Rowan (1983) suggested, 'myth and ceremony', drawing in a specific, if minimal, set of characteristics of formal organisation into the prevailing organisational arrangements.

Third, in terms of wider organisational space it also represented a statement of presence, of distinctive purpose and (in this case) constructive challenge to other, more or less established organisations in the field, of which many had more specific, connected and powerful institutions on which to rest. Formalisation has involved the creation of a visible, identifiable, regulated and accountable, and active set of arrangements distinct from but incorporating existing organisations.

The task, then, was to construct an organisational form which connects sufficiently to the institutional base and to valued change in that base that it can survive. The partnership has a constitution and formalised governance system. It has a budget, a Chairman, a designated half-time manager, and other roles including lead clinician and professional adviser roles (nursing, human resources, commissioners, academic). The practices of business management have entered the partnership. Work groups are now expected to submit business plans; the Steering Group assess and reconcile competing priorities. Leadership of the working groups is documented with objectives and milestones, against which progress is measured and chased. There are distribution lists and an increase in use of written communication. In short, the partnership has taken on certain important practices of its constituent organisations and, as such, is recognisable, deemed to be professional, legitimate.

The capacity of the partnership to speak on behalf of its constituency has been tested through presentations to health authorities and through the working groups. Beyond the gastroenterology business case and the written response to the regional review of CAMHS, it is starting to produce resources for its members – a web site carrying existing clinical guidelines for inspection, comparison and, potentially, reconciliation, a medical workforce strategy, a review of paediatric general surgery, an agreement to standardise diabetes databases and so on. These start to define and reinforce a formal organisational presence with value to the field.

Lawrence, Hardy and Phillips (1999) argue that the institutionalised practices, rules and technologies that structure organisational fields reward particular strategic positions and practices while sanctioning others, motivating those actors less privileged by existing rules to work to overcome them. Thus, commissioners, community trusts, the tertiary centres and specialist service trusts are now becoming engaged and implicated. Although the partnership remains vulnerable on each of its projects, the idea of a sub-regional network of linked services is now, service by service, capable of development, adjustment and insertion into the institutional framework which shapes the organisational arrangements. The stronger, more specific mandate for managed clinical networks, rather than the initial generalised call for 'partnership' is a potentially important symbolic resource.

DISCUSSION AND CONCLUSION

Collaborative working is regarded, instrumentally, as a means of achieving ends which would not (so readily) be achieved by organisations acting alone or in competition. It is a distinctive form of organising activity. Whilst not disputing this regard, this chapter has started from another point, which sees the process of construction of a multi-organisational venture as one of establishing value in a contested field. Not only is the field contested, but it is also sharply focused on the legitimacy of organisation, that legitimacy established by reference to institutions which shape the field. So much is proposed by institutional theory. Where the purpose of a organisational venture is to bring about change in that field and, by implication, in the institutions that shape it, the process of construction becomes critical and institutional theory has had less to say. Scott (1995) has suggested that the inertial, conformist pressures of institutions might be capable of challenge through collective action, and Partners in Paediatrics has provided a case of voluntary collaborative action intended to challenge certain institutions governing the organisation of health care services. It has been able to draw support and legitimacy from generalised mandates, or regulative forces, weak when set against more specific imperatives, but nevertheless sufficient to initiate a process of organising through which it has built value and legitimacy through appeal to normative and cognitive pressures.

A trajectory of institution-building is suggested by the case. Human and Provan's (2000) case analyses suggest two broad strategies – start from within and then move to build constituencies outside; or start with external interests and then add value within. PiP, it seems, has sought to keep both strategies going, although it has been more successful within. A second type of dynamic concerns movement through the elements of organisation through which value can be represented. Generalised mandates and professional norms provided the basis on which to establish legitimacy and value, initially in the expression of a shared purpose and, then, as a pooled capacity – the network of contributors spanning nine acute Trusts. Cementing this in the formalisation of the partnership commanded further capacity (new Trusts joining and interest from commissioners). The critical issue remaining is that of the partnership's fit within the wider framework of institutions which shape and protect the current arrangement of services and their organisations and its ability to shape that context through appeal to specific mandates to develop managed clinical networks.

Theoretical questions also arise. In such an institution-rich organ-isational field, Meyer and Rowan (1977) suggest the process of formal-isation would be relatively de-coupled from function: it would represent attention to the ceremonial demand of the institutions rather than the functional end of coordination. There is some evidence that the partnership has comforted itself and its constituents through the adoption of Trust practices of business planning; yet, the production of such a plan also seems to provide a device for activating the coordin-ation structure provided by the Steering Group and the work groups. The jury is out on Meyer and Rowan's proposition.

Tolbert and Zucker (1997) suggest that whilst legitimacy is generally given primacy as the end in institutional theory, it might be taken, instead, as a means to securing needed resources. In this sense, they argue, institutional theory closes up with resource dependency theory and legitimacy simply becomes another currency of exchange. Again, this question remains open. In practical terms, institutional theory offers a way of seeing and ordering pressures shaping organisations. It also suggests how, strategically and tactically, institution-building can be informed. The theory might also provide a means of reading where and how attempts to change institutions could most profitably focus energies. That is a demanding task for organisational behaviour research and for organisational practice: the theory provides crude categories of institutional pressure and limited insight into how they become separated, ready for change, or hopelessly entangled.

The case study points to issues of scale and scope in organising processes, the critical and recurrent question of boundary management and processes of integration into 'larger' and 'smaller' schemes. For this specific partnership, important questions have been raised about how to link the contributions of commissioners and providers in rela-tion to service planning.

The problems raised by the scale and position of the partnership area are evident: as well as the Trusts, organisations with a normal interest in children's health-service planning include two Regional Offices of the NHS Executive; children's tertiary centres, six health authorities and over 20 primary-care groups. Service providers of relevance extend well-beyond paediatric services, including specialist surgical and mental-health providers and primary-care professionals. In addition, social services and education services have very significant planning responsibilities for, as well as professional input to, children's health. The partnership is not a part of the 'natural order' of the NHS – for a source of innovation/critique, that is appropriate, but, even with the idea of clinical networks bringing change in what is legitimate, PiP does not fit comfortably within the prevailing institutional framework of (on the one hand) NHS Executive (Regional Offices) responsible for policy translation and specialist service commissioning and (on the other) District commissioning and service complexes. It is at these two levels that resources (including authority) and accountability for resources are currently concentrated. Primary Care Groups (PCGs) and especially Primary Care Trusts (PCTs) will start to fragment the latter.

The partnership will need to find many ways of accessing power and ways of concerting those efforts to achieve change without losing the starting agenda. One symptom is for pressure to extend membership of groups beyond original intentions, as Selznick's (1957) brand of institutional theory would predict. PiP will need to decide whether or when service issues are so important that it is willing to extend its activity beyond institutionalised understandings of its place. For 'broadband' services like paediatrics, by comparison with more specific services such as vascular surgery or cardiology for which networks across acute providers are forming, such boundary work will remain a challenge to institutional as well as to organisational integrities. This chapter has suggested that the way in which institutions and organisations can become aligned to enable rather than simply constrain change is an important task for research and practice. Although a basic framework for analysis has been proposed, much still remains to be done to explore, systematically, the questions raised.

That leads, finally, to wider questions of method. The analysis presented above fuses theoretical insight with a rich case study to suggest that there may be much to gain by taking in understanding organisational behaviour in health care through institutional theory. This chapter has focused on the attempt by a specific organising effort to draw legitimacy from the prevailing mass of supportive and open institutional forces. We began started with questions about the degree of difference or of similarity in organisational form that may be 'admissible'. Whilst longitudinal studies of organisational formation, change and continuity may continue to provide both theoretical, empirical and potentially policy insight, there is an important methodological challenge – to find ways of mapping and tracing tendencies towards conformity or variety across the organisational field: only then will it be possible to ask why observed patterns might be occurring and whether they are desirable.

References

Baker, C.D. and Lorimer, A.R. (2000) 'Cardiology: The Development of a Managed Clinical Network', *British Medical Journal*, 321: 1152–3.

Cropper, S.A. (1996) 'Collaborative Working and the Issue of Sustainability', in C.S. Huxham (ed.), *Creating Collaborative Advantage* (London: Sage): 80–100.

Cropper, S.A. (1999) 'Value Critical Analysis and Actor Network Theory: Two Perspectives on Collaboration in the Name of Health', in A. Mark and S. Dopson (eds), *Organisational Behaviour in Health Care* (Basingstoke: Macmillan – now Palgrave).

Department of Health (1997) *The New NHS: Modern, Dependable*, Session 1997–8; Cm 3807 (London: HM Stationery Office).

Department of Health (1998) *Partnership in Action: A Discussion Document* (London: Department of Health).

Department of Health (2000) *The NHS Plan; A Plan for Investment, a Plan for Reform* (Cmd 4818–I London: HM Stationery Office).

DiMaggio, P. and Powell, W. (1983) 'The Iron Cage Revisited: Institutional Isomorphism and Collective Rationality. Interest and Agency in Institutional Theory in Organizational Fields', *American Sociological Review*, 48: 147–60.

DiMaggio, P. (1988) 'Interest and Agency in Institutional Theory' in L. Zucker (ed.), *Institutional Patterns and Organizations* (Cambridge, Mass.: Ballinger): 3–21.

Edwards, N. and Harrison, A. (1994) 'Planning Hospitals with Limited Evidence: A Research and Policy Problem', *British Medical Journal*, 319: 1361–3.

Ferlie, E. and Pettigrew, A. (1996) 'Managing through Networks: Some Issues and Implications for the NHS', *British Journal of Management*, 7 (special issue, March): S81–99.

Gioia, D. (1998) 'From Individual to Organizational Identity' in D.A. Whetten and P.C. Godfrey (eds), *Identity in Organisations* (Thousand Oaks, Cal.: Sage): 17–31.

Greenwood, R. and Hinings, C.R. (1996) 'Understanding Radical Organizational Change: Bringing together the old and the new institutionalism', *Academy of Management Review*, 21: 1022–1054

Harrison, A. and Prentice, S. (1996) *Acute Futures.* (London: King's Fund)

Hoffman, A.J. (1999) 'Institutional Evolution and Change: Environmentalism and the U.S. chemical industry', *Academy of Management Journal*, 42: 351–371.

Human, S.E. and Provan K.G. (2000) 'Legitimacy Building in the Evolution of Small-Form Multilateral Networks: a comparative study of success and demise', *Administrative Science Quarterly*, 45: 327–365

Joint Working Party of British Medical Association, The Royal College of Physicians of London and The Royal College of Surgeons of England (1998) 'Provision of Acute General Hospital) Services: consultation document'. London: Royal College of Surgeons.

Klein, R. (1995) *The New Politics of the NHS*, 3rd edn (London: Longman).

Lawrence, T., Hardy, C. and Phillips, N. (1999) Collaboration and Institutional Entrepreneurship: the Case of Mère et Enfant (Palestine). Paper to

International Symposium: Linking Collaboration Theory and Practice, Melbourne, 14–17.

Meyer, J.W. and Rowan, B. (1977) 'Institutionalized Organizations: Formal Structure as Myth and Ceremony', *American Journal of Sociology*, 83: 340–363.

Mistry, P. (1997) *Rationalizing Acute Care Services* (Oxford: Radcliffe Medical Press).

Oliver, C. (1991) 'Strategic responses to Institutional Processes', *Academy of Management Review*, 16: 145–179.

Partners in Paediatrics (1999) Year 1: Report of the Conference held at Keele University: September 1998. Partners in Paediatrics, Mid Staffs NHS Trust, Stafford General Hospital.

Partners in Paediatrics (2000) Partners in Paediatrics: Report of Year 2 of the Partnership. Partners in Paediatrics, Mid Staffs NHS Trust, Stafford General Hospital.

Posnett, J. (1999) 'Is bigger better? Concentration in the Provision of Secondary Care', *British Medical Journal,* 319: 1063–5.

Ritti, R.R. and Silver, J.H. (1986) 'Early Processes of Institutionalization: The Dramturgy of Exchange in Interorganizational Relations', *Administrative Science Quarterly*, 31: 25–42.

Selznick, P. (1957) *Leadership in Administration: a sociological interpretation* (New York: Harper & Row).

Selznick, P. (1996) 'Institutionalism "Old" and "New"', *Administrative Science Quarterly*, 41: 270–277.

Scott, W.R. (1995) *Institutions and Organizations* (Thousand Oaks, Cal.: Sage).

Scottish Office (now Scottish Executive) Acute Services Review Report (Edinburgh, Scottish Office, 1998).

Singh, J.V., Tucker, D.J. and House, R.J. (1986) 'Organizational Legitimacy and the Liability of Newness', *Administrative Science Quarterly*, 31: 171–193.

Smith, R. (1999) Editorial: 'Reconfiguring Acute Hospital Services', *British Medical Journal*, 319: 797–8.

Stringer, J. (1967) 'Operational Research for "Multi-organizations"', *Operational Research Quarterly*, 18: 105–120.

Tolbert, P. and Zucker, L. (1997) 'Institutional Theory', in S. Clegg, C. Hardy and W. Nord (eds) *Handbook of Organization Studies* (London: Sage): 175–90.

West, P. (1998) *Future Hospital Services in the NHS: one size fits all?* (London: Nuffield Provincial Hospitals Trust).

6 Integrating Acute and Community Health Care: Integration versus Cooperation? The Case of Child Health Services*

Annette King, Naomi Fulop, Nigel Edwards and Andrew Street

INTRODUCTION

Integration of and cooperation between services has become increasingly important for service planning and delivery in the 'new' National Health Service (NHS) (Department of Health, 1998a). As the competitive culture of the NHS of the early 1990s has given way to a more conciliatory and cooperative culture, the different agencies and stakeholders in health and social care are now called upon to work in closer proximity and partnership. The focus has been on structural reorganisation to try to increase levels of integration and cooperation between services. It is hoped, for example, that the development of Primary Care Groups (PCGs) and Primary Care Trusts (PCTs) will promote higher levels of integration between primary and community health services. Further, proposals to establish Care Trusts which will be able to commission both primary and community health care, as well as

* The study on which this chapter is based was funded by NHS Executive London Region Organisation and Management R&D Group. We would like to thank the following people for their help: Phuong Huynh, from the University of Texas, who assisted with the study over a three-months period; Pauline Allen for comments on earlier drafts of this paper; and the audience at the second international research symposium 'Organisational Behaviour in Health care: Reflections on the Future' at Keele University (January 2000) for their useful insights on an earlier draft of this chapter. We are particularly grateful to all our interviewees and focus group participants who gave up their time to participate in the study. The views expressed are those of the authors alone.

social care, is an attempt to increase integration of services (Secretary of State, 2000).

Integration and working in partnership are not new ideas. The former Conservative government encouraged collaboration between primary and secondary care (Department of Health, 1996). However, the White Paper, *The New NHS* (Department of Health, 1998a), issued by the incoming Labour administration, stressed integration as a central policy objective. It emphasises the need for increased linkages of all services with primary-care provision and encourages the development of models for combined and cooperative service delivery across primary, secondary and tertiary health care.

The recognition that there is a need for a close working relationships between social and health care has led policy-makers to debate how the interlinkages may be strengthened, and common working practices developed. The key question is whether structural reorganisation is sufficient to promote integration of and cooperation between services. This chapter examines this question by focusing on the integration of and cooperation between child health services. Drawing on theories of integration and cooperation, and using the results of an empirical study of combined and separate acute and community NHS Trusts, we analyse the place of formal organisational structures and informal relationships as contexts for delivering integrated acute and community child health services. The evidence suggests that informal forms of cooperation and collaboration are as important as, if not more so, than organisational configurations in terms of providing integrated acute and community child health services. These findings have wider implications for the future development of the integration of services in the context of organisational change within the NHS.

In this chapter we first discuss theories of integration and cooperation which provide a framework for the analysis of organisational configuration as a means to promote integration. We then describe a research study which, using a range of methods, compares different organisational forms (combined and separate acute and community NHS Trusts) and their relationship to service integration. The empirical evidence used to address this question is analysed in relation to the theories, and the wider implications for service integration are drawn out.

THEORIES OF INTEGRATION

The study of service integration in health care has centred on integration of health care providers through *formal* horizontal and vertical integration, drawing on economic and organisational theories of the firm, for example transaction costs theories (Ferguson and Goddard, 1997). The role of *informal* forms of integration, in the form of cooperation and network relationships, has received less attention.

The concept of vertical and horizontal integration provides a framework for analysing formal organisational integration in health-services providers. Transaction-costs theories conceptualise organisational integration in terms of increasing the efficiency of the organisation through internal economies of scale, increased market power of integrated firms and increased information access (Williamson 1975, 1986; Oster 1994). Horizontal integration involves the formal merger of organisations providing the same types of products or activities (see for example Frances *et al.*, 1991). In British health care debates, mergers of NHS health care providers have been discussed largely in terms of reducing management costs and transaction costs (Crail, 1997; Street *et al.*, 2000; Hamblin 1998).

Through vertical integration, an organisation will integrate all or parts of the production process into the organisation as a measure of rationalising its operation and of increasing control over it. In forward (downstream) vertical integration the organisation buys up the distribution process, whilst in backward (upstream) vertical integration it buys up its suppliers (Oster, 1994: 195). Vertical integration has been particularly influential in developments in the US health care system, where for commercial reasons health care provider organisations have 'bought in' other areas of health care. It is exemplified by those Health Maintenance Organisations (HMOs) that attempt to provide a comprehensive range of health care and facilities (Aletras *et al.*, 1997). In England, prior to the development of PCTs, examples of vertically-integrated health care organisations have been found in the form of combined acute and community Trusts. In addition, 'mixed cases' of vertical integration combine numerous forms of integrative measures. US HMOs for example, have integrated acute, community and ambulatory services and cover all aspects of patient care (Robinson and Casalino, 1996). They have been a mixed success (see, for example, Robinson, 1996; Miller, 1996; Rauber, 1998).

While vertical integration emphasises the formal context of service integration in assessing the impact of financial and organisational management structures, this chapter also considers informal, cooperative relationships as an important dimension in service integration. For the latter, we utilise a second approach to conceptualising integration

in organisational economics network theory. Network theory emphasises the role of 'social relations rather than institutional arrangements'
in shaping organisational processes (Granovetter, 1985: 491). Network
approaches view organisations as complex social relationships, organised by patterns of recurring links between the different parts of the
organisation and based on social relations between individuals and
groups (Nohria and Eccles, 1992; Lincoln, 1982; Thompson, 1991;
Kickert and Koppenjahn, 1997). Cooperative and collaborative networks are the basis of integrative links across different parts of an
organisation and between organisations (Nohria, 1992; Lincoln, 1982).
Networks can operate on an informal basis, as relationships between
groups and individuals; or they can develop into formal networks in
the form of joint ventures or partnership programmes (Granovetter,
1985: 497). Some networks may develop into more formal organisations in the future (for a discussion of the transition from networks to
organisations see Sheaff, this volume). Formal and informal networks
operate on a number of levels and organisational contexts and are
important 'carriers' of stabilising and developing values and practices
in hierarchical organisations (Powell, 1991; Baker, 1992; Kogut *et al.*,
1992).

For an analysis of acute and community service integration, network
theory provides an opportunity to assess the impact of a range of
relationships and links between acute and community services beyond
the narrow context of formally integrated organisations. This chapter
uses the definition of service integration, which includes formally
integrated services where services have formally combined budgets
and management, and formal and informal networks based on cooperative relationships. Figure 6.1 presents an overview of the different
methods of integration in child health services (box C), formal organisational structures (boxes A and B) and forms of service integration
(boxes D and E).

In order to take account of the formal organisational configuration
of acute and community health care providers, this chapter compares
acute and community child health services in two Trust formations: (1)
in combined acute and community Trusts (vertically-integrated health
care providers), where child health service are managed formally by
one organisation (box A); and (2) in separate acute and community
Trusts, where child health services are formally managed by two
separate organisations (box B). In comparing formal and informal
forms of integration in the two Trust formations, we examine the
impact of the formal organisation of Trusts on service integration.

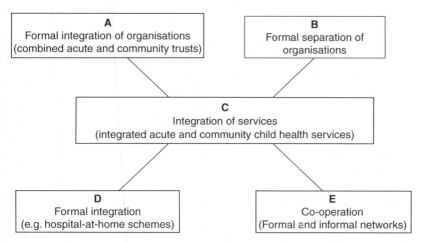

Figure 6.1   Overview of different methods of integration in child health services

We also examine informal ways of integrating services via cooperation in both types of Trust (boxes D and E).

THE RESEARCH STUDY

This chapter draws on data from a research study investigating the differences between acute and community services for children and older people in combined and separate acute and community Trusts. The question investigated in the research is whether vertically-integrated Trusts (combined Trusts) lead to higher levels of service integration. The study included an analysis of management costs using national data (Street *et al.*, 2000); a questionnaire survey of provider Trusts and Health Authorities in five NHS Regions; and data collected in six case studies using semi-structured interviews with health care managers and professionals, and focus groups with service users and carers.

The chapter focuses on services for children, using data from the survey of provider Trusts and data from the six case-study sites. The questionnaire survey of 106 provider Trusts was conducted between June and November 1998, and the case studies were conducted between February and October 1999. Survey data were used to gain an overview of integration and cooperation within and between Trusts. Six case studies were selected purposively (Bowling, 1997) from the survey to provide a range of levels of service integration (Box 6.1). Data from the case studies were used to develop a framework for comparison of integrated and non-integrated service organisation (Hartley, 1994). The approach to analysis is closer to that of Miles (1979) – who stresses the need for an early explicit, if tentative, organising framework – than the purely grounded-theoretic approach characteristic of Glaser and Strauss (1967). The theories described above provided an organising framework for analysis of the case studies: themes were drawn out from the case studies and a thematic profile of each Trust established. Second, cases were compared, and differences and/or similarities among the case studies were analysed. The theoretical approach taken is that of 'contextualism' which takes consideration of content, process and context of integration (Pettigrew *et al.*, 1985; Pettigrew, 1987).

Box 6.1   Summary of Districts and Trusts in case studies

Trusts and Districts	*Description*
District 1 combined Trust A	A combined Trust in a rural area. Acute and community services are managed in conjunction with neo-natal medicine and gynaecology. Community paediatricians participate in the acute hospital cover. Budgets are separate. The lead clinician of the service is a community consultant.
District 2 combined Trust B	An all-district Trust, covering a number of market towns. It is divided into a large number of directorates. Children's services is one of the smaller directorates. The business manager controls the budget. Acute and community services are located on different sites and clinics are held in various localities. The clinical lead is an acute consultant.
District 3 combined Trust C	A combined Trust, divided into a number of directorates. Children's services are combined

---

Box 6.1   *cont.*

Box 6.1 *cont.*

with women's and neo-natal medicine in one business directorate. Acute and community services retain separate budgets. Community services are located in a separate building, although clinics are sometimes held in the acute hospital. Community paediatricians are located in the acute hospital. The clinical lead for children's services is a community paediatrician.

District 4 acute and community Trusts P and Q

The Trusts are located in a medium-sized market town. Trust P has an integrated acute and community child health service, managed by a business directorate in the acute Trust. (services are located in the hospital, including most outpatient clinics). Professionals are located on the hospital site. Most PAM services are located in the acute Trust, although they are managed professionally by the community Trust.

District 5 acute and community Trusts R and S

Acute and community services collaborate through a series of clinics and through professional contact, although there are plans for greater integrated working. The community Trust has a strong mental health focus, while community paediatrics is only a small aspect of the service.

District 6 acute and community Trusts T and U

Acute and community services are closely interlinked. The paediatric home-care team is funded by the community Trust, but outreaches from the acute hospital. Community consultants are partly funded by the acute hospital, and they take sessions in the acute wards. The clinical lead is a community consultant.

The range of methods used in the study reflects the complexity of the phenomena of cooperation and integration. A 'mixed scanning' approach allows for the combination of higher level analysis (surveys) with detailed analysis of case-study material (Etzioni, 1967). Using a range of research methods also allows for data and methodological triangulation whereby data are collected from different people and groups using multiple methods in an attempt to limit bias (Denzin, 1989).

Findings from the Research Study

The Survey

The survey of child health services included 106 acute, community and combined Trusts in 5 NHS Regions. (The survey was conducted before the reconfiguration of the NHS Executive Regions in April 1999. The study was conducted in the following NHS regions: Anglia & Oxford, North Thames, South & West, South Thames, West Midlands). In North Thames Region, all combined, acute and community Trusts were included; in the other four regions, all combined Trusts and a randomly selected sample of acute and community Trusts were surveyed. The survey collected data on the organisation of acute and community services. The questionnaire provided a 'working definition' of integration and cooperation in order to allow respondents to distinguish between the two. Integration was defined as 'the formal linking of acute and community services resulting, for instance in combined management and/or combined finance arrangements between service units'. Cooperation was defined as 'more informal arrangements between services units and among staff and management including informal working relationships'.

Table 6.1 shows the response rate for children's services; 71 children's services returned questionnaires, an overall response rate of 67 per cent. Two major themes emerge from the survey. First, as Table 6.2 shows, the way acute and community services are organised reflectsTrust configuration: combined Trusts mainly provide combined acute and community services; while most separate acute Trusts provide only acute services and separate community Trusts provide only community services. As expected, 78 per cent (18/23) of combined Trusts provide both acute and community services. The majority of acute Trusts, 80 per cent (24/30), and community Trusts, 78 per cent (14/18), only provide acute or community services respectively. A significant minority of acute Trusts, 20 per cent (6/30), provide some combined acute

Table 6.1 Survey of children's services response rate

Trust type	No. of Trusts in sample	No. of responses	Response rate (%)
Acute	42	30	71
Community	29	18	62
Combined	35	23	66
Total	106	71	67

Table 6.2 Acute, community and combined Trusts: type of service

	Acute Trust (N = 30)		Community Trust (N = 18)		Combined Trust (N = 23)	
	Frequency	Per cent	Frequency	Per cent	Frequency	Per cent
Acute	24	80	–	–	1	4
Community	–	–	14	78	4	17
Combination	6	20	3	17	18	78
Missing	–	–	1	5	–	–

and community services for children. Secondly, cooperation and integration of acute and community services does not depend on the configuration of Trusts. Both Trust types have formally-integrated acute and community services, and both Trust types show similar ways of cooperating between acute and community services.

Formal Integration

Tables 6.3 and 6.4 summarise the frequency of integrated acute and community services in the different Trust types, which were formally

Table 6.3 Acute and community Trusts: integrated children's service

	Acute Trusts (N = 30)		Community Trust (N = 18)	
	No.	%	No.	%
Yes	16	53	6	33
No	14	47	11	61
Missing	–	–	1	6
Total	30	100	18	100

Table 6.4   Combined Trusts: integrated children's services

	No.	%
All services are integrated	9	39
No services are integrated	3	13
Some services are integrated	11	48
Total	23	100

integrated through combined funding or management. Fifty-three per cent (16/30) of acute Trusts and 33 per cent (6/18) of community Trusts reported providing some formally-integrated acute and community children's services (Table 6.3). It would have been useful to provide a direct comparison of integrated services in separate and combined Trusts. However, this may have led to double counting of integrated services in acute and community sister organisations. Data are therefore presented separately for integrated services in separate acute and community Trusts. The frequency of integrated services in combined Trusts is not as high as might have been expected. A total of 48 per cent (11/23) had some integrated services, but only 39 per cent (9/23) provided acute and community child health services which were fully-integrated (Table 6.4). A small number of combined Trusts, 13 per cent (3/23), continue to provide separate acute and community services, for example, by maintaining separate management structures and budgets.

Cooperation

In all Trust types, the most frequently mentioned forms of cooperation between children's acute and community services were as follows: standard methods of communication, defined as telephone conversations, exchanging of notes and letters; shared location of services; and care packages (the agreed provision of health and social care services following discharge) (Table 6.5).

The pattern of cooperation between acute and community services is similar in acute and combined Trusts. Sixty-one per cent (14/23) of services in combined Trusts and 53 per cent (16/30) of acute Trusts reported operating with these standard lines of communication. Shared location was used by 40 per cent (12/30) of services in acute Trusts and by 48 per cent (11/23) of services in combined Trusts. The exception is the use of care packages, which were reportedly used

Table 6.5   Forms of cooperation between acute and community services

Trusts	Standard lines of communication	Shared location	Care packages
Acute ($N = 30$)	16 (53%)	12 (40%)	11 (37%)
Community ($N = 18$)	7 (39%)	5 (28%)	3 (18%)
Combined ($N = 23$)	14 (61%)	11 (48%)	2 (9%)

by only 9 per cent (2/23) of combined Trusts, but were used by 37 per cent (11/30) of acute Trusts and 18 per cent (3/18) of community Trusts.

This analysis of the pattern of integration and cooperation suggests that for children's services, combined status does not seem to provide a clear advantage for developing an integrated service provision. Rather, service integration and cooperation occurs in all Trust configurations. Furthermore, all Trusts use a combination of formally integrated services and informal arrangements of cooperation for organising acute and community services. One of the limitations of the survey is that it cannot capture the complexity of formal and informal forms of integration. For example, the data on the forms of cooperation are likely to represent only a part of the complex cooperative arrangements in the Trusts. In the second part of the analysis, we explore integration and cooperation between different Trust types through the analysis of the case-study material.

The Case Studies

The case studies include three acute Trusts and their adjacent community Trusts, and three combined acute and community Trusts in six Districts (Table 6.6). Box 6.1 gives a brief description of each Trust. For children's services, data were collected from a total of 61 people (see Box 6.2 for further details). Semi-structured interviews were conducted with health care professionals and managers in Trusts and representatives of key agencies outside the Trusts (including health authorities, social services departments and PCGs). Four focus groups with parents of children with continuous healthcare needs were also conducted.

Interviews covered three broad areas of acute and community service organisation:

Table 6.6   Summary of Districts and Trusts in case studies

District	Trust	Status
1	A	combined
2	B	combined
3	C	Combined
4	P	acute
	Q	community
5	R	acute
	S	community
6	T	acute
	U	community

Box 6.2   Interviews – children's services

Managers and health care professionals in NHS Trusts	23
Health Authority managers	6
Local Authority social services managers	5
GPs and PCG representatives	5
Others 6	
Focus group participants (parents)	16
Total	61

---

1   The organisation of acute and community children's services, particularly discharge and continuity of care.
2   Service development plans and cooperation with other agencies.
3   Strategic developments and financial issues.

The focus groups explored the experiences and views of parents. In this chapter, focus group data are used to triangulate views expressed by professionals and managers.

Overall, among the three combined Trusts (A, B and C), only Trust B has a fully-integrated management structure for children's services, including the management of budgets. Children's community services in Trusts A and C retain separate budgets and are located outside the acute hospital. In both Trusts, a community consultant leads child health services.

The separate acute and community Trusts have developed a number of different patterns of working across acute and community services. Child health services are organised in a distinct way in District 4. Acute Trust P has an integrated child health service directorate. It manages acute and community child health services, while professions allied to medicine (PAMs) are managed professionally in the community Trust. In District 5 (Trusts R and S), the services cooperate on a case-by-case basis and each service is relatively separate. In District 6, the separate acute and community Trusts T and U have developed close informal working relationships between the services and a number of formally-integrated services. These include the shared post of lead consultant for children's services located in the community Trust and a paediatric community service which is located in the acute hospital.

The Pattern of Integration and Cooperation in Service Delivery

In the analysis of the case-study data, the categories of formally-integrated services, formal networks and informal networks were used to study formal and informal service integration. Table 6.7 summarises the relationship between acute and community services in separate and combined Trusts. The shaded areas indicate the strength of the links in the categories of formally-integrated services and formal

Table 6.7 Integration and cooperation of services in case studies

District	Trusts	Service integration and cooperation		
		Formally-integrated services	Formal networks	Informal networks
1	Combined Trust A			
2	Combined Trust B			
	Combined Trust C			
4	Separate Trusts P and Q			
5	Separate Trusts R and S			
6	Separate Trusts T and U			

Fewer   More

and informal networks, from an analysis of the case studies. Acute and community services in all Trusts work with a combination of formally-integrated services and formal and informal networks. Combined and separate acute and community Trusts have similar types of formally-integrated services. Child health services in all Trust types have developed patterns of working with their 'partners' at service level, whether internally with other clinical services such as surgery or pathology, across acute and community boundaries, or with departments in other Trusts and/or other agencies. Formal networks are particularly strong in District 3 (combined Trust C) and in District 6 (acute and community Trusts T and U). All Trusts have strong informal networks. The different methods of integration are discussed below.

The similarities between formal and informal integration in the case studies of combined and separate Trusts paint a different picture from the one indicated by some of the findings from the survey. For example, in the survey, more combined Trusts report having formally-integrated services and using other forms of cooperation than either acute and community Trusts (Table 6.4). A possible reason for this is that in the survey combined and separate Trusts have different perceptions about the level of formal service integration and informal forms of cooperation in their respective Trusts. Separate acute and community Trusts may be more 'cautious' in appraising their formal and informal forms of cooperation than combined Trusts. For example, in some of the interviews with representatives of combined Trusts, the assumption by some respondents was that the organisational structure of combined acute and community services already presupposed a high level of service integration. These perspectives were often qualified during the course of the interview or challenged through the inclusion of other stakeholder perspectives.

Formal Integration of Services

In all the case-study districts, hospital-at-home schemes are the most important integrated service. These involve combined funding and staffing between acute and community services and are used to shorten the stay in hospital and allow children with acute illnesses to be cared for at home. In District 6 this is a community funded service which operates out of the acute hospital:

It makes much more sense to organise it this way, because the community people know what is happening outside the hospital.
(Lead consultant paediatrician, Trust U, District 6)

Other forms of formally-integrated services include jointly-financed clinical posts and joint training rotations for paediatricians. Districts 3, 4, 5 and 6 also have coordinating acute and community nursing posts.

Acute services play a major role in providing comprehensive health-care for children with acute continuing (profound) health care needs, for example for children with life-limiting illnesses or severe disabil-ities. Services are organised through different forms of 'open-door' policies adopted by children's wards:

We have a small number of children, who we know very well and who come in quickly.
(Acute paediatric consultant, Trust B, District 2)

For these children, hospital is the first point of call: arrangements such as named paediatric consultants, immediate ward access and fast-lane referrals make acute services accessible at very short notice:

I only use the GP for repeat prescriptions. He doesn't really know about the condition and I think he is glad that he does not need to get involved. (Parent, District 3)

Formal Networks

Formal networks in all Trusts have become an increasingly important forum for raising additional funding for services. Paediatricians, managers and community nursing managers, in particular, are increas-ingly drawn into participating in bidding for additional funding as part of partnership initiatives (health and social services) and charity funding (such as Diana nurses). The common agenda to attract funding has brought services together and is a basis for cooperation and establishing closer links. Services in all districts report this as a positive development and are keen to pursue this in future, not only for the sake of being able to 'add' to the service, but also because of the opportunity to work across boundaries with different agen-cies:

We all have to do partnership working now. That is really good, you get to know people and we all have our bids in the draw now for the next time.   (Children's services manager, Trust A, District 1)

From a user perspective, formal networks of cooperation smooth the transition between services. For example, in District 6, parents comment positively on the cooperation between special education and health services in developing individual programmes at the local special needs school:

When my daughter started a new eating regime, after her hospital stay, the school was informed by the community paediatric service and we all worked out a programme together. It meant that everybody was doing the same thing. And I didn't have to push for it or to explain it all.   (Mother, District 6)

In Trusts A and B, where formal network cooperation is weaker, community paediatric services find it difficult to convene review meetings. Parents report that they often have to struggle to discuss their children's progress within a multidisciplinary setting.

Informal Networks

In all six case-study districts, informal networks bring together professionals and ease the work across service boundaries. The presence of formally-integrated services does not appear to make a difference to the significance of informal networks:

Occasionally, we have a particularly difficult case and need some urgent social work advice. I then simply ring the locality manager to get a quick decision.   (Lead consultant, Trust C, District 3)

Yes, of course, if I really felt that I needed the opinion from a psychiatrist for this child, I could give Dr.... a call, and he would try and see the patient, although officially there is no cover at night.   (Lead paediatric consultant, acute Trust R, District 5)

While informal networks are particularly important in 'smoothing' the transition between acute and community services, they cannot make up for every shortcoming in the service. In the focus groups, parents of children with continuing health care needs raised the issue of lack of support, training and equipment, and the constant battle for resources for community services as particularly problematic. Clinicians tended to share this view, pointing to the limits of service delivery caused by their increasing workload.

Overall, the combination of formally integrated services and formal and informal networks is effective in linking acute and community services. Trust configuration does not seem to have an impact. The case studies also show the importance of networks in facilitating cooperation between acute and community services. This finding is supported through the parent focus groups, where positive and negative experiences of service provision seem to be related to cooperation and integration at the service level rather than at the organisational level.

Internal and External Cooperative Relationships

Differences in Trust configuration come into focus when other cooperative relationships of child health services are analysed. The first concerns the position of child health services within the internal Trust hierarchy; the second concerns the strategic cooperative relationships child health services in Trusts can develop with other agencies, such as local authority departments of social services and education.

Table 6.8 summarises the internal and external cooperative links child health services have developed in separate and combined acute and community Trusts. The strength of these cooperative links is indicated by different shades. In two cases, the strategic links for a separate Trust are channelled through its 'sister' Trust. In the case of community Trust Q, strategic links are channelled through acute Trust P; and for acute Trust T, its strategic links are via community Trust U.

Except for Trust C, child health services in combined Trusts report that they have limited strategic links within the Trust hierarchy and they also lack strategic connections with agencies outside the Trust boundaries. In Trust C, strong strategic links have been established through the personal efforts of the lead clinician, who has a personal interest in participating in strategic forums, circumventing Trust management. In the separate acute and community Trusts, child health services have strong strategic relationships with outside agencies through at least one of the 'sister' Trusts. All separate acute and community Trusts also report strong links to their own Trust hierarchies.

Cooperative Links within Trusts

In the combined Trusts A, B and C, child health services perceive that they are disadvantaged in relation to more 'powerful' acute direct-

Table 6.8   Other cooperative relationships in combined and separate acute and community Trusts

District	Trusts	Strategic, cooperative links	
		Within the Trust	With outside agencies
1	Combined Trust A		
2	Combined Trust B		
3	Combined Trust C		
4	Acute Trust P		
	Comm. Trust Q	n/a	n/a
5	Acute Trust R		
	Comm. Trust S		
6	Acute Trust T		n/a
	Comm. Trust U		

Weaker links   Stronger links   n/a: not applicable

orates. The comparatively small size of the service reduces negotiating power for developing integrated services across departments:

> We don't have any influence on the elective surgery list of our colleagues. This makes it quite difficult for us to plan. . . . Orthopaedic and other surgeons will not accommodate children's services into their planning.   (Acute paediatric consultant, Trust C, District 3)

Having community services as part of the child health service provision does not necessarily strengthen the internal position of children's services in the overall Trust hierarchy: in some of the combined Trusts, community services are regarded as too costly by other departments. Professionals in child health services are concerned about the wider impact of internal restructuring in Trust on child health services, limiting the chances for service development:

> We have been challenged about the cost of our community budget. These consultants seem to think that community paediatrics is about giving a few injections, which should not cost much.
>   (Acute paediatric consultant, Trust C, District 3)

The professional divisions and the fights between the services are getting worse ... [On the acute side], there are more and more referrals to tertiary centres and there is an argument that the acute service could become even smaller.

(Community paediatric consultant, combined Trust B, District 2)

Over the last 10 years, my services have been decimated
(Lead paediatric consultant, combined Trust A, District 1)

In the focus groups, this lack of status in community services seems to filter down to the perception of parents about the quality and scope of community services. Parents in District 1 commented on the lack of facilities in the child health development centre and the lack of service development:

That centre, it really needs a lot of work doing to it. Ever since my son and I have been coming there, they have not had decent equipment. They don't even have the special drinking cups.

(Parent , District 1)

Staff do seem to change quite a lot, it is probably not very attractive for them here.

(Parent, District 1)

In the separate Trusts, community services are viewed as more progressive:

Yes they have done a lot in the last few years. There are a number of new initiatives, also for parents.

(Parent, District 6)

Strategic, Cooperative Links with Outside Agencies

In the combined Trusts, children's services perceive that they have little input into relevant commissioning bodies, such as the HA or PCGs, about strategic developments through their Trust management. Consequently, participation in partnership projects and cross-agency strategies is limited to the service-level initiatives. Wider strategic issues cannot be given enough attention:

I am invited to a lot of these steering meetings. I often cannot go because of my clinical work-load. And there is nobody else.

(Lead paediatric consultant, combined Trust A, District 1)

This is a sentiment repeated by all the combined Trusts, which cannot spare the management time to develop the links outside the service boundaries. This has a particular impact on links with education and social services – these are not developed systematically.

In contrast, in community Trust U, the established informal collaborative structures work so effectively that strategic responsibility for developing children's services has devolved to departmental level. In the separate acute and community Trusts T and U in District 6, strong collaboration at service level has evolved into independent strategic management role in the locality, circumventing Trust hierarchies. Health professionals themselves have taken on this role:

> I am getting involved in most of the discussions that are going on. We decide within our team, who will take on what.
> (Lead paediatric consultant, community Trust U, District 6)

Children's services increasingly negotiate independently across complex statutory interfaces and a multitude of agents, including social services and education, tertiary centres, GPs and voluntary organisations.

Strong cooperation between services, professional ties and shared care practices seem to reduce the perception of vulnerability to organisational change. The lead clinician in acute Trust P is confident that the PCG development will not affect the core of their service configuration:

> I know that they have extensive plans... however, as it works well here, there is no reason why we cannot carry on.
> (Lead paediatric consultant, acute Trust P, District 4)

Children's services in separate acute and community Trusts feel more secure, with the result that they are more willing to continue with developing services, and confident in participating in strategic planning of children services at the local level.

In contrast, in combined Trust C, children's services have to face the possibility of reconfiguration: community services are to be made part of the planned Primary Care Trusts, despite their professional objections. This may threaten the paediatric specialty in the Trusts as a whole:

> I would like somebody to explain to me how community paediatrics will fit into primary care... The fact that they do not work in the

hospital but outside it does not make them into a primary care service.

(Acute paediatric consultant, combined Trust C, District 3)

The community paediatric service is of particular significance in developing close strategic cooperation between health services and other agencies, because much of their work depends on developing informal cooperative working relationships across different organisational boundaries. Areas of community paediatrics, for example child development and child protection, bring the community paediatric service into close proximity with partner agencies. This makes them ideally suited to develop the partnership criteria:

When I sit on these panels, I am always surprised [at] how close community paediatricians are to our thinking. They also take a long-term view, have to take the population into account, rather than the individual patient.

(Manager, social services department, District 1)

There are some indications from the focus groups that strategic cooperative links have an impact on services in combined and separate Trusts. In District 6, the community paediatric service seems to have a central role in providing advice and connections to other services for parents:

If I need to know something I can always raise it ... they find out about things.

(Parent, District 6)

In the combined Trusts A, where strategic links with outside agencies are weaker, parents raised the general deficit in information as a serious problem:

I had to find out everything for myself. The hospital or the clinic did not seem to know anything.

(Father, District 1)

The exception is combined Trust C. Parents have access to an extensive information booklet, developed in cooperation between the child health services and social services. Parents regard it as a good resource book.

The lack of good cooperative managerial links within and outside the Trust structure in combined Trusts seems to have forced child health services into a defensive position in relation to organisational change from within and from the outside. This potentially limits the scope for development and further participation in partnership programmes.

DISCUSSION

Theoretical and Methodological Issues

The approach taken in this chapter allowed us to develop a framework of analysis which recognises informal forms of integration and cooperation as valid and significant in health-services integration. We would argue that network theory provides a sensitive approach in drawing out significant dimensions of integration in acute, community and combined Trusts, which would otherwise have remained obscured.

The study used a range of methods in order to analyse the complexity of the phenomena. A questionnaire survey was used to gain a broad picture of integration and cooperation in Trusts. However, these data should be treated with some degree of caution. For example, although respondents were provided with working definitions of integration and cooperation, these definitions are open to interpretation and it is possible that respondents may have used other definitions in the survey, depending on their perceptions of integration and cooperation. This may have introduced a bias into the survey results. However, the advantage of using case-study data alongside the survey data is that different perceptions of integration can be explored in more detail and validated by triangulating the different perspectives of stakeholders.

The research study described in this chapter outlines the importance of having an explicit theoretical approach when studying organisational issues (Ferlie, 2000), and using an appropriate range of methods to study these complex phenomena.

Implications for Organisational Change in Health Care

This chapter has considered the role that formal and informal forms of integration have in service integration of acute and community child health services. Evidence from this research study indicate that acute and community child health services can develop effective forms of informal and formal integration across acute and community services, regardless of the formal Trust configuration. The results from the survey and the case studies both show the continued significance of formal and informal networks in child health services. The research findings suggest that these are at least as important in service provision as formally integrated services. Community child health services, in particular, play a central role in developing these network links, because their work is embedded in multi-agency working, which requires cooperation across service boundaries. The analysis also points to the importance of formal networks in developing child health services across agencies. Developed as the result of statutory requirements, they have increasingly strategic significance for planning and developing children's services across agencies.

From the case studies, there is evidence that combined Trust status may threaten the development of cooperation between child health services and other agencies which provide services for children. The isolation of child health services within the overall combined Trust structure limits the capacity of services to develop more strategic cooperation and participation with agencies outside the Trust boundaries.

The research study highlights the importance of considering informal relationships in the analysis of integration in health services. This has wider implications in the context of the huge organisational change which the NHS has been, and is being, asked to implement. The focus in recent years has been on large-scale, structural change to organisations. From the creation of Trusts in the internal market in the early 1990s, to the creation of PCGs and PCTs more recently, the underlying assumption has been that these changes will result in improvements at the service level, including greater integration. The evidence set out in this chapter indicates that the level of service integration may be independent of organisational configuration. Instead, formal and informal networks, a key element of the integration of services, require incentives which may not necessarily be provided through organisational structures. However, changes to organisational forms may have unintended consequences, such as the finding that community services in combined acute and community Trusts may lose out to more powerful acute interests. Thus the possible unintended consequences of current and future organisational changes within the NHS need to be examined.

References

Aletras, V., Jones, A. and Sheldon, T. (1997) 'Economies of Scale and Scope', in B. Ferguson, T. Sheldon and J. Posnett (eds), *Concentration and Choice in Healthcare* (London: Financial Times Healthcare).

Baker, W.E. (1992) 'The Network Organization in Theory and Practice', in N. Nohria and R.G. Eccles (eds), *Networks and Organizations Structure, Form, and Action* (Boston: Harvard Business School Press): 397–429.

Bowling, A. (1997) *Research Methods in Health: Investigating Health and Health Services* (Buckingham: Open University).

Crail, M. (1997) 'Pain without Gain', *Health Services Journal* (18 September): 13.

Denzin, N.K. (1989) *The Research Act: A Theoretical Introduction to Sociological Methods*, 3rd edn (New Jersey: Prentice-Hall).

Department of Health (1996) *Primary Care: Delivering the Future* (London: HM Stationery Office).

Department of Health (1997) *The New NHS: Modern, Dependable* Session *1997–8*; Cm 3807 (London: HM Stationery Office).

Department of Health (1998) *Modernising Health and Social Services National Priorities Guidelines 1999/00–2001/02* (London: Department of Health).

Etzioni, A. (1967) 'Mixed Scanning: A Third Approach to Decision-making', *Public Administrative Review*, 27: 385–92.

Ferguson, B. and Goddard, M. (1997) 'The Case For and Against Mergers', in B. Ferguson, T. Sheldon and J. Posnett (eds), *Concentration and Choice in Healthcare*, (London: Financial Times Healthcare): 67–82.

Ferlie, E. (2000) 'Organisational studies and health services research', paper presented at NHS Service Delivery and Organisation R & D Methods workshop, Newbury, Berkshire, May.

Frances, J., Levacic, R., Mitchell J. and Thompson, G. (1991) 'Introduction', in J. Frances, R. Levacic, J. Mitchell and G. Thompson (eds), *Markets, Hierarchies and Network. The Co-ordination of Social Life* (London: Sage): 21–4.

Glaser, B.G. and Strauss, A.L. (1967) *The Discovery of Grounded Theory* (Chicago: Aldine).

Granovetter, M. (1985) 'Economic Action and Social Structure: The Problem of embeddedness', *American Journal of Sociology*, 91: 481–510.

Hamblin, R. (1998) 'Trusts', in J. Le-Grand, N. Mays and J.A. Mulligan (eds), *Learning from the NHS Internal Market A Review of Evidence* (London: King's Fund): 100–17.

Hartley, J.F. (1994) 'Case studies in Organizational Research', in C. Cassell and G. Symon (eds), *Qualitative Methods in Organizational Research: A Practical Guide* (London: Sage): 208–29.

Kickert, W.J.M. and Koppenjahn, J.F.M. (1997) 'Public Management and Network Management: An Overview', in W.J.M. Kickert, E.H.H. Klijn and J.F.M. Koppenjahn (eds), *Managing Complex Networks* (London: Sage).

Kogut, B. Shan, W. and Walker, G. (1992) 'The Make-or-Brake Decision in the context of an Industry Network', in N. Nohria and R.G. Eccles (eds) *Networks and Organizations Structure, Form, and Action* (Boston: Harvard Business School Press): 348–65.

Lincoln, J.R. (1982) 'Intra-(and Inter-) Organizational Networks', in S.B. Bacharach (ed.), *Resarch in the Sociology of Organizations*, Vol. 1 (Greenwich, CT: JAI Press): 1–38.

Miles, M.B. (1979) 'Qualitative data as an attractive nuisance – the problem of analysis', *Administrative Science Quarterly*, 24(4): 590–601.

Miller, R.H. (1996) 'Health System Integration: A Means to an End', *Health Affairs*, 15(2): 92–106.

Nohria, N. (1992) 'Is a Network Perspective a Useful Way of Studying Organizations?', in N. Nohria and R.G. Eccles, *Networks and Organizations Structure, Form, and Action* (Boston, Mass.: Harvard Business School Press): 1–22.

Oster, S.M. (1994) *Modern Competitive Analysis* (New York: Oxford University Press).

Pettigrew, A.M., Ferlie, E. and McKee, L. (1985) *Shaping Strategic Change* (London: Sage).

Pettigrew, A.M. (1987) *The Awakening Giant* (London: Basil Blackwell).

Powell, W.W. (1991) 'Introduction', in J. Frances, R. Levacic, J. Mitchell and G. Thompson (eds), *Markets, Hierarchies and Network. The Co-ordination of Social Life* (London: Sage): 265–76.

Rauber, C. (1998) 'Pulling up Stakes. Anthem's Ohio Exit May Signal Medicare Risk HMO Trend', *Modern Health Care*, 28(24) (15 June): 26.

Robinson, J.C., Casalino, L.C. (1996) 'Vertical Integration and Organizational Networks in Health Care', *Health Affairs*, 15(1): 7–22.

Robinson, J.C. (1996) 'The Dynamics and Limits of Corporate Growth in Health Care', *Health Affairs*, 15(2): 155–169.

Secretary of State, (2000) *The NHS Plan*, CM 4818–1 (London: The Stationery Office).

Sheaff, R. 'Fragile Alliance or Collective Actor? English PCGs Problematic Transition from Networks to Organisations' (this volume).

Street, A., King, A., Fulop N. and Edwards, N. (2000) 'Are Management Costs Lower in Areas Displaying Greater Concentration of Organisational Provision? Lessons for Horizontal and Vertical Integration' Paper submitted to NHS Executive London Region Organisational & Management R&D Group (February).

Thompson, G. (1991) 'Introduction', in J. Frances, R. Levacic, J. Mitchell and G. Thompson (eds), *Markets, Hierarchies and Networks. The Co-ordination of Social Life* (London: Sage): 71–2.

Williamson, O. (1975) *Markets and Hierarchies Analysis and AntiTrust Implications* (New York: Free Press).

Williamson, O. (1986) *Economic Organization Firms, Markets and Policy Control* (Brighton: Harvester Wheatsheaf).

7 Power Differentials and Professional Dynamics: Insights from the Experiences of Overseas Nurses and Doctors

Ian Brooks and Sandra MacDonald

INTRODUCTION

There has been a long tradition of immigration as a source of staffing in the NHS. Both doctors and nurses have been targeted and various countries have gained prominence as sources of staffing at different times. What is new in this case is the temporary nature of most of the appointments. The NHS Plan (Department of Health, 2000) states that by 2004 there will be 7500 more consultants, 2000 more GPs and 20 000 extra nurses. The aim is to fill these shortages by increasing numbers in training, but in the interim by international recruitment. The problems of nursing shortages are not new and run deeper than just numbers. Buchan *et al.* (1998) say that the number of nurses registering is declining and the nursing workforce is becoming older. Overseas-trained doctors currently comprise 24 per cent of the workforce (Medical Workforce Standing Advisory Committee, 1997), a propoition which is set to increase. Since the UK became part of the EU, migration flows have changed and the mutual recognition of qualifications has provided a framework for the movement of health care professionals between EU member states. However, little research has been done on the ways in which the organisation impacts on these immigrant workers. The relationship and power differential between professionals and other groups in the NHS are not static and studying the impact of the presence of immigrant health care professionals can illuminate the UK experience.

The research presented here uses the experiences of doctors and nurses from several countries, within and outside the European

Union, to explore some of the issues involved in expatriate work and organisational practices. We explore differences among and between doctors and nurses and the organisational responses to these new workers. The experiences of health care professionals were not uniform and the induction and socialisation processes were very different for doctors and for nurses. In this chapter we look at these differences in detail, concentrating on such issues as language, contracts, terms and conditions, induction and socialisation. Working practices themselves were found to differ widely, leading to much variation in the degree of responsibility allowed to a particular category of worker.

Using these sets of experiences, we draw out the implications for the organisation in terms of power and professionalism. We seek to understand how the presence of these expatriate workers fits into the dynamic processes through which professional boundaries are maintained. Insight into the contrasting experiences of doctors and nurses is developed with reference to the relevant literature on profession, power and gender. We explore the socially constructed nature of the occupations of nursing and medicine and the power-based differential which exists between them, using the lived experience of nurses and doctors from overseas.

PROFESSIONALISM, POWER AND GENDER

This research aims to contribute to an understanding of professionalism in healthcare. More specifically, it explores characteristics of, and highlights power differentials between, nursing and medicine. The experiences of overseas nurses and doctors both reflects the nature of these professions, while offering us illuminating insights, and serves to reinforces professional differentiation. The data provides ample evidence of professional differences in terms of status or power and gender. Nevertheless, the influx of overseas professionals into the NHS may also introduce challenge, tension and dynamism to inertia-ridden professions. Their very 'foreignness' introduces counter-cultural behaviours, expectations and values.

The literature defines a profession, in general terms, as an occupational group which provides an exclusive service involving the discretionary application of specialist knowledge (Forsyth and Danisiewics, 1985). Somewhat more robust and exclusive criteria are often used to differentiate occupational groups from 'true' professions, such as medicine and law. In this debate, nursing has been described as a 'semi-profession', a 'stunted occupational subspecies' (Salvage, 1988: 517), a label which reflects the consequence of its relatively powerless position. It is argued that following formation, professions develop knowledge bases and codes for constructing meaningful interpretations of events encountered within the professional world (Van Maanen and Barley, 1984). These include schemas, which are learned through formal education, and on-the-job socialisation which predispose individuals to cope in a 'professional manner' (Bourdieu, 1986).

In the context of this research, professionalism is viewed as a social construct with its definition grounded in symbols and artefacts, notably respondents' discourse and behaviours. As social systems, professions often comprise an amalgamation of dynamic sub-cultures. In nursing, nurse practitioners, health visitors and other specialists have enabled the profession to develop new knowledge and extend its cultural boundaries. On the other hand, organisational factors within some of these groups such as the sub-culture of permanent night nurses is considered a restraint on the profession's development (Brooks, 1999). However, professions also exist within an historical context which shapes the extent of their remit, their operating practices and professional codes, beliefs, values and ceremonies (Bloor and Dawson, 1994). This context ensures that nursing, medicine and other professions are 'anchored in the attitudes, perceptions, beliefs, motivations, habits and expectations' of their members (Katz and Kahn, 1966: 33): an 'anchor' which preserves professional differentials.

The changing power of professions (Carpenter, 1993; Elston, 1991; Johnson, 1972; Riza and Wegar, 1993) and the rise of 'new public management' (Ferlie *et al.*, 1996; Harrison, 1988) ensures that the National Health Service (NHS) provides a rich context in which to explore professional dynamics. What is more, in response to the Griffith report (DHSS, 1983) and subsequent NHS reforms, there has been a change from the dominance of professional power to the growth of managerial control. In this process, some have argued that nurses 'were deemed monumentally unimportant' (Clay, 1987: 57) while the dominant power of the medical profession is under constant challenge from government policy, managerialism and other health professions (Ashburner, 1996).

However, an understanding of professional power in healthcare is incomplete without a consideration of gender. The 1990 Equal Opportunities Commission survey revealed that most Health Authorities did not have adequate procedures and policies for attracting women with family responsibilities to higher-level managerial roles in the NHS.

Part-time work and lower-level jobs are dominated by women (Sly, 1996; Dex *et al.*, 1994) while in the UK about one-third of registered nurses work part-time (Smith and Seccombe, 1998) and 91 per cent are female (UKCC Register, 1998–99). Numerous research studies argue that women are excluded from higher-level roles or more prestigious and better-paid jobs in the NHS and elsewhere (Cockburn, 1985, 1991; Witz, 1992). Within both the nursing and medical professions senior positions, for example professional nurse managers and medical consultants, are disproportionately held by men.

The perception of a doctor's role as being the determination of clinical procedure and the application of advanced research-informed technical knowledge, as a masculine endeavour, contrasts with the essentially feminine nature of the caring and nurturing behaviour of nurses. (For further critical consideration of this position refer to Freidson, 1970a,b; Rueschemeyer, 1986; and Witz, 1992). Despite attempts within the nursing profession to embrace more practice and technical-based methodologies, its identification with caring behaviour ensures that it is undervalued relative to medicine (or management) and that the status of nurses is consequently undermined. Caring is often separated from the technical work (Carpenter, 1993) and, as such, is viewed as 'largely unproductive' (1993: 151). Additionally, many nurses pursue the traditional role of homemaker and primary carer (Brooks and MacDonald, 1999), and are increasingly required to work shift systems which 'are incompatible with family responsibilities that are still assigned to women in most societies' (Kazanjian, 1993: 165). Nursing struggles with professionalisation (Johnson, 1972) and in its attempts to gain occupational control or equity of treatment with 'competing' professions (for example, medicine) or from mediating processes, such as bureaucratisation or managerialism. Nurses' roles are changing in response to the needs of junior doctors in their attempts to reduce working hours, and in primary care with the shortage of GPs (Ashburner and Birch, 1999). Notable is the recent growth of the 'nurse consultant'. In the process, responsibilities are delegated from 'medicine' to 'nursing', but these are predominantly tasks not requiring a medical practitioner and doctors may be only too willing to have competent others take them on board. Rather than raising the status of nursing *vis-à-vis* medicine, this may merely preserve or reinforce power differentials.

What is more, the bureaucratisation of the professions has not impacted equally on all occupational groups in the NHS. The apparent 'commodity-like' nature of nurses' work appears to facilitate routinisation and lends itself to flexible working arrangements and managerial control. Nursing appears to invite the proletarianisation process by its inability to gain control over many aspects their work.

METHODOLOGY

The research presented in this chapter was based on a study carried out in a single hospital in the UK. Single case studies can provide rich data (Yin, 1989; Stake, 1994) which may be theoretically generalisable to other institutions with similar typologies. The case-study hospital, a medium-sized NHS Trust in the Midlands, with a full range of services was typical of provision outside urban centres. Lacking the prestige of larger teaching hospitals and the draw of inner-city facilities, the hospital faced difficult times in attracting and retaining nursing staff. A variety of methods were used to give different perspectives on the situation of the immigrant doctors and nurses. Key actor interviews were carried out with human-resource managers and other members of the management team; those who had responsibility for induction and socialisation of the expatriate workers were also interviewed. This gave the opportunity to explore the 'host-country' attitudes to the expatriate workforce and the reasons for recruiting staff from overseas. The recruitment process itself was explored through the views of management and of the expatriate workers themselves.

The researcher, as participant observer, visited the hospital and was given an insight into the hospital 'world'. Taking part in a visit to the site in the company of nurses from the USA, on a study tour, the researcher attended presentations on the hospital and its work and talked informally to staff. This visit included an overview of all hospital departments, giving an insight into the working environment in which the expatriates found themselves. In-depth interviews were carried out with doctors and nurses from the EU and other countries during 1999. In all, fifteen nurses and eight doctors were interviewed. Using complete transcripts of data, a comparative analysis of the answers from doctors and nurses was carried out and the differences and similarities between their responses identified. In the data presented here, we have grouped the responses thematically in order to foreground what we see as emerging themes for further investigation.

DATA PRESENTATION: NURSES

The nurses in our case study came from Finland, Germany, Australia, Canada and South Africa. All were female except for one male nurse from Finland.

Recruitment Process

Reasons for Coming to the UK

In the case of the Finnish nurses, job shortages had prompted them to take the opportunity to work in the UK, through an EU-funded programme. They hoped that this would enhance their job-seeking skills and give them work experience. Several had come for the opportunity to travel and to get experience of working in unfamiliar nursing environments. One nurse had come as the result of her husband's job relocation. Another was working abroad because of the shortage of nursing work in Canada; her intention was to return when there was a change in the employment situation. None of the nurses had come with the express notion of training and staying on in the UK but several were looking for a longer-term commitment than they were offered by the agency or the hospital.

Method of Recruitment

The nurses had either been recruited through an agency or were taking part in a short-term project arranged under the Leonardo scheme. The Leonardo programme is a European Union training programme aiming at improving the quality of vocational training systems and arrangements in Europe. Nurses from Australia, Canada, South Africa and Germany had come as individuals, all recruited through the same agency. In the case of some of the South African nurses, they were interviewed in their home country by a senior member of the UK hospital nursing staff. The Canadian nurses were interviewed by telephone; only one nurse applied for her job once resident in the UK. The nurses recruited through the agency did not arrive as a group, but the agency was committed to meet them and help them to find their way to the hospital. This was only partially successful – some nurses found themselves waiting at the airport and having to phone for instructions after a long international flight.

Adjustment Process

Accommodation

On arrival at their new place of work the nurses were all given accommodation on-site (except for an Australian nurse who lived with family) and their proximity helped in the adaptation to the new culture in which they found themselves. Having compatriots to share elements of 'culture shock' was seen as an important part of the learning process by the South African nurses who were surprised to find other expatriates from the same country already working in the hospital. Although many of the nurses were young and single, others had left husbands and family behind in the country of origin and were intending to return after the end of their short-term contracts. Family accommodation was not provided and married nurses were only accommodated if they came alone.

Induction

The process of induction started before expatriate staff reached the hospital. The recruitment agency undertook to arrange work permits, to 'meet and greet' nurses from overseas and to facilitate their arrival at the hospital. This produced uneven results. One South African nurse failed to be met at Heathrow despite the promise of the agency and was again let down the next day having to make her own way to the agency offices in Central London. Nurses were given an induction to the hospital on arrival. The Finnish nurses were inducted as a group and assigned a mentor to look after them on their wards. The South African and Canadian nurses were also given an induction to the hospital but this was much less structured as they did not arrive as a group. One Canadian nurse said that her induction was scheduled for the day she arrived but she was too tired to take part and so she went straight to her ward the next day. Further efforts were made on the part of the hospital to familiarise the nurses with their surroundings and duties. A focus-group session was held with nurses to give them a forum to discuss problems which had arisen. Through this it became clear that there were issues which the nurses would have liked to have had addressed. A South African nurse commented on this process as follows:

> She called a meeting and asked us what we thought, our suggestions. We all thought we should have had an induction into the way of life.

We were nurses back at home but we were told here, 'You don't touch that . . . you don't give I Vs'. It wasn't made clear initially.

Seminars on specific topics were arranged, for example on the bridging processes between social services and hospital care, and on how to read drug charts, which was a part of the daily routine which varied widely from country to country.

Language

The issue of language was mentioned frequently by respondents. This was not confined to those whose first language was not English; Canadian and South African staff also had difficulty in understanding 'hospital language'. Abbreviations were a key cause for concern because they could have different meanings in different countries, even when the common language was English. Nurses found that the names of drugs, often the trade names, used locally were different from those in their own country. Only the Finnish nurses, on the Leonardo project, were given language training. Three-days' training was provided by the hospital, but the nurses felt that this had been too 'conversational'. They would have preferred specific classes on medical language. Their preparation training in Finland had included language tuition but, in their view, this had not prepared them adequately for the experience of working in another country. Spoken language was not the only issue. Nurses reported having difficulty with written English, particularly when written as doctor's notes and when the doctor did not speak English as a first language either.

Cultural Differences

Nurses found differences both in the practice of nursing and in the role of the nurse in relation to patients and other health care workers. The nurses from Finland were surprised at the informality and extent of communication between nurses and patients. Nurses spoke of differences in methods of treatment, use of drugs and the conventions surrounding the delivery of drugs. Other elements of difference which could affect mood and thus work performance were the weather, the food and the built environment. One South African nurse commented:

The colours of the buildings. Way back home we have what we call bungalows. One storey and most of them you paint as you feel like it. Here you have to abide by the rules. Everything the same. My goodness. They couldn't believe at home when I told them – you just don't do things on your own.

The hierarchy of the hospital and the relationship between occupational groups was a surprise to some of the nurses. Nurses from Australia and Canada found it particularly difficult to adjust to, and had expected to call doctors by their first names and be 'part of a team'. One nurse commented:

> Doctors' rounds... when I first saw the consultant with this trail of people going around, I thought 'what are they doing?'

They were also surprised by the more 'traditional' uniforms. Although the uniforms were in a period of transition, quite a few blue dresses and belts were to be seen which was a contrast to the more informal dress worn in Canada and Australia. However, some nurses preferred it.

Some of the differences in the level of responsibility given to nurses gave cause for concern. One nurse expressed her dismay:

> When I got onto a respiratory ward the nurse said, 'Oh, you don't need to bring your stethoscope in, you don't use them. Doctors do that.' I was shocked. I thought we were supposed to work as a team and help each other.

This disregard for such an important badge of office clearly signalled to this nurse that she was not allowed to step over this particular professional boundary, in contrast to the inclusion which prevailed in her own country.

Professional Differences

Career Progress

A downward move was quite likely to have been made by nurses in coming to the UK. Those who had been out of work before coming were unable to work at the level of newly-qualified nurses, partly because of delays in registration and partly because of language barriers. Other nurses had taken a lower graded post, in particular the nurses from South Africa had to accept this as the price they paid for working in the UK. Although all nurses felt that they would take home a broader experience of nursing, no mention was made of it having helped to progress their career. No nurses were taking further education in order to advance their career, although two were considering registration on a degree course.

Retention

Nurses were on short-term contracts of a year's duration. Sometimes there was an option to stay on but several of the South African nurses had already gone back. Of those remaining, only a few were going to extend their contract while one or two were looking for jobs elsewhere in the UK. The contracts were arranged via the agency and if nurses were to be kept on then agency fees would have to be met. This was a strong disincentive to retention of nurses. Recruiting nurses from overseas was regarded as a short-term policy which could be put aside once the local labour market was more buoyant.

DATA PRESENTATION: DOCTORS

The doctors in our case study were all Senior House Officers, within a number of specialisms. Two of our interviewees were women and there were other women expatriate doctors in the hospital. Although the human-resources department did not keep records by gender, our observations and the comments of other doctors would point to a preponderance of male expatriate doctors. The doctors we interviewed were from Spain, India and Russia.

Recruitment Process

Reasons for Coming to the UK

All the doctors had strong career-based reasons for coming to the UK. The training which was available in the UK was regarded by the doctors as being a 'passport' to working in their chosen specialism both in the UK and outside it. However, there were many reasons, both personal and relating to the structure of the profession, which led them to choose the UK. For example, a Spanish anaesthetist explained:

> I always knew that I like to come here because I knew that anaesthetics in England is very good training. I have some friends here in England and they always explained that here is the training, here is the job.

Another Spanish doctor made it clear that the structure of the medical profession in Spain had influenced the decision to move to the UK for advancement:

> It sounds a bit crazy, but Spain is a crazy place. So I, like other people who want to get rid of that system, come here . . . We have to pass exams too, but in some way you have the chance to work in what you like, or you have the chance to fight and try to get a post where you like. Whereas in Spain if you don't pass the exam you will never get a chance to do what you like.

The emphasis from the outset was on furthering a career, the first step being a short-term contract at a hospital in the UK. In most cases it was hoped that this could be extended, if not further short-term opportunities would be sought in the UK.

Method of Recruitment

The doctors had all found jobs through the *British Medical Journal* and one had attended a privately-run language school, specialising in medical staff, which also provided job-search skills training for the medical profession. In contrast to the nurses, the doctors had long-term career plans which included a period of training in the UK. Some were intending to return to their country of origin, others intended to make a life in the UK.

Adjustment Processes

Accommodation

Accommodation for doctors was provided on-site in most cases, although one or two commuted from a nearby city. Accommodation was also provided for married doctors and those whose wives joined them during the period of their contract.

Induction

Doctors underwent a one-day induction to the hospital in general. The hospital site was not large, although spread out and this caused some of the 'on-call' doctors problems because of the difficulties of finding their way around. They were not always sure where they had to go when their bleeps sounded. This was compounded by communication problems, under the stress of urgency, combined with initial language difficulties. Further induction was not given to doctors.

Language

Heavily accented speech could cause communication problems and this was made worse when speaking on the telephone. One Spanish doctor remarked:

> I had quite a bad time with the phone, for example. I had to survive. It was all right, otherwise I would not have survived.

This particular doctor had taken the initiative to improve his language skills and was having private English lessons once a week. In order to take up posts doctors had to demonstrate their fitness to communicate by taking a language test. Doctors can also enrol on private courses run specifically to prepare doctors to fill in application forms for posts in the UK and to improve their medical vocabulary. One doctor had undertaken such a course and found it:

> Really, really useful. I think without this help perhaps you know, you can feel so alone, in hotel or in bed and breakfast without any help how to fill in these, sometimes complicated applications.

Cultural Differences

The existence of cultural differences even between those from other EU countries is illustrated by the story of one Spanish doctor. Remarking that his friends in Spain now found him to have become '*English*' after 18 months in the UK, he explained that this was due to his '*acquired behaviour*'. He had '*learned*' how to queue and this was a matter of amusement to his Spanish friends when he returned to Spain.

Doctors also commented on the differences in the way the hospital was structured. The bay system on wards is not a worldwide phenomenon. For doctors coming from countries where there are two patients to a room, with their own bathrooms, the system of bays on a large ward was a shock. The lack of privacy on wards presented them with difficulties. One Spanish doctor remarked that:

> You go in the middle of the night to somebody with a cardiac arrest and nobody will sleep at night. [and] There is no privacy. Doing

rounds I might stay an hour and a half in the ward to explain things like we have found a growth in your lung and everybody is hearing that.

The relationship between patients and their visitors also differs in comparison to similar relationships in the doctors' home countries. For example, visiting hours may be shorter or longer than in the UK and the amount of attention paid to relatives may be greater or lesser. An Indian doctor pointed out that fathers were not expected to be present at births in the hospital where he worked previously and that the 'first time you saw your child might be when it arrived home from the hospital'.

Despite such diversity in the cultural setting, professional practice was not seen to diverge from country to country. A doctor from Russia who had done his internship in Israel pointed out:

There isn't much difference. For example, I'm thinking of the clinical roles. In Israel medicine is quite advanced and basically they use the same drugs and procedures. The hospital was a bit smaller. Things were less organised. Otherwise there are similarities.

Another doctor, from India, describing his career path (four moves) since registering in the UK two years' previously said:

You have to move from one place to another. Once you go somewhere you have to acclimatise, where you are working. You have to know what the consultants want.

When asked if he had to undertake new learning every time he moved, he replied:

You have to settle down. I would not say new learning. The things are the same, but you need some settling down time.

However, these differences were in the system of working, not in what had to be done. He went on to say:

We have not much difference in treatment. Sometimes a consultant wants this. Sometimes that. There is personal choice. Every system is a bit different. But when you go there you will have to adjust with the system that already exists. You can't make your system. We can't make any systems. You have to abide by the system that is there.

Professional Differences

Career Progression

The doctors had all come specifically to further their careers, and some held the view that training in their specialism was superior in the UK to that available in their home country. Although difficulties in finding suitable employment were also critical factors for the Spanish doctors, they were positive about the training they were undergoing. Several had taken a decision to stay on indefinitely and partners had also moved to work in the UK. The possibility of working in other countries beyond the home country and the UK was also mentioned as another avenue of career progression.

Careers were regarded in terms of very long term prospects. A doctor from India, explained:

> because I don't have any limits to staying in this country, because I am married to a British citizen and I will be a British citizen, so I will stay for eight to ten years. That is enough knowledge and experience and then I might go back.

His career trajectory was not limited by difficulties surrounding residency in the UK, but even for those who had to continually renegotiate their right to remain (a doctor from Russia, for example) there was the intention to improve career prospects through the UK experience.

For some, the process was facilitated by contacts already in the UK. One doctor from India explained:

> Because my wife's relatives are also doctors, one is a dentist and one is a GP and before I came to this country [UK] they found out what I need to do before I start working here. They phoned me before I came to this country. I was well aware about exam techniques and what do I need to do. Everything was straightforward when I landed in this country.

Retention

The common practice of having a six-month contract and then trying to get it extended prevailed in this hospital as it does throughout the UK. Several doctors were hoping to stay on for a longer period and one or two had already successfully negotiated this. These doctors are expected to be mobile, even when they have not successfully obtained a 'rotation'. The doctor quoted above was in the second month of a six-month contract and hoped to be able to extend it. Since doctors apply individually to advertisements, no agency fees are required in their case, as it is with the nurses.

DISCUSSION

We have compared the responses from nurses and doctors and have attempted to draw out differences and similarities which have significance in terms of the two professions. Although nurses from all countries pointed out the differences in the relationship between the two professional groups, doctors did not mention nursing at all. Their comments on differences, which were fewer, related to the visiting hours, the layout of the hospital itself, the relationship with patients, but not with nurses or other care workers.

Nurses saw role differences and differences in practice which were not evident to the doctors, who concentrated on similarities in practice and adjusting to the individual 'style' of consultants rather than to a whole new way of working. In describing their 'shock' at some of the differences, the nurses' discourse revealed the constructed nature of their, and other's, professionalism.

The problems with medical terms and 'hospital language' were often cited by both nurses and doctors. Further problems with the use of language in written form and when using the telephone were also barriers to successful job performance and could be related to successful adjustment. These differences are part of the 'culture shock' experienced by expatriates and can even lead to their return home (Hardill, 1998: 12).

The perceived problems with language held another possibility in terms of adjustment. The doctors we interviewed had all embarked on long courses of training that they felt would enhance their position when they returned to their home country. However, in the competition for places on highly-prized courses or rotations, doctors from overseas may be at a disadvantage. Harvey and Buckley (1997: 40) maintain that:

[a guest] manager may have English as a second language, may not understand the culture of the organisation and, therefore, may be perceived by subordinates, in particular, as being less qualified for this new position in the domestic organisation.

In choosing a specialism doctors may be put off by what they perceive as racial and gender discrimination. The interviewer remarked on the greater number of women in anaesthetics and was told that it was difficult for overseas doctors to get into some specialisms (for example surgery) particularly if they were female. Doctors from overseas may be marginalised within the NHS and less valued than doctors from the UK.

The acclimatisation period for doctors and for nurses may be similar in that both groups struggle with unfamiliar terms and abbreviations. However, doctors have to pass a professionally approved language test, whereas the nurses in our study did not have to undergo any industry-standard test of language ability. The Finnish nurses had some language training prior to arrival and during the course of their training programme, but this was not typical. Since language is such a key element in acclimatisation to another culture, the implications seem to be that for nurses there is no need to provide training over and above the basics because they are not going to stay for long or to progress in their careers. However a case could be made for saying that nurses require high levels of language skills as they are expected to talk to patients in carrying out their 'caring' roles. Although doctors also need to talk to their patients in some specialisms, for example anaesthetics, one anaesthetist pointed out that they were given a 'check list' or 'questionnaire' to give to patients prior to operations which meant that they did not have to rely so heavily on their own language skills.

For doctors, adjustment was sometimes facilitated by having strong links with the UK. No nurses had such strong links; they were working in a different tradition, not based on professional links in the way that the doctors were. Nurses moving abroad to work tended to be young and single. Because recruitment is focused on single women, the problems attendant on dual-career families working abroad (Hardill and MacDonald, 1997; Harris, 1995) do not become a matter of concern for the organisation. While single accommodation only was provided for nurses, doctors were able to access 'married quarters'. Nurses, therefore, have no incentive to come as a family unit and have less emotional support than those who have other family members with them or waiting to arrive. Since nursing is such a highly feminised profession this differential treatment reinforces gender-based power differentials between the occupations.

Since doctors were more likely to be staying for the long term, they could be said to have a stronger motivation to make the experience work for them. Most of the doctors were married and had either come with a partner or waited for a short 'settling-in' period before being joined by a partner. Caught in the pattern of short-term contracts, this could further reinforce the gender-based stereotyping of nurses as uncommitted.

Another indication of the differences in the way in which each professional group is perceived in the organisation is the degree of involvement of the human-resource department in the recruitment and induction process. For doctors, the human-resources departments played an active role while the nurses were recruited by individual directorates. Their induction, training and acclimatisation were not dealt with at the same level of organisation.

CONCLUSIONS

Doctors are seen to be here for the long term, using the experience to enhance their careers. Nurses are seen as, or used as, temporary employees. There are financial barriers to retention of nurses because of the method of recruitment, and there is no career progression for them, in fact there is downgrading for some of those who are well-qualified. The expectations are that they will go back to their country of origin without acquiring further qualifications.

Organisational expectations of doctors are structured to provide established career paths and routes into further professional qualifications. These processes reinforce gender-based power differentials between the professions, and reflect attitudes to nursing as a 'semi-profession' as opposed to a professional elite. The relative status of the two professions is also underlined by the differential organisational involvement in their recruitment and retention.

The dynamic nature of the relationship between the professions can be seen in the views of nurses from countries which practice a more team-based version of caring for patients. When expectations are not met, as to the status of the two groups, will this be a force for change within the NHS? The range of national differences in attitudes to illness and death, amount of privacy due to patients and other deep-seated values point up the essentially socially constructed nature of medicine as a profession. Do such espoused values help to marginalise expatriate doctors and nurses within the NHS? If increasing numbers of health care workers are recruited from other countries, what will be the impact on the professions? Will the attitudes of these immigrant or expatriate workers alter the relationships between nursing and medicine?

This study is a beginning, it explores an area which is very little researched. Health care in the UK is facing staff shortages which may mean an increase in the numbers of workers from other countries, so that examining the organisational response to these workers is of particular relevance. The NHS Plan sees international recruitment of both doctors and nurses as a short-term measure. However, there are clear indications that the system used to attract nurses ensures that it is difficult for them to stay beyond their initial contract, often only for one year, whereas for doctors it is easier for those that choose to, to stay. Given that an additional strategy in addressing medical shortages is the substitution of physicians by other staff, especially nurses, then current patterns of recruitment of international nurses is unlikely to make a significant impact on nursing shortages in the long term.

References

Ashburner, L. (1996) 'The Role of Clinicians in the Management of the NHS', in J. Leopold, I. Glover and M. Hughes (eds), *Beyond Reason? The National Health Service and the Limits of Management* (Aldershot: Avebury).

Ashburner, L. and Birch, K. (1999) 'Professional Control Issues between Medicine and Nursing in Primary Care', in A. Mark and S. Dopson (eds), *Organisational Behaviour in Health Care: The Research Agenda* (Basingstoke: Macmillan – now Palgrave).

Bloor, G. and Dawson, P. (1994) 'Understanding Professional Culture in Organisational Context', *Organisation studies*, 15(2): 275–95.

Bourdieu, P. (1986) *Distinction* (London: Routledge).

Bourdieu, P. (1988) *Homo Academicus* (Cambridge: Polity Press).

Brooks, I. (1999) 'For Whom the Bell Tolls: An Ethnography of a Night Nurse Sub-culture', *Studies in Cultures, Organisations and Societies*, 5(2): 347–69.

Brooks, I. and MacDonald, S. (2000) 'Doing Life: Gender Relations in a Night-Nursing Sub-culture', *Gender, Work and Organisation*.

Buchan, J., Seccombe, I. and Smith, G. (1998) *Nurses Work: An Analysis of the UK Nursing Labour Market* (Aldershot: Ashgate).

Carpenter, M. (1993) 'The subordination of nurses in health care: towards a social divisions approach, in *Gender, Work and Medicine*, E. Rizka and K. Wegar (eds) (London: Sage).

Clay, T. (1987) *Nurses: Power and Politics* (London: Heinemann).

Cockburn, C. (1985) *The Machinery of Dominance* (London: Pluto).

Cockburn, C. (1991) *In the Way of Women* (London: Macmillan – now Palgrave).

Department of Health (2000) *The NHS Plan: A Plan for Investment, a Plan for Reform* (Cmd 4818-I London: HM Stationary Office).

Dex, S. Lissenburgh, S. and M. Taylor (1994) 'Women and Low Pay: Identifying the Issues. *Research Series No 2*, Equal Opportunities Commission, Manchester.

DHSS, (1983) *NHS Management Enquiry* (London: HMSO).

Elston, M.A. (1991) 'The politics of professional power: medicine in a changing health service' in J. Gabe, M. Calnan and M. Bury (eds) *The Sociology of the Health Service* (London: Routledge).

Ferlie, E. Ashburner, L. Fitzgerald, L. and Pettigrew, A. (1996) *The New Public Management in Action* (Oxford: Oxford University Press).

Freidson, E. (1970a) *Professional Dominance: The Social Structure of Medical Care* (Atherton Press: New York).

Freidson, E. (1970b) *Profession of Medicine: A Study of the Sociology of Applied Knowledge* (New York: Harper & Row).

Forsyth, P.B. and Danisiewics, T.J. (1985) 'Towards a Theory of Professionalisation', *Work and Occupations*, 12(1): 59–76.

Hardill, I. (ed.) (1998) 'Abroad Alone: Gender Perspectives on Professional International Migration', paper presented to conference, IGU Regional Meeting, Lisbon, Portugal (27–29 August).

Hardill, I. and MacDonald, S. (1997) (eds) 'Choosing to Relocate: An examination of the impact of expatriate work on dual-career households', *Women's Studies International Forum*, 21(1): 21–29.

Harris, H. (1995) 'Women's role in international management', in A.L. Harzing, and J. Van Ruyesseveldt, *International Human Resource Management* (London: Sage): 229–51.

Harrison S. (1988) 'The workforce and the new managerialism', in R. Maxwell (ed.), *Reshaping the NHS* (London: Policy Journals).

Johnson, T.J. (ed.) (1972) *Professions and Powers* (London: Macmillan – now Palgrave).

Katz, D. and Khan, R.L. (eds) (1966) *The Social Psychology of Organisations* (New York: Wiley).

Kazanjian, A. (1993) 'Health manpower planning or gender relations?' in *Gender Work and Medicine, op.cit.*

Medical Workforce Standing Advisory Committee (1997) *Planning the Medical Workforce: Third Report* (London: Department of Health).

Riza, E. and Wegar, K. (eds) (1993) *Gender, Work and Medicine* (London: Sage).

Sly, F. (ed.) (1996) 'Women in the labour market: results from spring 1995 labour force survey', *Employment Gazette*, 104(3): 91–113.

Smith, G. and Seccombe, I. (1998) 'Changing Times: A survey of Registered Nurses in 1998', *The Institute for Employment Studies* Report 351 (London).

Stake, R. (1994) *The Art of Case Research* (Thousand Oaks, Cal.: Sage).

UKCC. (1998) *Statistical Analyses of the UKCC's Professional Register, 1 April 1997 to 31st March, 1998* (UKCC, London).

Van Maanen, J. and Barley, S.R. (1984) 'Occupational Communities: Culture and Control in Organisations', in: L. Cummings and B.M. Staw (eds), *Research in Organisational Behaviour* (Greenwich: JAI Press): 287–365.

Witz, A. (1992) *Professions and Patriarchy* (London: Routledge).

Yin, R. (1989) *Case Study Research Design and Methods* (Thousand Oaks, California: Sage).

Department of Health (2000) *The NHS Plan; A Plan for Investment: a Plan for Reform*, Cmd 4818-I (London: HM Stationery Office).

8 Promoting User Involvement in Health Care Development: Challenges Demonstrated by Maternity Services Liaison Committees

Diane Berrow and Charlotte Humphrey

INTRODUCTION

The inclusion of user representatives in committees and groups is one of several forms of user involvement in the health service. There are several groups that presently include user representatives in their membership, relating to various aspects of the health service. For some years lay members have been included in research ethics committees and in general-practice patient groups. More recently, some of the research advisory groups involved in setting NHS research priorities have included user representatives (NHS Executive Research and Development Directorate 1998) and, at a local level, Primary Care Groups have been required to have lay membership (NHS Executive, 1997).

The inclusion of users in such groups reflects a philosophy of user involvement that users should be involved alongside health professionals in the decision-making process. This contrasts with the degree of user involvement that occurs through most consultation exercises where the user input is separate from where the decisions are made and where the results are fed into the process. The inclusion of users in the research advisory groups and Primary Care Groups provides evidence of the government's commitment to this philosophy – at least in principle (NHS Executive, 1998).

However, there have been reports of problems with regard to establishing user involvement in many of the forums. Some Primary Care Groups were found to have delayed the appointment of user members

(Smith and Dickson, 1998) and, while some research advisory groups included users, others excluded them because health professionals were concerned about the dangers of involving an unrepresentative user and what would happen if users identified different and incompatible priorities to themselves (NHS Executive Research and Development Directorate, 1998). User members involved in forums have reported problems with tokenism, isolation and not being taken seriously (NHS Executive Research and Development Directorate, 1998; Rigge 1994; Liberati, 1997).

The danger is that faith in the potential of multidisciplinary structures to provide an effective form of user involvement ignores the very real challenges that face people involved in the process. This chapter draws on the findings of a qualitative study of Maternity Services Liaison Committees – a specific type of user involvement forum – to identify some general challenges to user involvement through multidisciplinary groups. It focuses on five features of the structure and process of MSLCs.

Maternity Services Liaison Committees (MSLCs)

MSLCs were set up in each district in the early 1980s to bring together all the professionals involved in maternity care with lay representatives for the purpose of agreeing procedures and monitoring their effectiveness (Department of Health, 1993). They were set up in response to concern about perinatal mortality rates and the wide variation in these around the country and between social groups (Department of Health, 1982). They have representation from health care professionals who provide maternity care, the health authority and local users. Health care professionals include midwives, consultants, health visitors and general practitioners. Health authority professionals include public health doctors and commissioning managers. Users come from various user organisations including the National Childbirth Trust and Community Health Councils.

MSLCs are interested in the quality and availability of a wide range of maternity services. They contribute to the design of written information for local women about local services, and they are also concerned with wider service developments such as the implementation and evaluation of team midwifery – a way of organising midwives to promote continuity of care. The MSLCs provide an environment where all those involved can discuss progress being made by the unit or health authority in relation to health care initiatives, and one where members can raise problems with services and expect some response. In some topics the MSLC has a more central role and coordinates the actual work, for example in reviewing antenatal screening.

There have been a number of initiatives aiming to improve the functioning and effectiveness of MSLCs, many of which were instigated by user organisations such as the National Childbirth Trust, and the focus has been on empowering user members and reducing their isolation (Fletcher, 1996; Cowl, 1997; Key, 1997). Recently there has been a growing emphasis on the importance of team-building and learning research appraisal skills (Crowe, 1997). Participants have found the initiatives useful as a source of support and a chance to find out about the work and problems of other committees. However, there has been little systematic study of the functioning and effectiveness of MSLCs. Information that is available is from questionnaire surveys of MSLC members which were largely restricted to user members. The surveys found widespread concerns about the effectiveness of MSLCs and the extent to which they allow users to participate (Newburn, 1992; Gready and Newburn, 1997; Fletcher *et al.*, 1997). Users reported a lack of confidence in challenging other members and felt that their committees were dominated by health care professionals.

In 1996, in response to concerns about the effectiveness of MSLCs, the NHS Executive launched guidelines for MSLCs which provided detailed suggestions for how they could develop their structure and remit (NHS Executive, 1996). Encouraged by these guidelines, many MSLCs spent time reviewing their own structure and effectiveness, their relationships with the health authority and Trusts, and they have tried to develop more systematic and proactive input to the planning and monitoring of maternity strategy and the development and review of health care policies. Many have increased the amount of information they receive in these areas, but their influence in these matters remains limited or unclear.

METHODOLOGY

The study on which this chapter is based was a qualitative evaluation of the structure, process and impact of MSLCs. It combined longitudinal observation of committee meetings with in- depth interviews to promote understanding of the process of meetings and features of the interaction between users and health professionals. Previous research by others had been limited to questionnaire surveys of members. Combining observation and interview methods enabled an understanding of respondents' views in the context of the work of the MSLC and the behaviour of members.

A purposive sample of eight MSLCs was chosen to provide maximum variation on characteristics likely to be relevant to functioning including whether or not they were accountable to the Trust or health authority and the size of the committee. The meetings of the eight committees were observed over a one-year period in order to study how topics progressed over time and to establish how the work of the MSLC linked in with annual commissioning and monitoring activities in the health authority and Trust. An unstructured approach to observation was taken. What was said and what happened at meetings was recorded as comprehensively as possible using shorthand. Impressions of meetings and the behaviour of members were also noted. In total, 34 meetings were observed: between four and six in each MSLC.

Semi-structured interviews were conducted with a cross-section of members in the second half of the observation period. The primary aim of the interviews was to find out about the respondents' experiences of membership and their views on the functioning, effectiveness and value of their committees. Forty people were interviewed: eight user members, seven health authority personnel. 13 hospital-based midwifery managers and consultants, two GPs, one health visitor, one community midwife and eight chairpersons. The observation notes and interview transcripts were analysed by a combination of manual and computer methods.

FINDINGS

The findings in relation to five aspects of MSLCs which had an impact on user involvement are described. These are: user representation, 'ownership' of the MSLC, access to information, how health professionals respond to problems raised by users, and the adequacy of available resources.

User Representation

Membership

The NHS guidelines suggest that user representatives should comprise at least one-third of the membership. Half the MSLCs achieved this goal for some of their meetings, but most MSLCs also had meetings with only one or two user members present. This was due to a low baseline of user membership to start with, poor attendance by some users, or both these factors.

There was evidence of resistance on the part of some health care professionals to increasing the user membership. They had concerns about how representative user members could be and one consultant explained that if new users were recruited, he would feel unable to speak freely at meetings. Those who were committed to appointing more users found it difficult to recruit new members in spite of widespread advertising and the efforts of existing user members to recruit members through their networks with local women. There were particular difficulties recruiting members to represent minority groups. The NHS Executive guidelines suggest existing members can put across the interests of minorities, but the extent to which this is feasible or acceptable is debatable.

It seemed that while many users were interested in describing their experiences to existing user members, most were not willing or able to take part in the MSLC. It was interesting that, despite the fact that they appeared composed and confident, some user members thought meetings were intimidating and found participating nerve-racking. Even those with substantial experience of committees and campaigning described a degree of apprehension in relation to putting forward views that were different to those expressed by health professionals. Some MSLCs had or planned to develop user subgroups where recent users of maternity services met to discuss the care they received and raise problems. User members of the MSLC formed a link between the subgroup and the main committee, and these groups were seen as a way of involving a larger number of women. However, there is a potential hazard if these groups are used as an alternative to user membership. They provide feedback on services but do not promote user involvement in decisions made on the MSLC.

The Diversity of User Members' Interests

In their drive to increase user membership and avoid charges of tokenism, many MSLCs did not take into account the differences in users' interests in maternity services and user involvement. The way they participated in meetings was influenced by these interests. Some were primarily interested in specific aspects of maternity services or in the opportunities to raise problems experienced by local women. Others were more concerned with the role of the MSLC as a body that enabled users to be involved in the planning and monitoring of maternity services on a wider or strategic level.

This distinction between users was not articulated at MSLC meetings and not apparently accommodated in recruitment plans (except in one case where the MSLC had explicitly chosen to recruit a particular non-executive director of the Trust because of her knowledge and experience of the health service). The fact that users who might want to be involved are not an amorphous group and are not necessarily interchangeable is a significant, but unacknowledged issue.

Concerns about the Representativeness of User Members

Some health professionals questioned the representativeness of user members. They were critical that user members only represented fringe interests – those associated with white middle-class National Childbirth Trust members who want natural or home births. They saw users as out of touch with the typical user – the type of user that they should represent. Some health care professionals felt that they gained a good understanding of what local women want from day-to-day contact with them in the course of their own work and considered this to be a more valid source of information on what users want than user members' views. Their reservations led them to doubt the relevance of problems raised by users.

However, the idea that there are typical users can be challenged. Users fall into many subgroups in terms of their needs and wants. Middle-class NCT members might be one subgroup with respect to certain interests; disabled women and teenage mothers might be others. It might be that the planning and provision of centralised and standardised services to a population within a limited budget requires health professionals to focus on the commonalities between women rather than the differences. This demonstrates a potential tension between organisational goals and the multiple and possibly contrasting requirements of various subgroups of users. This was shown in one MSLC when user members pushed for improvements to be made to access for disabled users. Even though some changes were eventually made, the midwife member was quite antagonistic towards the user members as she felt that their narrow focus on disability access demonstrated a lack of appreciation of the wider problems and challenges facing the unit.

Some of the problems to do with representation may reflect the tendency to focus on *form* at the expense of looking at the *function* of user representation. When MSLCs looked at increasing the number of user members they did not discuss this in the context of a wider strategy of user involvement.

'Ownership' of the MSLC: How Independent is Independent?

The guidelines describe MSLCs as 'independent advisory bodies' that should be formally accountable to health authorities. However, there is an issue of how independent these groups are and can be. Most MSLCs were originally chaired by consultants and had little input from the health authority. Most have now changed to lay chairship and have more formalised health authority input and in part these changes were instigated in response to concerns about medical domination of the committees.

The independent nature of MSLCs does not accurately reflect the degree of influence that the health authorities had on the way MSLCs worked and subsequently on how users participated. Some health authority MSLC members were responsible for the MSLC as part of their jobs. In some of the committees the health authority representatives guided the MSLC reviews and took the lead on producing committee documents. Moreover, some of the lay chairs were appointed by the health authority and looked to the health authority representative for advice and support.

Health authority representatives focused on strategic issues. They were interested in monitoring the Trust and less interested than user members in the process of how the units actually meet their targets. Encouraged by the guidelines, many MSLCs were trying to develop a more strategic role in maternity services and this, combined with the influence of health-authority representatives, limited the opportunities for users to raise the problems reported to them by local women. In one MSLC, for example, the health-authority representative explained on several occasions that the problem raised by a user related to an operational matter and therefore did not fall within the remit of the MSLC. While this was in keeping with the new terms of reference of the MSLC, user members were left wondering what they should do and why they were on the MSLC.

The issue is not necessarily that people deliberately swayed the work of the MSLC in a manipulative manner, but that they naturally focused on the interests of their organisation or the demands of their jobs. While the commitment of individuals in the health authority may be critical in ensuring that the MSLC has influence in maternity services, the danger of losing the user perspective was not recognised.

Access to Information

User members of MSLCs were reliant on health professionals to inform them about what was going on in maternity services. Without adequate information they could not keep local users informed about policies and practices nor participate effectively or confidently in decisions that related to the planning or monitoring of maternity services. There were several factors which contributed to how well-informed users were.

The Attendance of Health Professionals

Rates of absenteeism for consultants were so high that MSLCs were without consultants at some meetings. The fact that consultants in some MSLCs – albeit a minority – did turn up to meetings regularly, provided some indication that the attendance of doctors was as much a function of commitment as it was of convenience. The absence of consultants reduced the opportunities for users to find out about clinical policy and practice and to obtain explanations for problems with obstetric care reported to them by local women. Agenda items and MSLC projects were held up because of a lack of information on clinical practice.

The Extent to which Health Professionals were Proactive

There was variation in how proactive health professionals were about informing MSLC members about relevant initiatives going on in maternity services. For example, while some MSLCs were told about the local audit of the Audit Commission, others were not. The extent to which health care professionals consulted the MSLC for their input to the development or review of health care guidelines also varied and was generally not systematic. Much of the MSLC input to guidelines arose as a consequence of user members requesting this.

The Extent to which Health Professionals were Open about Practices and Problems

There was variation between health care professionals in the extent to which they provided a comprehensive picture of health care practices.

While some provided accounts of practice which showed the problems as well as the progress, others made reports that seemed more like public-relations exercises, skating over any difficulties. For instance, in reporting on progress with promoting breast-feeding, midwives in one MSLC reported great success and provided a wholly positive and trouble-free picture. User members were suspicious because this information did not correspond with what they knew through their own contact with local women and other midwives. The reluctance of health care professionals to provide honest accounts of practice might be due to concern to show the unit in the best light, but it might also reflect a lack of commitment to the MSLC or user involvement.

The Appropriateness of Information for the MSLC

Within the health authority or provider Trust, information is compiled in a format suitable for a specific purpose – for instance, clinical protocols are written for the medically qualified person to understand and act upon. Rewriting or explanation might be required for a different audience, and providing such information is dependent upon the time available and commitment of health professionals.

The organisational isolation of MSLCs means that users are dependent upon those inside the health service to bring in information. This is in itself highly dependent upon the commitment of the health care professional to the MSLC. Some user members had their own contacts within the health service from whom they obtained relevant information, but many did not have this facility.

How Health care Professionals Respond to Problems Raised by Users

For some users one of the main motivations for getting involved with the MSLC was to be able to raise problems that they or local women had experienced and see that they are taken seriously by health professionals. A substantial amount of the interaction between users and health care professionals in some MSLCs related to this purpose. Aspects of the behaviour of health care professionals influenced how problems were discussed and acted upon.

Reluctance or Refusal to Discuss the Details of Cases

Health care professionals were sometimes reluctant to discuss the details of problems in relation to individual cases where it might be possible to identify the woman concerned or the staff who provided her care. They did not think it acceptable that individual staff or users might be identifiable and felt there was a danger of this even if the staff or user were not named if the case was sufficiently unusual. They were concerned not to breach their duty of confidentiality to women. In addition, some problems raised by users were the subject of complaints made by users to the provider unit. These were particularly difficult for health care professionals to respond to as they were not at liberty to discuss the details of such cases. They felt they were at an unfair disadvantage – user members could say whatever they wanted, but they could not defend themselves.

The difficulty for MSLCs was how to capitalise on the feedback user members provided while at the same time appreciating the problems from the perspective of health care professionals. The guidance suggests individual case studies could be useful for checking the quality of the service as they provide sufficient detail with which to make an assessment, but this does not accommodate the problems for health professionals.

The Degree to which the Problem is Accepted and Considered Important

Some problems were raised and discussed and action was taken as a result to investigate or resolve them. However, in many other instances the health care professionals did not accept the problem existed or did not consider it necessary to take any action. Comments from health care professionals such as 'That shouldn't happen', or 'That was an atypical experience – most unusual', resulted in a premature end to some discussions. In some cases they were sceptical about the accuracy of what had been reported by the user; in other cases they sought to reassure the user that the policy or practice was adequate. For instance, a user asked for clarification of the Trust's policy on providing scans at night because a local woman had been unable to obtain one. The head of midwifery explained that the policy was to provide scans and the problem should not happen. This kind of reaction had the effect of circumventing a full discussion of the problem to assess if any action needed to be taken. On other occasions the problem was accepted but the significance of it was minimised. The response was that some shortfalls in practice are unavoidable and not worth investigating.

Some user members thought the midwives were deliberately minimising the implications of the problem because of their lack of commitment to user involvement. In other cases they attributed the response to the health care professional's ignorance of what was really happening on the ground – midwives on the MSLC were mostly from managerial positions.

From the perspective of health care professionals, the problems raised by users were by their nature critical of the service and sometimes of individual health care professionals. Some health care professionals felt bombarded by criticism. They did not feel that the user members appreciated that the vast majority of women were completely satisfied with the service.

Access to Resources

Most MSLCs did not have a budget and were therefore dependent upon the health authority or provider unit to provide them with certain resources. The lack of money made it difficult to get satisfactory administrative support, limited the dissemination of published information, and restricted what costs could be reimbursed.

Lack of Administrative Support

Members of half the MSLCs found the level of administrative support inadequate. While some had the support of experienced committee administrators from the health authority, others relied upon secretarial support from the provider unit which only provided the service of taking minutes. In some committees, the user chairpersons were doing much of the work preparing papers and coordinating the work between meetings. They explained that there was a limit to what they could do without help and that this had an impact on what the MSLC could achieve. The health authority and provider units reported that there was a general lack of administrative support in their own organisations, and that unfortunately there was none to spare for secondment to the MSLC.

Limited Dissemination of Published Information

The cost of photocopying was absorbed by the health authority or provider unit. However, the lack of a budget made it difficult if not impossible for some MSLCs to disseminate published information to members. There was an expectation that members would get hold of the documents through some other route. Some user members were willing to spend their own money on documents, but such documents were not always easy to obtain or immediately available. They felt they were at a disadvantage in discussions as they did not have sufficient background knowledge of the topic area.

Restricted Reimbursement of User Members' Costs

The health authority or provider unit reimbursed travel expenses for users, but there was no provision for crèche facilities or childcare costs. In the absence of a budget, travel expenses had to be claimed retrospectively and the process was in some cases lengthy and bureaucratic. Many user members were out of pocket to some extent, although they considered themselves fortunate to be able to stand these costs and recognised that for some women this would not be feasible. They did not make a fuss about this issue, and seemed to expect to make sacrifices for the cause of user involvement.

When the lack of funds was discussed it was with a degree of resignation that nothing could be done. Health professionals suggested it might be better if the MSLC did not make a fuss about this issue lest the health authority or Trust realised what they already spent on the MSLC. Whatever the justifications for furtive arrangements, it was unfortunate that the situation appeared to reflect a lack of commitment within health authorities and provider units to the MSLC and by implication user involvement. It indicated that health professionals see user involvement as being more for the benefit of the user members rather than for the good of maternity services and therefore not worthy of investment. The fact that some user members were too embarrassed to claim their travel costs reflected this.

CONCLUSION

There are no other groups quite like MSLCs in the health service. However, their experiences are arguably relevant to any groups which bring together health professionals with user representatives, both those concerned with health care such as audit groups and those concerned with planning and development such as Primary Care Groups. Most of the problems are not easily resolvable because they demonstrate some fundamental differences between user representatives and health professionals with regard to what they expect or want from user involvement and show how dependent such groups are on the commitment and behaviour of health professionals. Accommodating the potentially diverse wants and needs of users did not sit well with their task of providing a centralised service. The barriers reflect the way user involvement has developed as an add-on activity within the health service rather than as an integral component of planning and monitoring. User involvement takes place one step removed from the decision-making.

The intention of this chapter has been to provide some insight into the challenges that face such groups and takes the discussion beyond a focus on training-up or empowering user representatives or improving or promoting team-working. The problems experienced by MSLCs demonstrate the extent to which health professionals are in control of health care, have a variety of ways of moderating user input, and are empowered to do this by the structure of the health service and its general approach to user involvement.

References

Cowl, J. (1997) 'Maternity Services Liaison Committees – Making Them Work', *Changing Childbirth Update*, issue 8 (March).

Crowe, S. (1997) Final Project Report. *CASP for MSLCs: A Project Enabling MSLCs to Develop an Evidence-based Approach to Changing Childbirth* (Oxford: University Institute of Health Studies).

Department of Health (1982) *Maternity Care in Action*, Part 1, Crown Copyright.

Department of Health (1993) *Changing Childbirth: The Report of the Expert Maternity Group*, Part 1 (London: HMSO).

Department of Health (1997) *The New NHS: Modern, Dependable* Session 1997–8; Cm 3807 (London: HM Stationery Office).

Department of Health (1998) *Partnership in Action: A Discussion Document* (London: Department of Health)

Fletcher, G. (1996) 'The Voices Project – Training and Support for Maternity Service User Representatives', *Changing Childbirth Update*, issue 5.

Fletcher, G., Buggins, E., Newburn, M., Draper, J., Wang, M. and Gready, M. (1997) *Report of the Voices Project* (London: National Childbirth Trust).

Gready, M. and Newburn, M. (1997) *Report of the Second Phase of the Choices Project*, unpublished (London: National Childbirth Trust).

Key, E. (1997) 'Local Review Day for MSLCs', *Changing Childbirth Update*, issue 8 (March).

Liberati, A. (1997) 'Consumer Participation in Research and Health Care: Making it a Reality', *British Medical Journal*, 315: 499.

NHS Executive (1996) *Maternity Services Liaison Committees: Guidelines for Working Effectively* (Leeds: NHSE).

NHS Executive Research Development Directorate (1998) *Research: What's In It for Consumers?* First Report of the Standing Advisory Group on Consumer Involvement in the NHS R&D Programme to the Central Research and Development Committee, Crown Copyright.

Newburn, M. (1992) 'Participation in Policy Making: The Maternity Service Users', in G. Chamberlain and L. Zander (eds), *Pregnancy Care in the 1990s*, Proceedings of a Symposium held at the Royal Society of Medicine (Lancaster: Parthenon).

Rigge, M. (1994) 'Involving Patients in Clinical Audit', *Quality in Health Care*, 3, supplement: 2–5.

Smith, K. and Dickson, M. (1998) 'Silent Majority', *Health Service Journal*, 17 December: 33.

9 A Problematic Transition from Networks to Organisations: The Case of English Primary Care Groups

Rod Sheaff

ENGLISH PRIMARY CARE GROUPS: HIERARCHIES IN EMBRYO?

Hierarchies and networks are usually contrasted as alternative governance structures (Thompson *et al.*, 1991; Kooiman, 1993). Various writers have argued, however, that the differences between networks and organisations should not be exaggerated. Powell (1992) notes the network-like character of organisations. Granovetter (1985) and others emphasise that formal relationships in both networks and hierarchies are 'embedded' in wider networks of informal relationships. Some writers implicitly regard networks as a durable form of governance where organisation is impossible but markets fail (Börzel, 1998). Others note that networks are sometimes a transitional form between markets and hierarchies (Powell, 1987). Certainly networks can consolidate into an organisation (for example proposed airline mergers, fusion of political parties and so on) although such transitions tend to be difficult and uncertain.

During the 1990s general practitioner (GP) fundholding in English National Health Service (NHS) primary care stimulated the formation of a range of primary health care networks. Some extended fundholding (for example Total Purchasing Pilot projects, which extended it to a wider range of services; multifunds through which fundholders managed their funds collectively), others were devised as alternatives to it (such as Locality Commissioning Groups, in which fundholding and non-fundholding GPs jointly advised Health Authorities on the purchase of hospital and community health services). GP cooperatives providing out-of-hours services also began to spread after 1993. The 1997 NHS (Primary Care) Act permitted new providers to enter NHS primary care, and existing organisations to combine into networks bringing together general practices, community health service NHS trusts (CHSTs), voluntary bodies and social services. It also permitted GPs to shift from a standard national contract to a more flexible, locally-negotiated contract. The current policy of creating Primary Care Groups (PCGs) generalises this network-forming approach across the NHS. As Labour's successor to GP fundholding, PCGs involve all the GPs in a locality in commissioning secondary and community care services. PCGs are to develop through four stages. Stage 1 and 2 PCGs are very much network entities; their Boards are dominated by GPs' nominees, and they influence local general practices who are still mainly independent contractors, through a mixture of budget payments and professional controls ('clinical governance'). PCGs will play an increasing role in commissioning community health (and hospital) services. Current health policy expressly intends that PCGs will develop into independent Primary Care Trusts (PCTs) but is unclear about PCT governance structures. One possibility is that the PCTs will remain networks, but more tightly organised networks based either on subcontracting or upon stronger forms of the arrangements which PCGs have used. The word 'Trust', however, also hints that PCTs could become hierarchical organisations similar to existing NHS hospital or community services Trusts (Sheaff, 1999).

These circumstances raise the question of what conditions promote or retard the transitions between loose network, more tightly coordinated closed network, and organisation? By 'organisation', organisational theorists generally refer to hierarchical organisations rather than such organisations as partnerships, peer-groups or cooperatives. By 'network' they generally mean a durable coalition of organisations and individuals who collaborate in pursuit of common goals. Using the case of English PCGs, this chapter therefore attempts to analyse what conditions facilitate, and which obstruct, the process of consolidating networks into organisations. The analysis predicts which types of PCGs are likely to find the transition easiest and therefore complete it sooner.

METHOD

A two-stage research method is therefore required. First one adumbrates a theory of how PCGs will make the transition from network to hierarchy; then one tests it against the available evidence. The preliminary theory step is to decide which theoretical characterisations of organisations and networks to use. For organisations, the classical, Weberian model of hierarchical organisational structures is the common point of departure for much subsequent theory. It is also a fundamental analysis because an organisation's formal structure (on which it focuses) is the presupposed framework around which the other, informal aspects of organisational behaviour occur. It is possible to accept this much Weberian theory without accepting two of its further, normative assumptions about the rationality of hierarchical organisation. We do not have also to accept that hierarchy is the governance structure *a priori* preferable to all others; nor that relationships within hierarchies are always beneficial or non-exploitative for all their individual members, least of all those at the bottom of the hierarchy. It is harder to pinpoint a single founding theory of networks. To characterise networks, the following argument makes assumptions which are widely accepted among network analysts notwithstanding their different categorisations and explanations of networks. The contrast between network and hierarchy implies what tasks confront those converting networks into hierarchies. (We do not have to assume that the evolution from network to hierarchy is smooth and even, or that it is irreversible.) A statement of the task then implies predictions about what conditions assist or impede the transformation from loose network to tightly organised network to hierarchical organisation. On this basis we can predict which characteristics of PCGs are likely to promote or retard their transition into PCTs, implying in turn which PCGs are likely to make the transition soonest.

Ideally one would use a longitudinal analysis to test these predictions, comparing how far and quickly PCGs with different organisational characteristics evolve from networks to hierarchies over the seven years (from 1998) that the process is likely to take for the slower-developing PCGs. Meantime, the only available method is cross-sectional analysis of data about the early stages of PCG formation. The data used here come from exploratory studies of PCG and PMS formation during 1997–98, earlier published research on the formation of precursor networks to PCGs, and the first year's (1999) data from an annual survey of a stratified random sample of 72 of the 481 PCGs. The cross-sectional analysis is made by selecting group survey variables relevant to the predictors identified in the theoretical analysis below, and a group relating to signs of PCG integration. For each group a score is then constructed (see Table 9.1), which allows correlations between predictor scores and signs-of-integration scores to be tested. In each test the null hypothesis is that the predictors being tested have no significant effect on the relevant signs-of-integration score. The significance level for rejecting the null hypothesis is set at the customary $p= 0.05$.

Insofar as the association is falsified, that is evidence against either the theory of tasks and conditions outlined above, or the underlying elements of Weberian and network theory from which they were derived. A falsificationist methodology is thus being used. These methods are still relatively rare in organisational studies compared with qualitative, especially historical, approaches. Because the tasks of transition are predicted from the general characteristics of networks and organisations, one would expect the predictions made here to apply to networks in general, but further research would be neces- sary to substantiate that claim for other contexts. Since 'organisation' is here taken to mean 'hierarchy', networks' evolution into other entities such as cooperatives or partnerships requires further, separate research.

FROM NETWORK TO HIERARCHY: A THEORY OF TRANSITION

A hierarchy essentially consists of a number of individuals working towards a common set of goals under the control of those individuals who control its resources and therefore compliance systems. Their defining feature is a social division of labour between those members whose main role is directly carrying out its mundane, practical tasks in pursuit of these goals and other members whose main role is to coordinate and direct them. Those higher in the hierarchy control the organisation's resources; depending on the case, a combination of physical means of production, knowledge, money, legitimation and use of physical coercion. Control of these resources gives those higher in the hierarchy a dominant role both in formulating the organisation's objectives and, above all, in controlling the productive activity of members lower down the hierarchy.

Depending on the different individuals' own particular interests, bargaining power and persuasive skills these objectives may be spon- taneously shared objectives or be emergent, compromise objectives negotiated between members, or simply the imposed objectives of the most powerful individuals or coalitions. Where individual members' objectives do not coincide spontaneously, those who control the organ-isation's resources can apply incentives (such as payments, coercion) to make them coincide artificially. Then, artificial incentives supple-ment the spontaneous rough convergence of objectives found amongst members of, say, a charity or pressure group. For its members the effect of negotiating objectives and of such incentives is to make work-ing to realise the organisation's objectives a means – even if a rather limited or inefficient means – of meeting their own prior personal objectives. Whatever conflicts there may be between the organisation's objectives and its members' (other) desires and interests is resolved in favour of the organisation's objectives.

To achieve these objectives the controllers of a hierarchy require sufficient technical resources (for example for activities such as trans-port provision, which requires substantial physical, indeed industrial, resources) besides those for the compliance system. Increasingly, even work such as medicine relies on scientifically based technical know-ledge as a resource.

Although networks and organisations alike pursue common goals, the relationship between goals and members differs between the two forms of governance structure. Its constituent organisations preexist the network; they face incentives which predate the network and indeed provide their reason for joining and participating in the net-work. Network membership and activity serves the prior purposes of its constituent organisations. They are subordinate to the constituent organisations' goals as means – often one among many – to realise the constituents' prior goals. Further, these prior goals will not necessarily even be amongst the main objectives of the constituent organisations. But if circumstances bring the network's objectives into conflict with those of the network constituents, the constituents are likely to give their own prior objectives priority. Constituents join or leave networks (Smith, 1993), sometimes only temporarily. Thus network objectives are means to constituent organisations' objectives, and the latter (as outlined above) are means to individual organisational members' objectives. Network objectives thus stand in a more indirect, mediated relationship to those of the individuals who are members of the net-work's constituent organisations.

Network constituents are often functionally differentiated (Rhodes, 1988), each making a specific contribution to the network's activities. For example, there exist NHS primary care networks which involve public bodies (NHS Trusts), private individuals (independent practi-tioners), voluntary (for example patient groups) and local government departments. In networks, however, there is a greater risk than within an organisation of duplication or gaps between different members' contributions to realising their common objectives. For networks are integrated and managed mainly by informal mechanisms such as brokerage (bringing problems, solutions and actors together; Kickert and Koppenjahn, 1998) and *ad hoc* problem-solving. Networks are consequently based on wide variety of resource exchanges. Depending on the case, the types of resource exchanged include financial, informational and political resources (legitimacy, status, influence) (Rhodes, 1988) besides help in kind.

Although they are not hierarchical, many networks have inner and outer circles of constituents who play more or less active roles respectively in the network activity and in coordinating the network constituents' activities (Smith, 1993). The more influential constituents hold so-called 'modal positions' in a network (Kickert and Koppenjahn, 1998). Depending on the case, this network-level role can be taken on by an existing member organisation, by an existing external body (for example one general practice taking on administrative tasks on behalf of a whole group of practices) or by specially constructing a new, internal 'focal organisation' for it (Klijn, 1998). Depending upon whether the network centre plays a weak or a strong role, we can speak of loosely and of tightly organised networks respectively. Thus the English medical profession is a relatively tightly organised network; patients' organisations constitute more loosely organised ones. Like organisations, networks require a common belief system and discourse (knowledge, values, rules) as means of coordinating and legitimating their everyday collaboration (Börzel, 1998).

Six interdependent tasks therefore have to be accomplished to change a loose network first into a tighter network, then a hierarchy:

1 Induce network constituents to pool resources with each other.
2 Prioritise the hierarchy's objectives over the network constituents' prior objectives by constructing compliance mechanisms within the new hierarchy.
3 Establish and resource a compliance system controlled by the core body
4 Establish a technical division of labour for achieving the hierarchy's objectives
5 Give the core body control over the resources necessary for achieving the common objectives
6 Legitimate the above

The agent of this transition can be either existing network constituents or an external body (for example government). One would expect transitions motivated by an external body to be at greater risk of encountering conflict between network constituents, hence delays or failures of formation.

Two incentives are available to allay network constituents' fear of ending up in asymmetric, exploitative relationships with the higher levels of the hierarchy (Powell, 1987). Once-off 'joining incentives' can be exchanged for the constituents' resources (for example a buy-out, official recognition etc.). Routine incentives can be made permanently available after joining, and these have to be no less attractive than the alternative. A negative example is the group of Leicester GPs who collectively withdrew from PCG activity because (they held) they were insufficiently paid for the time and work it demanded of them. Both kinds of incentive can include non-material benefits (such as legal recognition, influence) and negative incentives, that is less-bad consequences of joining than not joining the new hierarchy. For example, GPs contemplating joining CHS Trusts as salaried doctors in the first wave PMS pilots had as routine incentives a reduction in administrative load and guarantees of personal and practice income; offset (in some cases) by loss of pension rights and the claim. Parts of the GP press provided a disincentive to join by arguing that salaried status would reduce GPs' clinical autonomy and financial independence.

So far as possible the hierarchy-builders have to remove any underlying conflicts between members and make any existing incentives within or between network constituents compatible with the new incentives. This can be done by incorporating network constituent organisations' existing incentive systems whole, as branches of the new compliance system or as intermediate link within it, thereby internalising them to the organisation; or by actively circumventing and weakening them. The positive aspect is of replacing the negotiative, *ad hoc* compliance strategies in networks (Rhodes, 1988) with routinised compliance systems, concentrating the disposal of legitimacy, money, physical resources, knowledge and coercion in the hands of the core body. Similarly, constructing a technical division of labour necessitates replacing *ad hoc* 'reticulist' decisions about functional roles and task allocations with permanent, specialised role allocations and durable, complementary, mutually-agreed working practices. Lastly, it is necessary to legitimate the new relationships, giving the new organisations' objectives and activities a stronger justification than any conflicting prior goals of the constituent bodies could claim.

The foregoing implies what conditions and network characteristics are likely to make it easier, quicker and cheaper for loose networks to become tight networks and then hierarchies. Providing incentives for network constituents to join the new organisation is likely to be easier where:

1   Participation in the organisation offers those who join access to new resources, economies of scale, scope or administrative costs (Coase, 1937; Williamson, 1985), the chance to create larger risk pools or to relieve constituents of difficult, marginal or onerous tasks (e.g. managing staff, operating budget systems, dealing with taxation etc.).
2   The costs of joining are low.
3   Network constituents have few or no alternative ways to realise the objectives which transition to organisation would promote.
4   Those forming organisations can choose which network constituents to include and can differentiate the routine and joining incentives for different actors (cf. Kickert and Koppenjahn, 1998).
5   The people forming the network into organisations are skilled in negotiation.
6   Excluded network constituents have no reason to obstruct the transition, or cannot. As a negative example, some GPs who opposed their colleagues' shift to the new, post-1997 form of contract did so because they feared that less money would then remain in the pooled budget used to finance their own, old-style contracts.
7   There is lower 'organisational density' (Oliver and Ebers, 1998); that is, fewer constituents, hence less negotiating involved in combing the network constituents and less risk of competition for roles within the new organisation. So for a given size of clientele, locality or service it is easier to assemble few larger constituents into an organisation than many small ones into an organisation. Among NHS Total Purchasing Pilot projects, the smallest (20 000 to 50 000 population covered) were the most successful at acting collectively (Robinson, 1998).

Constructing a hierarchy is likely to be easier where 'entrepreneurial' professions or groups exist, willing to take control of the modal positions (Hanlon, 1997) and exhibiting managers' characteristic 'expansionary bias' (Niskanen, 1971). Establishing a compliance system is likely to be easier where conflicts amongst constituents' prior interests and with those of the network are fewer, more transient, and more marginal to the constituents. This is likelier to occur when network constituents are more homogenous constituents in terms of occupational mix, objectives, incentives faced (financial interests), working practices (Börzel, 1998). It is also likelier to be easier, the more resources those in the modal positions can gain control of; and when network constituents are responsive to cheap, simple compliance systems such as appeals to technical expertise or legitimacy rather than (say) payments or coercion.

It is likely to be easier for constituents to agree complementary working practices and to establish a technical division of labour when, firstly, they are not competing for roles. (Thus it would be easier to integrate doctors and dentists than psychiatrists and clinical psychologists.) One way in which these conditions obtain is when there is no duplication of roles among network constituents or, if there is duplication, competition between them is weak (for example because of an undersupply of their services or because they already operate anti-competitive practices). Another way is when certain constituents or their members can promote their occupational interests by functional allocation of roles, for instance by monopolising a role by *force majeure* (medicine is a classic example). However, constructing new legitimations is likely to be easier where constituents' prior belief systems are mutually consistent, and their material interests converge rather than conflict.

PCGS: OBSERVATIONS AND PREDICTIONS

We can now operationalise these general predictions for the case of PCGs. Variation in these factors across PCGs should, on the theories recounted above, predict PCGs' speed of transition through the second and later stages, ultimately to hierarchy.

National policy, which guarantees GPs' right to remain independent contractors if they wish, besides guaranteeing GPs' dominance of PCG Boards, are common to all PCGs. So is legislation governing such matters as nurse prescribing, certification of illness and death, the statutory roles of directorial boards and managerial committee in PCTs and the legitimations of, and objections to, PCGs advanced in the mass media and professional press. All PCGs and PCTs are geographically based. Membership is mandatory for all GPs in their territory, as is the exclusion of commercial providers from NHS primary care (Jenkins, 1999). These common factors cannot be used to predict variations in PCGs' progress towards closer networks and hierarchy, but there is one apparent exception. All Health Authorities (HAs) are in an ambivalent position regarding PCG formation. On the one hand they face performance management pressures to develop PCGs and establish PCTs swiftly. On the other hand, they have an interest in delaying and minimising the loss of their budgets and functions to PCGs and PCTs. How HAs resolve the dilemma can be expected to vary from place to place.

One would therefore expect to see a faster transition, the more of the following predictive conditions obtain:

P1   In PCGs with fewer PHC providers, that is PCGs with smaller populations, and those where concentration of general practices into group practices had gone furthest before PCG formation began (that is, those with the fewest practices rather than fewest GPs *per se*).

P2   Incentives for joining a closer network or organisation are stronger and the disincentives weaker.

P3   There are few conflicts of interest between PHC providers. Amongst general practices the main current source of conflict is redistribution for non-fundholder use of extra resources which GP fundholders acquired during 1991–98. One would expect such conflicts to be smallest in PCGs with either a very high or a very low proportion of ex-fundholders, and sharpest where about half the GPs were fundholders. One would also expect fewest conflicts in PCGs where no groups of practices or GPs were obviously excluded from the Board.

P4   There is a higher per-GP 'unified' (overall) budget, in particular a higher management budget or where the PCG is below its target budget, hence likely to be gaining budget in coming years. This enables it to offer relatively large joining incentives and create compliance structures.

P5   PCG/T formation would help solve specific health or service provision problems. These problems both legitimate the transition and are common tasks around which to organise a coherent, integrated division of labour. On grounds both of the inverse care law (Tudor Hart, 1971) and the factors predicting demand for services (Jarman, 1980) one would expect such problems to be more prevalent in PCGs serving poorer populations; that is,

PCGs with the highest underprivileged area (UPA) score. These PCGs tend, for instance, to be those with the greatest problems of GP recruitment and retention.

P6   In the case of externally-sponsored formation of tighter networks and organisations, local political actors (HA, LMC, 'entrepreneurs', other professional bodies) support the formation of a tighter network or an organisation, especially it their support extends beyond permission and legitimation to the offer of physical resources or cash.

The above theory implies that PCG-with-PCG mergers would have an ambivalent effect on the transition. *If* PCG/T mergers can produce economies of scope and scale – as yet there is little evidence either way – one would expect PCG mergers to facilitate the transition because these economies could be used to provide benefits of integration. What is more certain, though, is that mergers of PCGs with other PCGs would increase the number of constituents and interfaces to integrate across. That would tend to make the aforementioned tasks more difficult.

In some places PCG members already have experience of creating the larger, tighter networks mentioned above, putting them in a position to form tighter networks and organisations sooner than the others. Nevertheless, making an earlier start is itself an outcome of the factors noted above, not an additional factor promoting the formation of networks or hierarchies. For this methodological reason it should not count as a predictor of integration. As signs of the transition outlined above one would expect to observe:

S1   Transition from stage 1 to 2 PCG, to stage 3 PCT, then stage 4 PCT.

S2   A strengthening PCG/T role as the focal organisation (network centre), reflected in a shift from informal resource exchange to governance structures based on sub-contracts and, eventually, employment as the PCG becomes the apex of a hierarchy. Initially one would expect to see an increasing proportion of GPs sub-contracted to the PCT under the new local contracts instead of the old national contract; and, later, an increasing proportion of GPs become the salaried employees of the PCT (not to be confused with increasing employment of salaried GPs by general practices). Concomitantly, one would expect to see an increasing proportion of all PHC staff being salaried PCG/T employees and greater tendency to share technical support and other common-user resources at the PCG/T level.

S3 More integrated technical working arrangements such as common clinical protocols and homogeneous, integrated information systems.

S4 Mergers of PCGs with CHS Trusts, or parts of them

S5 Restratification of professionals, with some spending an increasing proportion of their time on PCG/T managerial work and others a decreasing proportion.

Table 9.1 shows how a scoring system was constructed for these two groups of variables. The theory outlined above predicts that the total scores for P1–P6 will correlate with the total scores for signs of integration S1–S5.

Table 9.1   Factors predicting integration and signs of integration in PCGs

Predictors	Scoring criteria
P1 Small number of interfaces	
A number of general practices	1 point = in lower quartile
B number of GPs	1 point = in lower quartile
P2 Incentives	
A PCG manages own over-and underspends?	1 point = yes
B whether PCG can bank underspends	1 point = yes
C all groups of GPs represented on PCG Board	1 point = yes
D practices keep part or all prescribing savings?	1 point = yes
P3 Compatibility of interests	
A agreement within PCG Boards	Score = 1/3(3 − number of controversies*)
B no reduction of GP fundholders' services?	1 point = no reduction
P4 Resourcing	
A total unified budget, per practice	1 point = in upper quartile
B whether IM&T budget appears adequate	1 point = yes
C management budget, per practice	1 point = in upper quartile

Table 9.1   *cont.*

Table 9.1   *cont.*

Predictors	Scoring criteria
P5 Policy tasks	
A ratio of highly deprived patients to marginally deprived patients per 1000 population	1 point = in upper quartile
B deprivation payment per 1000 population	1 point = in upper quartile
C mix of ex-fundholding practices and others 1 point if between 25% and 75%	former fundholders
P6 Main actors' support	
A working relations with HA	1 point = 'good' or 'very good'
B HA views on Trust status	1 point = 'HA supports' or 'HA promotes'
C proportion of GPs who support PCG	1 point = 50% or more
D proportion of nurses who support PCG	1 point = 50% or more
S1 Moves to next PCG stage	
A PCG decision on when to seek PCT status	1 point = by 2002
B level of PCT anticipated	1 point = level 4
S2 PCG/T Board as modal organisation	
S2N Network tightness	
A Board's sense of common purpose, vision	1 point = above mid-point of scale
B jointness of Board's decision-making	1 point = above mid-point of scale
C number of nurse networks within PCG	Score = (8 − number checked) 1/8
D GPs' willingness to share resources, equipment, premises	1 point = above mid-point of scale
S2Q quasi-market formation any PMS practices	1 point = yes
S2H hierarchy formation	
A number of PCG directly employed staff	1 point = in upper quartile
B any salaried GP principals	1 point = yes
S3 Integrated technical working	
A proportion of practices sharing use of healthy living centre, PC resource centre, OOH centre,	1 point = mean of over 50% of practices share

Table 9.1 *cont.*

Predictors	Scoring criteria
minor injuries centre, walk-in PHC centre and other shared resources (mean of 6 scores)	
B level of dedicated administrative support for clinical governance	1 point = above mid-point of scale
C joint clinical governance activity with CHS trusts	1 point = yes
D information availability	1 point = above mid-point of scale
E use of shared prescribing data	1 point = yes
F use of shared prescribing guidelines	1 point = yes
G use of shared disease guidelines	1 point = yes
S4 Provider collaborations	
A any multi-practice PMS schemes	1 point = yes
B proportion of practices in OOH cooperative	1 point = 50% or more
C any discussions about merger with NHS trusts?	1 point = yes
D any PMS partnership(s) with NHS trust?	1 point = yes
S5 Professional restratification	
A full time clinical governance and/or prescribing professional support	1 point = yes

* Respondents were invited to list up to three 'controversial subjects' at PCG Board meetings during 1998–99.

RESULTS

Correlations between the total (summary) predictor scores and the total (summary) scores for signs of integration were analysed using two standard tests for non-parametric data; Spearmans *rho* and Kendall's *tau* (both two-tailed). For comparison, a simple logistic regression (OLS) analysis was also made, on the generalised linear model (Hutcheson and Sofroniou, 1999). All three tests indicate a modest but significant correlation between the predictor scores and the signs-of-integration scores. Using Kendall's *tau*, the correlation coefficient is 0.221, significant at $p = 0.008$. Using Spearman's *rho*, the correlation coefficient is 0.298, significant at $p = 0.011$. The OLS standardised correlation coefficient is 0.322 (95% confidence interval 0.1 to 0.712; the constant B = 3.564), significant at $p = 0.006$.

These preliminary results suggest that the factors noted above do partly, but certainly not entirely, predict differences in PCGs' tightness as networks. There are three possible reasons why the correlations are relatively modest. Firstly, the foregoing theoretical account of what factors determine the transition from loose network to tight network may still omit some important factor or factors. Further, qualitative empirical research would be required to discover what these may be. Alternatively, the above theory may include some relatively unimportant factors which could be omitted from the analysis with little loss of explanatory power. At the time of writing, work continues to analyse what each predictive factor contributes to the correlations. Preliminary results suggest that the most influential factors are the number of practices, the lack of conflicts, management budget size and good relationships with the HA. Work is also continuing to analyse relationships among the predictors and among the signs of integration. Thirdly, the first year's data were collected at a very early point in the transition, reflected in low mean scores for both the total predictor scores and the total signs-of-integration scores. The mean total predictor score was 4.86 out of a possible 18 (SD = 1.93; range = 1.00 to 9.33). The mean total signs-of-integration score was 5.53 out of a possible 22 (SD = 2.43, range = 2.43 to 11.63). The theory above implies that both scores would rise as the construction of PCGs and PCTs progresses, possibly raising the correlations in doing so. Supplementary, longitudinal analyses to test this conjecture will become possible as second and subsequent years' data become available.

CONCLUSIONS AND POLICY IMPLICATIONS

On the evidence of English PCGs, the foregoing model of how networks evolve into tighter networks and eventually hierarchies appears to be on the right lines but with scope for refinement by identifying which are the most powerful predictors to concentrate on in future research. As more years' data accumulate, longitudinal analyses both of the overall model and to identify the strongest predictors will also become possible. It would also be valuable to supplement and interpret the foregoing analyses through further qualitative research.

Certain factors which promote organisational formation are beyond policy-makers' reach. These include what network constituents already exist, their membership and, in the short term, what processes of production they use. Neither can policy-makers necessarily influence whether other organisations or coalitions (for example professional bodies, trades unions, pressure groups, consumer organisations and so forth) oppose the evolution of networks of their transition into organisations. Although it does not apply to the NHS, national policy-makers cannot influence any foreign members of networks either.

Insofar as the above theory has a limited validity, it implies that policy-makers can promote the formation of tighter networks and organisations in various ways. One is by extending and deepening existing networks rather than reconstructing new networks from scratch (for example because policy-makers misconceive them as alternatives or obstacles to current policy). This includes tolerating or encouraging spontaneous, 'bottom up' collaboration among network constituents in the form of informal or semi-formal groupings alongside the construction of more formal organisational structures. Likewise, relational rather than classical forms of service contract promote extra-contractual, informal relationships and trust that strengthen working relationships between network constituents (Sheaff and Lloyd-Kendall, 2000).

Additionally, such policy-makers might promote the creation of pathways of care, service protocols or production procedures (for example common referral systems, information sharing, common sources of raw materials and so on) across network constituents' boundaries. Not least, it is necessary to give the occupants of modal positions the means to produce voluntary compliance (incentives and legitimation) to ensure that network constituents get permanent nett benefits from joining an organisation; or failing that, to make joining cost-neutral to them. Tolerating or promoting professional restratification enables the entrepreneurial elements in the professions to spend more time managing, to acquire the necessary management and coordinating skills to fulfil a buffering role between the rest of the network and the world outside it, and to extend this into a 'colonising' role (Broadbent and Laughlin, 1992), whereby the entrepreneurs transmit policy-makers' objectives and beliefs into the rest of the network.

These findings are still rather provisional, but at least one methodological conclusion is clear. To refine and qualify our understanding of the transition for loose networks to tight networks to hierarchy requires a combination of theoretical and empirical research and, in the empirical domain, a combination of quantitative (cross-sectional and longitudinal) designs with the qualitative methods more familiar to researchers in organisational behaviour. Lastly, the transition from loose network to hierarchy is one thing; the transition from loose network to cooperative or partnerships may prove to be quite another, requiring its own theory and research.

Acknowledgements

The National Primary Care Research and Development Centre's PCG database was created by Deborah Baker, Mark Hann and Andrew Wagner, collaborating with Robert Barr, Justin Hayes and Neil Matthews of the Department of Geography, Manchester University, UK. The Centre's Tracker Survey core team are Brenda Leese, Keri Smith and David Wilkin.

References

Börzel, T. (1998) 'Organizing Babylon – On Different Conceptions of Policy Networks', *Public Administration*, lxxvi(2): 253–73.
Broadbent, J. and Laughlin, R. (1992) 'Contractual Changes in Schools and General Practices: Professional Resistance and the Role of Absorption and Absorbing Groups', in R. Flynn and G. Williams (eds), *Contracting for Health. Quasi-markets and the National Health Service* (Oxford: Oxford University Press).
Coase, R. (1937) 'The Nature of the Firm', *Economica*, 4: 386–405.
Granovetter, M. (1985) 'Economic Action and Social Structure: The Problem of Embeddedness', *American Journal of Sociology*, lxxxi(3): 481–510.
Hanlon, G. (1997) 'Professionalisation as Enterprise: Service Class Politics and the Redefinition of Professionalism', *Sociology*, 22(2): 43–63.
Hutcheson, G. and Sofroniou, N. (1999) *The Multivariate Social Scientist* (London: Sage).
Jarman, B. (1983) 'Identification of Underprivileged Areas', *British Medical Journal*, 284: 1705–9.
Jenkins, C. (1999) 'Personal Medical Services pilots – New Opportunities', in R. Lewis and S. Gillam (eds), *Transforming Primary Care* (London: King's Fund).
Kickert, W.J.M. and Koppenjahn, J.F.M. (1998) 'Public Management and Network Management: An Overview', in W.J.M. Kickert *et al.* (eds), *Managing Complex Networks* (London: Sage).
Klijn, H.E. (1998) 'Policy Networks; An Overview', in Kickert, W.J.M. *et al.* (eds), *Managing Complex Networks* (London: Sage).
Kooiman, J. (1993) (ed.) *Modern Governance* (London: Sage).

Niskanen, W. (1971) *Bureaucracy: Master or Servant?* (London: IEA).

Oliver, A.L. and Ebers, M. (1998) 'Networking Network Studies', in Kickert, W.J.M. *et al.* (eds), *Managing Complex Networks* (London: Sage).

Powell, W.W. (1987) 'Hybri'd Organizational Arrangements: New Form or Transitional Development', *California Management Review*, XXX(1): 67–87.

Powell, W.W. (1992) 'The Social Embeddedness of Getting into Print' in Zey, M. (ed.), *Decision Making: Alternatives to Rational Choice Models* (London: Sage).

Rhodes, R.A.W. (1988) *Beyond Westminster and Whitehall* (London: Unwin Hyman).

Robinson, R. (1998) 'Primary Care Groups as Managed Organisations', NHS 50 conference, Brighton University.

Sheaff, R. (1999) 'The Development of English Primary Care Group Governance: a Scenario Analysis', *International Journal of Health Planning and Management*, 14: 257–268.

Sheaff, R. and Lloyd-Kendall, A. (2000) 'Principal-agent Relationships in General Practice: The First Wave of English PMS Contracts', *Journal of Health Services Research and Policy* v(3): 156–163.

Smith, M.J. (1993) *Pressure, Power and Politics* (Hemel Hempstead: Harvester).

Thompson, G. Frances, J. Leva R. and Mitchell, J. (1991) (eds) *Markets, Hierarchies and Networks: The Coordination of Social Life* (London: Sage).

Tudor-Hart, J. (1971) 'The Inverse Care Law', *The Lancet* (27 February) 401–12.

Williamson, O.E. (1985) *The Economic Institutions of Capitalism* (New York: Free Press).

10 Clinical Governance: Is NICE the Right Word?

Marie L. Thorne

INTRODUCTION

This chapter uses a discourse analysis of clinical governance to explore the changing nature of power relationships between government, doctors and managers in the NHS. Clinical governance was selected because

> Medicine is so central to modern society that doctors have emerged as perhaps the key profession. The extent to which they are regulated, and the nature of any governmental involvement in that regulation, is thus a matter of widespread interest and concern.
>
> (Moran and Wood, 1993: viii)

As clinical governance was only introduced in April 1999 the chapter focuses on the public discourse generated by the three key groups crucial to its enactment – the regulators (government), the implementers (managers) and the regulated (doctors). The introduction of clinical governance may be usefully compared with the introduction of clinical management which generated a number of models as it evolved in practice. Typically these were based upon the dominance of either management or medicine or some form of collaborative partnership where the power dynamics of each group shifted according to the issue in question (see Exworthy and Halford, 1999). Discourse analysis is used as means of identifying the power relationships between the groups.

The chapter is in three parts: the first section introduces discourse analysis. Section two presents statements from public documents from government, doctors and managers to interpret their discourse of clinical governance. The final section draws together these views to make sense of their meanings and their relationships using the concept of monological and dialogical discourse (Keenoy *et al.*, 1997). This approach is used to identify if a new 'dialogue' has been created

184

through a community of collaboration or whether the discourse is primarily a government 'monologue' reflecting a new form of hegemony in the management of professionals.

DISCOURSE AND POWER

Language is central to the concept of discourse as it is through language that ideas and practices are communicated and appraised (Thomas, 1997). Language has both use (or meaning) and function as words are used to 'do' things as well as make statements (Hoenisch, 1998). This capacity creates what Wittgenstein (1974) called the 'language game' where language itself is an activity or a form of life. The language and discourse of clinical governance raises the question of what each group of actors means by the term and what they might want it to do.

Discourse according to the work of Foucault is not simply a way of seeing but is always embedded in social practices which reproduce that way of seeing as the 'truth' of the discourse (Knights and Morgan, 1991). The power of discourse is illustrated by Gee and Lankshear (1995: 11) who define it with a capital 'D' to show its importance in providing insight into the ways of 'thinking, believing, acting and interacting, speaking, listening and valuing... to signal membership of a particular social group.'

Each profession, managers, politicians and clinicians is embedded in its own community that is maintained or embedded through its social practices whilst divided according to its client group and praxis (Kogan, 1996). Complex sites of social practice, such as the NHS, bring together people with very different discursive traditions and when this happens meanings, which are socially constructed (Berger and Luckmann, 1967) and embedded, may become contested in ways that have social, political and moral implications. As Fairclough (1992: 3) said, 'Discourses do not just reflect or represent social entities and relations, they construct and constitute them.'

The concept of power is central to discourse analysis. Clegg (1994) describes how Foucault (1977) focused on the power of professional discourses to limit define and normalise 'vocabularies of motive' that are available in specific sites or contexts for making sensible and accountable what people should do, can do and consequently do. Here power is normalised through the discursive formation of knowledge which is why Foucault argued that power and knowledge are inseparable as knowledge, through its creation, reproduces particular discursive practices: discourses are the means by which power is constituted. As Foucault (1984: 110) said:

Discourse is not simply that which translates struggles or systems of domination but is the thing for which and by which there is a struggle, discourse is the power which is to be seized.

If discourse is power, who is trying to seize the discourse and power of clinical governance? Foucault's dynamic view of power sees it as shifting and unstable manifesting itself through networks and alliances that are constantly created and recreated. There are three ways power is viewed within discourse (Fairclough, 1989). Firstly, some parts of discourse become standardised giving some forms of language far greater power than others and enabling those who use it to assume more powerful positions. Secondly, certain types of discourse embody and sustain power relations by constraining the way in which discourse takes place – or where it originates. Thirdly, power limits access to discourse itself.

Whilst discourse embraces a plethora of power knowledge relationships which are communicated and embedded in a range of social practices, meaning making can be viewed as contested as well as negotiated and embedded as some social contexts will promote some meanings and limit others (Foucault, 1980). Wetherell *et al.* (1987) illustrate how any organisational discourse is constructed out of a myriad of contradictory and conflicting views as any given discourse reflects a stage in a number of intersecting relationships which involve power and power struggles, understandings and misunderstandings, acquiescence and resistance, complementary and contradictory elements.

Language is constructed, embedded and contested and often indeterminate. Discourse is inevitably a locus of conflict as some benefit from its use whilst others lose out. Consequently some may want to actively promote a particular form of discourse whilst others resist it or try to dissolve it (Parker, 1992). This chapter draw attention to the discourses of clinical governance, how they are constructed and the system of power that surrounds them (Knights, 1992). Any discourse will capture both the advantaged and disadvantaged in its web of power relations (Phillips and Hardy, 1997). The relationship between these two forces is complex, for as Clegg (1994) points out there is not a discourse of power on one side and a discourse that runs counter to it on the other – rather there can be different and even contradictory discourses within the same strategy or rhetoric. Yet wherever there is power there will be resistance. However, if we accept the social construction of a web of institutions and discourses and believe that social actors are free to maintain or reject discourses, discourses themselves are neither inherently oppressive nor omnipotent (Giddens, 1984). Often the issue in political or institutional discourse is the articulation and display of an *authoritative voice* to hegemonise the discourse (Alvarez-Caccamo, 1996).

Discourse Analysis

Having reviewed the role and nature of discourse analysis how might the text be analysed or interpreted? Alvarez-Caccamo (1996) suggests a number of attributes to consider – the nature of the actors and audience; the range of terminology and the ambiguity surrounding it; the range of permissible behaviours left for the audience and the responses expected – have the audience been silenced? Who will benefit and who will lose from the introduction of clinical governance and what resistance exists?

It is important to understand the power of silence and the difference between monological and dialogical discourse to determine whose discourse dominates. Identifying silence and 'din' encourages us to ask who is doing the ignoring and excluding (Hearn, 1996)? What remains unwritten or unsaid may be more powerful and provide greater insights into the nature of the discourse than that which appears or is spoken. Accessing the space between words or silence is difficult as silence can also be interpreted in a number of ways – from assent through aggressive resistance to a simple lack of interest.

How do some discourses become dominant? Keenoy *et al.* (1997) suggest that where there is a dominant group discourse is invariably monological – where one story is viewed from the perspective of a dominant group (Boje, 1995). The monologue need not be restricted to one group or set of views, but it must be coherent. Invariably most analysts find it easy to construct one coherent story of events making the monologue the most common form of analysis. In contrast, dialogical discourse recognises and legitimates multiple meanings and interpretations. Independent voices and autonomous discourses which make up a plurality of meanings or plurivocal interpretations are also legitimated.

Although people and organisations change in response to their environment they rarely change in a way that fulfils the intentions or plans of a single group of actors (March, 1984) such as government. The next section analyses the discourse of clinical government using material presented by the government, doctors and NHS managers.

GOVERNMENT DISCOURSE

The Context: Modernising and Change

The published material on clinical governance used here is from three documents: the White Paper *The New NHS: Modern and Dependable* (Department of Health, 1997); The New NHS Modern, Dependable, popular version (MD), the discussion document *A First Class Service* (Department of Health, 1998); and the NHS Executive guidance document, *Clinical Governance: Quality in the New NHS* (Department of Health, 1999). *Modern and Dependable* presents the government's agenda for reform using the rhetoric of 'Modernising' and based upon Labour's 'Third Way'. Ham (1999) describes how the Third Way emerged from a debate within the party between the modernisers and the traditionalists which may explain a discourse that appeals to both groups. Marrying history and tradition with modernity and change pervades government language Dott 1997 Chapter 2 as it states its commitment to 'building on what has worked, but discarding what has failed' introducing an NHS built upon 'partnership and driven by performance' based upon six key principles: a *national service* based upon *local responsibility* working in *partnership* to drive *efficiency*, guarantee *excellence* and rebuild *public confidence*. These principles provide the context for clinical governance.

Modernising, like 'new', is now universally applied by government throughout the public services and is central to Labour's lexicon. This blanket usage reflects the rhetoric of management fads or fashion – words and concepts that create bold promises and promises of quantum leaps in productivity and efficiency (Kieser, 1997). Both terms reveal a tension between the need for change and continuity as the Prime Minister's Foreword to the White Paper (DoH, 1997) states:

Creating the NHS was the greatest act of modernisation ever achieved by a Labour Government. It banished the fear of becoming ill that had for years blighted the lives of millions of people. But I know that one of the main reasons people elected a new Government on May 1st was their concern that the NHS was failing them and their families.

Modernisation, synonymous with renewal, updating and rejuvenation is presented as an historical tradition by transposing the current discourse onto a different historical era. Reinventing the creation of the NHS as an act of modernisation enables Blair to appropriate its earlier success into his new discourse. This creates positive connotations that authenticate and legitimate an 'authoritative voice' for a dominant government discourse. One strand of rhetoric reflects the New Public Management discourse of empowering the 'consumer'. However, pledges and appeals for patients' and the public's involvement in decision-making may also be seen by cynics as a rhetoric employed to legitimate government changes.

Clinical Governance

Clinical Governance: Quality in the New NHS (DoH, 1999) provides 'developmental guidance' with an 'action' framework for implementation. It defines clinical governance as:

> A framework through which NHS organisations are accountable for continuously improving the quality of their services and safeguarding high standards of care by creating an environment in which excellence in clinical care will flourish.   *(Ibid.: 3)*

The definition uses positive language to combine increased accountability with security and excellence. Superficially this seems uncontentious. However, combining two very different terms – 'clinical' and 'governance'– is symbolic of the government's desire to integrate two separate organisational domains. The term governance was explicitly appropriated from corporate governance and the CEO's statutory financial responsibility, and combining it with a statutory 'clinical' duty addresses the criticisms that the NHS is too driven by financial performance. Clinical governance is meant to restore a balance by bringing clinical performance 'to the top of the NHS agenda' (DoH, 1998: 6) putting quality 'in its rightful place at the heart of the NHS' (*ibid*.: 33) and making it clear that quality is 'everybody's business' (*ibid*.: 34).

Clinical governance is described as the 'linchpin' of the government's strategy as it 'applies to all sections of the NHS', sits in the 'centre of quality' and is 'crucial to the overall success of the agenda' (*ibid.*: 2,3). The language constantly reinforces its importance and the need for its success. The tone of the discourse is also normative as the NHS Executive state that there is a need for a 'fundamental shift in the culture of many NHS organisations' to implement it successfully although government recognise that it 'cannot be implemented overnight' (*ibid.*: 2,4). They will also seek demonstrable evidence of its 'successful introduction' in both the short and medium term. Simply introducing clinical governance is not enough: it *must be successful*. How will this be achieved? Government has created the National Institute for Clinical Excellence (NICE) (to provide guidelines on clinical and cost-effectiveness) and the Commission for Health Improvement (CHI) to 'support and oversee the quality of clinical services at local level' (DoH 1997 3:2). CHI has the power to affect both doctors and managers and its 'dual role' as supporter /inquisitor is revealed in the way it is described as

> able to intervene by invitation or on the Secretary of State's direction where a problem has not been gripped.
>
> (DoH 1997: 6 *Popular version*)

Where clinical governance is failing, there will be 'rapid investigation and intervention' to deliver improved performance through the NHS Executive or CHI. Although clinical governance is about changing the culture from 'blame to learning' (DoH, 1999: 5) the rhetoric of accountability suggests paradoxically that clinical governance may well induce a blame-centred culture.

Managers and particularly CEOs are now accountable with a statutory duty exercised on behalf of the Trust Board to assure the quality of their services and provide the Board with regular reports on quality, integrating all senior managers into the clinical domain. Earlier reforms placed clinicians into the managerial and executive hierarchy; now CEOs as non-medical managers have a legitimate claim to the clinical domain through accountability for clinical performance. The discourse directed toward managers specifically is directive about their role and style of operation imposing both structures and expectations of performance. Whilst there is some flexibility for 'local interpretation' there are four common core steps: leadership; assessment; development; and assessment.

Clinical governance is an imposed top-down change. CEOs and Boards need to 'sign up to the need for change and drive it forward through the whole organisation.' They (and clinicians) need 'strong leadership'. Their style is further circumscribed by the need for more 'open communication and collaboration' and to ensure the 'total involvement of staff in shaping services and planning change' (DoH, 1998: 75). There also needs to be 'free access to the CEO and Board where problems or barriers to progress arise'. Moreover, the emphasis on providing a 'searching and honest analysis' of strengths and weaknesses is monitored in a veiled threat that those Boards who do not identify problems will be deemed to be failing:

The content of the Board's agenda will send a powerful signal to the whole organisation, to the local media, the public and to the health organisation's partners. The more substantial and searching the issues the board discusses, the more it will be concluded that clinical governance is taken seriously.

(Clinical Governance DoH 1999: 18)

Increased openness increases accountability and surveillance from inside and outside the organisation; and managers are both under surveillance and part of the 'monitoring group'. Demands on CEOs are considerable as they must possess a wealth of attributes to implement clinical governance, through the government designated leadership style, structures and processes.

The changes of structure and professional accountability are even greater for doctors. Every Trust CEO must nominate a 'lead clinician' responsible for clinical governance, and create a Trust Board clinical governance sub-committee. All hospital doctors must now take part in national clinical audits and confidential enquiries (DoH, 1999: 14) and assume joint responsibility for the delivery of multi-agency services. The 'drive' for clinical governance has to be supported through 'workforce issues' including staff training and the development of new skills and competencies. Government are tightening up and integrating professional self-regulation with clinical governance to cope more effectively with poor clinical performance. Doctors' 'right to self-regulation' is balanced by the need to 'modernise it' to restore 'public confidence'. The language switches subtly from a divisive to inclusive stance – 'If this confidence is to be restored, *our* systems of professional self-regulation must be modernised and strengthened' (DoH, 1998: 47) This section identifies the need for openness and responsiveness to change and increased public accountability to maintain standards. A General Medical Council listing of the duties of a doctor also appears on the page – why? Is it to reinforce the message, identify the similarity in the discourses or reassure the profession? Strong language is used to ensure that doctors 'stop performing' if their performance is unacceptable (*ibid.*: 38). An interesting insight is revealed in the change in reporting relationships *proposed* in the discussion document and dropped or postponed in the final guidance. The *First Class Service* document (*ibid.*) identifies that the 'lead clinician' will be 'accountable to the CEO and Board', but in the final guidance this has been 'fudged' suggesting the structure is not finalised and will emerge from a paper on self-governance and clinical governance produced only for doctors. Direct organisational accountability for clinical performance to a non-clinical manager may have met with too much resistance from doctors.

DOCTORS' DISCOURSE

Only medical journals are used as data sources (*British Medical Journal* and *Clinician in Management*) for the discourse analysis. A position justified by their explicit role to 'influence the debate on health' (Smith, 1999) and the public nature of their text. Clinical governance has created a 'din' of different voices offering alternative interpretations of its meaning and impact which use a range of styles from the practical (Scally and Donaldson, 1998; Wattis and McGinnis, 1999) to the literary (Douglas, 1999) to support it (Scally and Donaldson, 1998; Lee and Mythen, 1999) question it (Smith, 1999; James, 1999; Cunningham, 1999) or 'debunk' it (Goodman, 1998; Thompson, 1999; Light, 1999). Although doctors accept clinical governance is inevitable their discourse is struggling with what it *means* both philosophically and practically to the profession. The polyphonic voices of doctors reflects their professional fears and their desire to gain or appropriate the power created by the discursive space of clinical governance. Defining its meaning is the first step in the power struggle.

The Meaning of Clinical Governance

Goodman (1998) recognises the power of clinical governance because it carries a statutory duty, but complains it is difficult to grasp as it lacks any 'intuitive meaning'. Although Scally and Donaldson (1998) claim to spell out the meaning of clinical governance they focus more on an aspiration of how clinical governance should be

> rigorous in its application, organisation wide in its emphasis, accountable in its delivery, developmental in its thrust, and positive in its connotations   (*ibid.*: p. 61)

rather than what it is.

Goodman (1998: p. 1725) attacks their description as 'meaningless rhetoric' saying that:

> Clinical governance emerges as a mixture of the blindingly obvious (people should lead well and work well in teams) and the unproved (clinical audit),

whilst Douglas (1999) goes even further; his 'short story' describes it as, 'It's crap. Jus' words... it's jus'words. Crap.'

Goodman's public 'debunking' of Scally and Donaldson resonated throughout the profession culminating in questions being raised about the authenticity and authorship of the article (Walshe, 1999). Interestingly the article's ambiguous status may have been due to its appearance in the Christmas edition of the *BMJ* as it has a tradition of publishing seasonal 'jolly' or 'spoof' articles. Publishing a critical view of clinical governance opened up the debate, allowing others who were equally sceptical to voice their views without fear of undue disapproval. Its publication created and legitimated a space for resistant or critical discourse that might otherwise not have emerged in public.

However, Cunningham (1999) suggests that the debate and differing discourses presented by Goodman and Scally and Donaldson created 'confusion, uncertainty and not a little embarrassment for the rest of us', suggesting that a rhetoric of fundamental resistance to clinical governance was both unexpected and unwelcome.

Doctors were anxious about the CEO and Trust Board accountability for clinical quality. The BMA described the arrangement in concrete terms drawing on *A First Class Service* as the 'authoritative voice' to legitimate their claim that the government has *recommended* that the *responsibility* for implementing frameworks for clinical governance should be *delegated* to lead clinicians (Beecham, 1999), thus appropriating the territory and discourse of clinical governance into the medical domain. Scally and Donaldson (1998) separate the strategic and operational issues explaining that 'final accountability' rests with the CEO, whilst daily responsibility lies with the 'lead clinician'. This interpretation is more than simple semantics if clinical governance is now 'enshrined' as the key to clinical performance (Hopkinson, 1999).

The medical discourse(s) can be crudely categorised into three rhetorics: relationships with management; fear of and or resistance to clinical governance; and practical implications for the delivery of services. As this chapter is concerned with the power relationship between doctors and managers it concentrates on the first two strands.

Talking about Management

As government focuses on partnerships to deliver clinical governance, how far do doctors see themselves in partnership with managers? The language of partnership appears primarily when implementation is discussed; here the language is collaborative, presenting a coherent strand as part of a monological discourse. Doctors recognise the need for clinicians and managers to 'develop a shared vision' jointly owned (Wattis and McGinnis, 1998: 16), 'drawing together' professional endeavour and management commitment to create a 'cohesive programme of action' (Scally and Donaldson, 1998).

Despite managers' accountability for clinical governance, doctors describe themselves as 'the' 'leaders' (Lee and Mythen, 1999). It is interesting how the term *lead* clinician reinforces this relegating managers to a supporting role and arguing that the managers' culture has to change to accommodate the complexity of clinical governance (Wattis and McGinnis, 1998). Managers' enhanced power should also be used to benefit clinicians by liberating them from bureaucratic tasks,

> Managers will need to appreciate their role in supporting and contributing to clinical governance....managers will need to support the development of a knowledge infrastructure and find ways of liberating highly skilled clinical staff from inappropriate repetitive paperwork.   (Wattis and McGinnis, 1998: 17)

increasing funding to ensure data collection for clinical governance (Black, 1999), and ensuring doctors' workloads are within prescribed levels of safety (Sandeman, 1999).

However the most powerful discourse is not the fear of managerial power but the refusal to recognise its existence, to reframe it in subordinate terms or to overtly indicate how clinical governance can increase medical power. James (1998) describes how a commitment to clinical governance will reduce patient anxiety, restore public confidence and enable clinicians to reduce 'interference' in their professional activities – ultimately enabling them to regain greater professional control. Anyone outside the profession entering professional territory is defined as 'interfering' suggesting they should not be there. Douglas (1999: 287), perhaps somewhat tongue in cheek, captures the flavour of this opportunistic discourse beautifully when the haematologist in his story interprets the medical versus management position for her medical colleagues:

If you look at the things that management can actually manage it comes down to the laundry, the porters, the cooks and the crèche if they're lucky. They can't get near the real stuff, the things we do. They really need our help... it's an opportunity for us. A kind of partnership. We could do things our way.

This reinforces the all-powerful medical fantasy where partnership means control and the medical turf remains sacrosanct.

The Language of Fear and Resistance

Many clinicians are 'suspicious' of clinical governance, and the recipe to overcome their fears according to Wattis and McGinnis (1998: 17) is to 'engage as many clinical staff as possible' and confront their suspicions when they arise. Resistance is another matter. Some doctors take 'pleasure and relief' in the discourse of opposition to the rhetoric of clinical governance (Light, 1999) as it clarifies their feelings of 'desperation' at how it is being handled (Thompson, 1999). Both Goodman (1998) and Douglas (1999) use piercing narrative styles to either challenge (Goodman) or expose (Douglas) the emptiness of the rhetoric. Douglas, an author as well as a doctor, uses a narrative vignette or short story to present stereotypical medical views of clinical governance. Its humour and style enable him to be extremely piercing and cynical in a way which would be unacceptable if presented as a 'typical' *BMJ* article. In contrast, Goodman's article made him both hero and villain amongst the medical community. Light (1999: 735), a supporter of Goodman's views, also identifies the reasons why medical resistance to government initiatives is relatively low key these days and how the covert agenda in most of the government strategies is to gain control of doctors.

I was beginning to believe we had all lost our critical facilities or were too intimidated or exhausted to protest at the latest con trick to keep us in line.

Yet any attempts at control of doctors by non-doctors will invariably be fraught with problems as clinical governance depends upon doctors' judgements and they have the power to 'subvert' the system (Smith, 1998). However, resistance may have to be voiced within the rhetoric and framework of clinical governance as not 'being part of the development' can only lead to 'fruitless opposition' (James, 1998: 94) where the discourse itself is challenged. Defining the space for medical resistance is important, and those who may be silent in this discourse but will resist the changes cannot be ignored so may have to be 'won over' (Wattis and McGinnis, 1998: 17) as the government sees 'fighting with doctors' as a waste of time whilst trying to modernise the NHS (Smith, 1998). Currently there is no evidence of strategies to 'win over' the resistors other than the threat of an even worse scenario (Smith, 1998; Simpson, 1999).

MANAGERS' DISCOURSE

The data on managers' discourse is drawn primarily from a 'policy document' produced by the Institute of Health Service Managers (IHSM) (Bloor and Maynard, 1998). The document reveals that IHSM also have a 'Think Tank' on clinical governance suggesting that managers have devoted both time and resources to examining the issue. However the paucity of articles in the *Health Service Journal* devoted to clinical governance is in stark contrast to those in the *BMJ*. Why are managers remaining silent on an issue central to their role and government policy?

The Meaning of Clinical Governance

Bloor and Maynard (1998: 2) interpret clinical governance literally as 'the control and direction of behaviour with authority' that is not 'solely a medical issue' as it 'requires regulation not just of the medical profession but clinical teams and those that manage provision of services'. This broad and literal definition embraces words that managers would feel comfortable with – such as control, direction and authority – as these suggest clear lines of accountability and power structures. It also 'goes beyond' the medical profession to encompass services more generally. For Jones (1999) clinical governance is 'essentially a management intervention' but one that may be fraught with difficulties for managers. He likens governance to 'steering' rather than 'rowing' but recognises the difficulties in steering the NHS when the rowers (doctors) also control the tiller!

However, the managerial perspective reinforces the legal duty of CEOs that will provide the control and authority necessary to ensure they can exercise their accountability for delivering 'quality' health care through the new government frameworks (Bloor and Maynard, 1998).

Concerns about Clinical Governance

One of the main concerns expressed by managers is their fear that clinical governance, like audit, will be 'captured' by doctors and perceived as 'doctor driven'. Bloor and Maynard (1998: 7) go on to say that if doctors capture the discourse and colonise clinical governance, it is likely to be 'ineffective'. This suggests that doctors may want to use their medical power to interpret and reinterpret clinical governance through their culture. The current clinical hegemony of medicine suggests doctors would subjugate other professions, limit ownership and access to the process and restrict patient involvement. These are all criticisms levelled at doctors by Phillips (1999) who describes the power struggles between doctors, managers and other professions in the NHS as unevenly weighted in favour of doctors.

Managers' discourse expresses this power struggle overtly in two ways: doctors' refusal to work through 'managerial hierarchy' or authority structures – which is central to the accountability structures inherent in clinical governance; and the control they exercise over the clinical arena using their expertise to exclude other professionals and patients.

Jones (1999) describes how doctors refuse to work through line management, even where clinical directors are put in place to exercise that authority. His solution is to give clinical directors more power to limit the practice of subordinate staff if their audit standards are unacceptable. The managerial view is concerned with the discourse of discipline for the incompetent, rather than the development or improvement of performance. Yet if doctors refuse to accept the managerial discourse and praxis of managerial hierarchy this will prove very difficult to enact. An alternative response is to 'managerialise' audit, removing it from the purely clinical domain by imposing managers in the audit cycle or through management monitoring of the process. Managerialising the audit process through both language and behaviour is a way of colonising that arena to prevent exclusion as new levels of managerial accountability are imposed.

It is also difficult for managers to gain access to the clinical domain and discourse as they lack the expertise to guide and shape clinical standards (Jones, 1999: 90). Yet Phillips (1999: 27) argues the persistence of the 'medical model' is the problem, not the solution, as it reinforces medical power and excludes the voices of the disadvantaged to their further disadvantage:

> If the powerful and respected perpetuate oppressive language and attitudes, second rate services are provided – often in a negative or patronising way.

Defining clinical and non-clinical managers' roles becomes important in marking out territory and power relations. Bloor and Maynard suggest that managers should be involved in decisions about identifying priority areas of variability, where uncertainty is a problem and where new interventions have major impacts on budgets or patient care. Yet identifying variability is central to clinical turf, an area where doctors may feel threatened. Managers should also 'disseminate standards' and 'interpret national standards' locally suggesting that their power will come from the translation of the discourse into the organisation and the communication of standards throughout the organisation. The question remains open about what language managers will use to convey this material either within the organisation or across its boundaries.

Finally, managers seem to have ignored the thrust of clinical governance that set out to remove a culture of blame. Perhaps managers fear the blame will shift from the doctors to managers. Rather than focus on the potential dismissal of inadequate doctors the concern is on the use of managers as scapegoats for situations they cannot 'control'. Bloor and Maynard identify the potential managerial problem of being held 'responsible for clinical performance without sufficient power to influence clinical practice' (1998: 15). Continued 'self regulation' by doctors limits the impact managers can make, making the 'dismissal of managers an incomplete remedy for poor clinical practice' (*ibid.*). Although managers are legally accountable their power to regulate doctors is limited to exercising 'influence' often through the lead clinician to create a 'partnership between clinicians and managers' (*ibid.*: 17) and perhaps dissipate blame?

CONCLUSIONS

This chapter has examined the discourse of clinical governance from the perspective of the government, doctors and managers to reveal the power struggles inherent in its introduction in the NHS. What conclusions can we draw? Musson (1999: 317) questions the nature of power and power relations:

Is clinical governance about managing (guiding or supervising) or about controlling (commanding and overruling) clinical activity? And either way, who is the controller in this process of destroying sacred cows – who exactly is to be the governor in clinical governance?

Some interesting and perhaps unexpected insights emerge when the three strands of discourse are synthesised and analysed. Although the evidence is itself contestable three main conclusions can be drawn about clinical governance:

1   The discourse is monological (Keenoy *et al.*, 1997).
2   The discourse is contested as doctors, government and management struggle to impose their meaning through implementation, but doctors are overtly trying to seize, colonise and appropriate the discourse to retain professional power.
3   The discourse, rather than encouraging openness, honesty and partnership, may be spawning a defensive discourse of blame and inter-professional conflict.

Each of these issue is discussed in turn.

Support for a monologue of clinical governance is revealed through the authoritative voice (Alvarez-Caccamo, 1996) of government in the clarity of the rationale, aspirations and structures it imposes. Government will use their words functionally to 'do' things (Hoenisch, 1998) in NHS organisations which managers and doctors cannot resist. The criticisms of managers and doctors are framed within that discourse recognising its legitimacy and authority rather than resisting the discourse itself through the creation of an alternative dialogue. Patterns of resistance revealed major differences between doctors and managers. Doctors would have liked to be able to contest the discourse but recognised it was fruitless and those who resisted it created confusion, uncertainty and embarrassment for the rest of the medical profession. Doctors are contesting the meaning of clinical governance and its cultural and practical implications. In contrast, managers remained remarkably silent. What does this silence reveal (Hearn, 1996)? Alvarez-Caccamo (1996) explored why audiences may be silent and applying his ideas suggests government may have constructed a discourse in which the permissible behaviours of managers, as implementers of government policy *is* to remain silent – at least in public. Is silence a form of public assent by managers or are they afraid to show dissent to their paymasters? Giddens (1989) argues that people have the choice to resist a discourse, but in this case they would also have to accept the personal and career consequences that followed. How can government claims to increased openness be sustained if managers can only 'talk in private'?

Doctors are trying to 'seize' this new discourse (Foucault, 1984) and embed it in their existing culture and praxis (Kogan, 1996) by constructing (Fairclough, 1992: 3) a 'medical model' of clinical governance that reinforces their 'authoritative voices' and power of clinical self-regulation and power over other professionals including management. Doctors reinterpreted collaboration and partnership with management as 'doctors leading' and managers supporting them. If successful, their strategy would subvert any government intentions (March, 1984) to gain control of the medical profession. The medicalisation of clinical governance is also more likely to make it unsuccessful according to managers. Although government discourse places a statutory duty on CEOs, managers recognised their lack of expertise and ability to gain access to the clinical domain.

The government model espouses partnership, strong leadership by managers and searching and honest analysis on clinical quality for the public. Yet behind this, the interprofessional discourse of managers and doctors reveals increased rather than reduced tensions. As the section above demonstrates, doctors have yet to assimilate the radical culture change and managed clinical practice the government expects. Managers, silenced in their criticism of government, have instead turned their attacks towards doctors. Doctors were perceived as trying to capture clinical governance, posing a threat to its successful implementation and the jobs of CEOs where clinical governance is failing. Managers' discourse revealed negative fears such as becoming organisational scapegoats for clinical failure outside their expertise and control.

Although interprofessional power struggles are 'are self-evident to anyone who has set foot in general practice or hospitals' (Phillips, 1999), the government discourse explicitly focuses on culture change and cooperation and partnership between doctors and managers. As 'rhetoric and enacted practices are equally real' (Legge, 1995: 60) hostile managerial discourse is unlikely to foster a culture of collaboration or success! Despite the upbeat discourse of government, managers focus on fear of failure and blame using paradoxically precisely the rhetoric that clinical governance is meant to dispel.

Finally, what has the language of clinical governance done (Hoenisch, 1998)? It seems to have induced a series of paradoxes. The threatened restraint on doctors is seen by them as an opportunity to increase rather than reduce their power. Increased power for managers has created problems of increased dependency on doctors to deliver clinical governance. And a thrust for increased partnership, collaboration and success may ultimately result in increased blame, interprofessional conflict and failure.

References

Alvarez-Caccamo, C. (1996) 'Building Alliances in Political Discourse: Language, Institutional Authority and Resistance', in H. Kotthoff (ed.), *Folia Linguistica*, XXX (3/4) Special Issue on Interactional Sociolinguistics: 245–70.

Beecham, L. (1999) 'Consultants Receive Guidance on Clinical Governance', *British Medical Journal*, 318: 1081.

Berger, P.L. and Luckman, T. (1967) *The Social Construction of Reality* (New York: Doubleday).

Black, N. (1999) 'Clinical Governance: Fine Words of Action?', *British Medical Journal*, 316: 297–8.

Bloor, K. and Maynard, A. (1998) 'Clinical Governance: Clinician, Heal Thyself?' IHSM (Institute of Health Service Managers) Policy Document.

Boje, D.M. (1995) 'Stories of the Storytelling Organization: A Postmodern Analysis of Disney as Tamara-land', *Academy of Management Journal*, 38(4): 997–1035.

Clegg, S. (1994) 'Weber and Foucault Discourse: Social Theory for the Study of Organizations', *Organization*, 1(1): 149–78.

Cunningham, W.F. (1999) 'Clinical Governance in General Practice', *British Medical Journal*, 26 January.

Department of Health (1997) *The New NHS Modern and Dependable*, Cm3807, Session 1997–98 (London: The Stationery Office).
Department of Health (1998) *A First Class Service: Quality in the New NHS* (London: The Stationery Office).
Department of Health (1999) *Clinical Governance: Quality in the New NHS* (London: The Stationary Office).
Douglas, C. (1998) 'Clinical Governance Made Simple', *British Medical Journal*: 285–7.
Exworthy, M. and Halford, S. (eds) (1999) *Professionals and the New Managerialism in the Public Sector* (Buckingham: Oxford University Press).
Fairclough, N. (1992) *Discourse and Social Change* (Cambridge: Polity Press).
Foucault, M. (1980) *Power/Knowledge: Selected Interviews and Other Writings, 1972/1977* (New York: Pantheon).
Foucault, M. (1984) *The History of Sexuality: An Introduction* (Harmondsworth: Penguin).
Gee, J.P. and Lankshear, C. (1995) 'The New Work Order: Critical Language Awareness and "Fast Capitalism Texts" ', *Discourse: Studies in the Cultural Politics of Education*, 16(1): 5–19.
Giddens, A. (1984) *The Constitution of Society* (Oxford: Polity Press).
Goodman, W. (1998) 'Clinical Governance', *British Medical Journal*, 317: 1725–7.
Ham, C. (1999) 'The Third Way in Health Care Reform: Does the Emperor Have Any Clothes?', *Journal of Health Services Research and Policy*, 4(3): 168–73.
Hearn, G. (1996) 'Deconstructing the Dominant: making the one(s) the other(s)' *Organization*, 3(4): 611–26.
Hoenisch, S.M. (1998) 'A Wittgensteinian Approach to Discourse Analysis', *www.Criticism.com*
Hopkinson, R.B. (1999) 'Clinical Governance: Putting it into Practice in an Acute Trust' *Clinician in Management*, 8: 81–8.
James, A.J.B. (1999) 'Clinical Governance and Mental Health: A System for Change' *Clinician in Management*, 8: 92–100.
Jones, G. (1999) 'Clinical Governance: A Customisation of Corporate Principles. Will it Work?' *Clinician in Management*, 8: 89–91.
Keenoy, T., Oswick, C. and Grant, D. (1997) 'Organisational Discourses: Text and Context' *Organization*, 4(2): 147–157.
Kieser, A. (1997) 'Rhetoric and Myth in Management Fashion', *Organization*, 4(1): 49–74
Knights, D. (1992) 'Changing Spaces: The Disruptive Impact of a New Epistemological Location for the Study of Management', *Academy of Management Review*, 17(3): 514–36.
Knights, D. and Morgan, G. (1991) 'Corporate Strategy, Organizations, and Subjectivity: A Critique', *Organization Studies*, 12(2): 251–273.
Kogan, M. (1996) *Diversification in Higher Education: Differences and Commonalities*, Paper for the Sixth National Symposium of Higher Education Research in Finland, University of Jyvaskyla, 22–23 August.
Lee, J.L. and Mythen, M. (1999) 'Think Again: Clinical Governance', *British Medical Journal*, 30 January.
Legge, K. (1995) *Human Resource Management: Rhetorics and Realities* (London: Macmillan – now Palgrave).

Light, L. (1999) 'Emperors, New Clothes', *British Medical Journal*, January 4.
March, G. (1984) 'How we Talk and How we Act: Administrative Theory and Administrative Life', in T. Sergiovanni and J.E. Corbally (eds), *Leadership and Organizational Cultures* (Urbana: University of Illinois Press): 18–35.
Moran, M. and Wood, B. (1993) *States Regulation and the Medical Profession* (Buckingham: OU Press).
NHS Executive (1999a) *Clinical Governance: Quality in the New NHS*, Health Service Circular (March) (Leeds: NHSE).
NHS Executive (1999b) *Clinical Governance: Quality in the New NHS*, Summary (Leeds: NHSE).
Musson G. (1999) Who is the Governor in Clinical Governance?, *British Medical Journal*, January 2S: 317.
Parker I. (1992) *Discourse Dynamics* (London: Routledge).
Phillips, A. (1999) 'Fair Game' *Health Service Journal*, May 20: 26–27
Phillips, N. and Hardy, C. (1997) 'Managing Multiple Identities: Discourse, Legitimacy and Resources in the UK Refugee System', *Organization*, 4(2): 159–185
Sandeman, D.R. (1999) 'Will Clinical Governance Make a Difference', *British Medical Journal* 318: 1085.
Scally, G. and Donaldson, J. (1998) 'Clinical Governance and the Drive for Quality Improvement in the New NHS in England', *British Medical Journal*, 317: 61–65.
Simpson, J. (1999) 'Defining Moments in Medicine', *Clinician in Management*, 8: 58.
Smith, R. (1998a) 'All Changed, Changed Utterly', Editorial, *British Medical Journal*, 316: 1917–1918.
Smith, R. (1998b) 'Regulation of Doctors and the Bristol Inquiry', *British Medical Journal*, 317: 1539–1540.
Smith, R. (1999) 'NICE: A Panacea for the NHS', *British Medical Journal*, 318: 823–824.
Thomas, P. (1997) 'Researching Strategy Discourse as Social Practice', paper presented at the British Academy of Management conference.
Thompson, R.A. (1999) 'Bravo', *British Medical Journal*, January 4.
Walshe, K. (1999) 'Clinical Governance', *British Medical Journal*, January 7.
Wattis, J. and McGinnis, P. (1999) 'Clinical Governance: Making it Work' *Clinician in Management*, 8: 12–16.
Wetherell, M., Stiven, H. and Potter, J. (1987) 'Unequal Egalitarianism: A Preliminary Study of Discourses Concerning Gender and Employment Opportunities', *British Journal of Social Psychology*, 26: 59–71.
Wittgenstein, L. (1974) *Philosophical Investigations*, trans. G.E.M. Anscombe (Oxford: Basil Blackwell).

11 Organising Emotional Health

Annabelle Mark

The purpose of this chapter is to think about and start to map the role of emotion in health care organisation; to set out some parameters by which its consideration should inform the future, in order to establish and maintain the emotional health of the organisation and its workforce, and ensure that it can continue to deliver services to the community which meet their needs for the twenty-first century.

INTRODUCTION

In setting the scene it is necessary to identify the reasons why this issue is emerging at this time; what the current evidence is for its importance; what definitions are available which can determine the approach, and finally to consider what that approach might be. As a starting point a small-scale set of in-depth interviews with a group of professionals working in health care have been undertaken to clarify some of the issues and perspectives which have been emerging during this analysis, and these have both amplified and clarified key points. At the outset no more than the dictionary definition of emotion was assumed, that is 'an instinctive feeling as opposed to reason' (Sykes, 1982), because the concept of emotion itself is subject to interpretation and contention (Calhoun and Soloman, 1984). This interpretation is also that most easily grasped when thinking about emotion, as it does not require a definition of what are and are not emotions or emotional states. Furthermore, in health care the philosophical dualism between reason/rationality and emotion/affect is the basis upon which so much of the discussion with professionals begins.

ORGANISATIONAL EMOTION IN HEALTH

Developing an understanding of the role of emotion in health care organisation is necessary for a number of reasons. The first is the role of emotion and its effect on processes and relationships within organisations; for example a recent literature review (Keren, 1996) indicates that certain hedonistic motivators like desire could influence decision-making and distort claims to rationality because lower-order needs linked more closely to the emotions have to be met before higher ones can be activated. Such visceral effects suggest that the organisational iceberg, which shows emotions such as fear, anger, liking, desire and despair below the water line (Herman, 1984), may finally bring organisations shuddering to a halt if they are not now explicitly considered as both part of the detail and the strategic map of organisational life, as for example work on the effects of change and redundancy are now showing (Worrall, Campbell and Cooper, 2000). Likewise, relationships within health care can be constructed for a range of reasons both rational and emotional in origin, although disentangling the motivation for these can prove more complex than at first appears as Cassell (1998) has found. Her research on problems that women surgeons face suggests that the emotive basis for the interpretation by all players of the surgeon's role as gender-specific, is located historically in the male role because of the nature of the task. Without some attempt to disentangle these motivators, little change to current behaviours is possible and these continue to militate against this particular group of women in medicine. New avenues are, however, opening for women where the nature of the task is changing through the development of non-invasive technologies like laser surgery.

The second is the relationship between the organisation and its environment in health care. This has to be seen in its social context, where peer group (Mestrovic, 1997) rather than political or organisational control may become paramount because of the instability of organisational forms, and the increasing disillusionment (Fineman, 1997) with manipulation of emotions to serve organisational purposes (Ralston, 1995). If in future the peer group is located through a profession rather than an organisation, attempts by organisations to challenge professional role boundaries may be doomed. Professions have developed strategies to protect themselves from organisations and these are external and emotional rather than rational in origin, based as they are, on a need to belong. In contrast, organisations in health care increasingly cannot assume that they can control the external reference points or domains (Mark and Scott, 1992) for individuals, notwithstanding the ever-tighter grip of audit and governance within health organisations. Further areas of concern are the international and scientific context of health care, the former changing expectations for provision and the latter changing expectations for intervention. Both are driven by fear and a desire for happiness and fulfilment, both emotions which are utilised to advantage by commercial organisations and the professions who have reason to drive these two agendas forward.

The third is the context that the organisation attempts to provide for the relationship between patient and professional in responding to the needs of both to interact rationally, socially and emotionally in the pursuit of health. Managing the boundaries of access to the system often demonstrates a rational response to an emotional request (Mark *et al.*, 2000) which is itself problematic, and added to this is the idea that the context of these interactions is changing, certainly at primary care level, from one of relationships to encounters (Gutek, 1997). Such encounters mean that emotion is increasingly managed in a more transitory and impersonal way, often mediated by rationalising technologies like computer-aided decision support.

Developing Interest

The developing interest in emotion is apparent across a number of disciplines. The reasons for this are somewhat speculative but would, for example, include gender and the role of women in the workplace (Brewis and Linstead, 2000), as well as the development of a female discourse which is now changing the shape of organisations (Itzin and Newman, 1995; Martin, Knopoff and Beckman, 1998; Rothschild and Whitt, 1986). In addition, there is an increasing disillusionment with purely rational approaches (Hassard, 1993; Fineman, 1993) both within and between organisations, which requires new approaches and have led to a developing interest in the role and purpose of emotion (Ashforth and Humphrey, 1995). This interest is still bedevilled by a lack of research (Argyris, 1957; Fineman, 1993) which, where it does exist, is often predicated on a rational perspective which purports, even at its most qualitative (Hammersley and Atkinson, 1995), to provide explicit descriptors of relationships between process and object. This approach suggests that the research constructs themselves need reframing, and that the use of postmodernist and poststructuralist (Hassard and Pym, 1993) approaches have a further contribution to make or that new theoretical methods (Genosko, 1998) which challenge existing methodological boundaries must be explored. Such perspectives should concentrate on the meaning of the whole perspective rather than an analysis of its parts. In the same way that the laws of perception allow us to make sense of incomplete visual information through the concept of closure, so too research methods may need to concentrate on the whole perspective, however incomplete, and the information derived across it rather than just the sum of individually analysed parts.

Such an approach echoes the work of the Gestalt school of psychology whose chief contributor to organisation theory was Kurt Lewin (1951) whose work on change theory continues to inform health care organisations today. In health care such an approach would also reflect the growth in holistic approaches to health itself. Postmodernist approaches (Kilduff and Mehra, 1997) reinforce a disparateness of interpretation which may well reflect on the lived experience in UK health care in recent years (Dent, 1995). However, this perspective does not necessarily contribute to an understanding of how emotion helps in linking such events for the individual (Goleman, 1996) to make sense of such experiences (Weik, 1995). Poststructuralism, however, allows for an exploration of meaning in a way that provides some useful tools for analysis (Cropper, 1999; Lupton, 1998). However, while such approaches are persuasive within their own theoretical contexts, they are still an anathema in health care research (Mark and Dopson, 1999) where the acceptance of qualitative techniques have yet to make a significant breakthrough into the dominant paradigm (Bradley *et al.*, 1999) based as it is on a rationalist reductionism.

What is perhaps less well-understood, but may support this dichotomy, is that while quantitative research can be accessed through transferable skills found within statistical methods, the expertise necessary for good qualitative research is more dependant on cumulative tacit knowledge (Polanyi, 1962) being present within the researchers, making its replication and interpretation by others more difficult.

Health Methods

Reasons given for the schism in methods within health care usually start with reference to the supposed Cartesian separation of mind and body 'I think therefore I am' (Burkitt, 1998); but perhaps, within health care in particular, this separation has a further purpose. This is that the reliance on knowledge based on reason is implicitly valued in the organisation for its *emotional* role. It sets the scene for the very necessary trust which must exist between patient and professional; reason is in effect the third-party agent used as a justifiable tool to persuade both organisations and individual patients to set aside emotional responses such as fear, in order to allow extraordinary actions and interventions to occur in the name of health care. This separation of the objective and subjective feeling state (Ashforth and Humphrey, 1995) is reinforced further because the study of medicine has long been able to relate emotion to physiological process, thereby defining its relevance as fundamentally biological.

This perception of emotion in medicine, as reducible to rational analysis, is then organisationally and professionally reinforced by, for example, the relative status of the neuro-physiologist to the psychiatrist (Cassell, 1998); the former enjoying high status in dealing with physiological manifestations, the latter considerably lower in the medical hierarchy dealing with more nebulous psychological manifestations of mind–body relationships. Yet the link between emotion and its manifestation can be unreliable if the physical response alone is used as an indicator of the presence of an emotion, and its relationship to consciousness is only just beginning to be explored (Damasio, 1999). Furthermore, the physiological responses to events manifesting in fear or laughter can now be generated by manufactured experience, seen at its most extreme in experiences with 'virtual reality'. Manipulating these responses has for a long time been at the heart of what Hochschild (1983) defined as 'emotional labour', and which in health care operates in various ways (Ashforth and Humphrey, 1995) to protect both professional and patient from much of the emotional trauma inherent in health care processes.

Finding Out

The problem at the outset is thus one of credibility for a research agenda in relation to emotion in health, which will be acknowledged and accepted as relevant to the future organisation of health care and all its key stakeholders or actors (Downing, 1997). Definitions of what is an emotion, what do we mean by emotion and what definitions might be used in research are summarised by Lupton (1998), who concludes that emotion should be a foundation question for any social science discipline, but that definitions themselves fall into categories specific to the discipline exploring them. Indeed, when searching through certain literatures it is the word 'affect' rather than emotion which produces the relevant research (Ashforth and Humphrey, 1995). In health care organisational terms a literature review reveals that much of the relevant material is found by looking for specific emotional responses (Wilkinson, 1995); searching for physiologically-based emotions such as happiness, fear, anger and depression produces evidence (Kempner, 1987) which demonstrates the perceived separateness of these experiences from a professional perspective, rather than the relationships between them.

Two things are manifest from these approaches. First is the need to understand the interplay between emotional states, as manifested physically and psychologically, and emotional action – the transition process remains unclear. These can be interpreted differently depending on whether, for example, a social-constructionist (Suttie, 1988) or cognitive theory (Frijda, 1988) approach is applied. The former focuses on emotion as largely learnt rather than inherited behaviour, while the latter concentrates on the interrelationship between physical responses and what individual recognition does with this in different contexts. Secondly, emotional states which appear separately as experiences in the individual and are validated by their physiological manifestation, are often therefore assumed to appear as separate organisational experiences, when in fact the organisational consequences are often complicated by the simultaneous presence of a whole range of emotional states manifested by both individuals, groups and the organisation as a whole (Ashforth and Humphrey, 1995; de Vries and Miller, 1984).

In health care the presence of emotion is integral to both the definition of purpose and its implementation to a degree which can result in both individual and organisational dysfunction, as a study of a London teaching hospital has suggested (Holden, 1991), leading to ontological, spiritual and moral anxiety. Therefore, developing an understanding of the shared meaning of emotion as something more than the dualistic opposite of rationality, which is at the heart of the scientific basis of knowledge (Czarniawska, 1997), is becoming essential to an understanding of why current methods, based on rational reductionism, only provide half the story (Bradley *et al.*, 1999) when examining health outcomes.

Looking In

The health of the NHS as an organisation is also threatened by the emotional dysfunction of many of its key players (Williams, Michie and Pattani, 1998) as recent surveys have suggested; yet such issues have not been adequately addressed by either health care organisations or the research agenda of the academic community. The focus in health care on problems of the interface between the organisation and the consumer/patient often start from the assumption of a state of wellness in the organisation and its workforce, when the contrary is often true (Williams, Michie and Pattani, 1998). Such assumptions, while understandable, can often interfere with the outcomes of encounters at the interface on an emotional level; for example busy primary-care doctors seeing an emotionally-distressed patient may behave in a way which provides appropriate clinical care, but may be counterproductive in terms of the process and eventual outcome of care (Roter *et al.*, 1995), because they fail to deal appropriately with the emotional consequences of the encounter for the patient. Dealing with the psychological well-being facilitated to the patient by such an encounter does not ameliorate the normative needs assessment which clinical training engenders as a first priority, but does as Roter *et al.* (1995) suggest affect outcomes of both specific treatments and long-term relationships between the patient and the health care organisation.

The failure to recognise the emotional context of such encounters exhibits what Ashforth *et al.* (1995) describe as the organisational strategies for neutralising emotion, where role obligations inhibit expression of emotion. The proposals that Roter makes to change the response of these doctors moves the issue forward to what Ashforth then describes as prescribed emotion, which is similar to Hochschild's (1983) idea of emotional labour. Yet the training of doctors in such skills lags behind that of nurses (Novack *et al.*, 1997), and the division between care and cure that the respective roles represent is perhaps symbolic also of the organisational need to separate these two responses in order to manage them more effectively. Such issues require further research.

Changing Contexts

The utilisation of emotions within the wider society for instrumental purposes (Hochschild, 1983; Mestrovic, 1997) has had a corrupting effect on their original purpose as a signalling device. Manipulation of this signalling device may have led to an existentialist loss of self, a sense of alienation for both users and providers of health care which interferes with the communication necessary for understanding between patient and provider to allow successful interventions to occur. The consequences of this corrupting influence in society is seen in the breakdown of trust in general between the public and those seeking to influence or persuade them, whether as politicians or professionals (Beck, 1992).

Such trust is essential to the doctor–patient encounter and will become more so when the genetic revolution takes off (Jones and Zimmern, 1999); as the signs which prompt the lay perspective to engage with health care professionals will be absent, the diagnosis will be dependent on signs apparent only through the professional expertise of science. The patient will have no visible indication of a problem and must accept that intervention is necessary and beneficial in the long term. The patient will therefore need to trust the doctor to an even greater extent, and this relationship may need to be built on a new understanding of how to achieve trust in the absence of a perceivable link, for the patient, between the mental concept or the signified and its signifier or material aspects (Saussure, translated by Harris, 1983).

The explicit discussion of emotion has been neglected, and some might say hidden, within health care and its organisation; in part because much of the emotional activity of health care is labelled as caring and dismissed as a largely reactive feminine activity, with little attempt made in the UK to relate emotion to health itself (Stewart Brown, 1998). Furthermore, changes in the organisation of health care during the 1980s and 1990s have cast aside attempts to provide a caring organisational context in which care and cure roles and activities are undertaken, and has set up emotive dissonance (Hochschild, 1983) for many both giving and receiving health care. This dissonance between what is experienced and what is known and expected is the emotional impact of redrawing the political map of health care policy in the UK. Some attempts to redress this imbalance have been seen in the organisational moves towards understanding values and culture, and developing missions and visions for the future; but it is with a return to collaborative rather than competitive working as set out in *The New NHS – Modern and Dependable* (Department of Health, 1997) that a current understanding of emotion, within a UK context, may become possible.

Developing Health Care

The NHS as an organisation was predicated on what Kempner would describe as primary emotions; it removed fear of the problems of access and affordability (Rivett, 1998) which are apparent in market-led systems (Gold, 1999). However, its recent manifestation under the Conservative administrations of the 1980s and 1990s led to an approach which sought to provide consumer responsiveness through markets. This alternative perspective suggests that there is a transfer from a response to reducing fear, towards an attempt to meet a desire for happiness by providing what patients want rather than just what they need. This has been further reinforced by private-sector approaches to advertising health which eschew references to basic emotions in favour of an appeal to secondary, socially-constructed emotional responses (Huang, 1998); this is seen, for example, in private health care adverts which appeal to matters of convenience and comfort rather than clinical excellence. However, the development of the New Public Management philosophy and its context as part of the Third Way in British politics demonstrates that a complete return to the past is neither appropriate nor possible (Ferlie, 1999; Wilkinson, 1995). A new more sophisticated awareness is required of what the NHS can deliver and what the patients and public might expect. However, at the heart of this what remains is the principle of removing fear, and when the NHS fails in meeting this primary emotion the impact leaves politicians and managers impaled on their own rhetoric.

Emotion as a developing agenda across a number of disciplines has allowed for interpretations which can sometimes seem inappropriate to the possible outcomes; especially when methodological understanding is maintained within a rationalist paradigm, for example quantifying economic effects in relation to caring (Michele Issel and Kahn, 1998). Nevertheless the poverty of rationality in identifying new ways of developing health care and its organisation is now being revealed and explicitly discussed in its own heartland (Stewart Brown, 1998; Bradley *et al.*, 1999); an analysis of the role of emotion in the organisation and delivery of effective health care is beginning to be understood both in the UK and the USA, (Fineman, 1993; Pennebaker, 1995). The organisation of health systems through the rational process continues unabated and is most recently demonstrated in the evidence-based medicine (EBM) movement (Gray, 1996). Its purpose has, however, been bedevilled not by its content, but rather by the barriers to implementation aroused because of fear that it will remove autonomy and flexibility in the professional role (Dopson and Gabbay, 1996; Dunning *et al.*, 1997). While this may not be the original intention (Davidoff *et al.*, 1995), the fear of many has been its use by the organisation of health care for such a purpose. Rationality in the form of EBM has stumbled upon the uncertainty at the heart of organisational action where shadow systems (Stacey, 1996) are used to confound progress until they can be absorbed and interpreted within acceptable parameters by the various interest groups.

Orienteering the Future

New perspectives are now required if the development of health care is to be maintained and contained in a way appropriate to the community it serves. Such perspectives, however, can be shown to have different agendas depending on the organisational, cultural, social and historical context in which they are entrenched.

In health care it is suggested that some emotional mapping needs to take place if the relationships between individual and organisational emotional dynamics are to be understood. A first step to understanding is to answer the question: *what organisational and professional barriers to human potential* (Seedhouse, 1991) *might exist for those working within and those receiving services from the organisation?* Research is also needed on the emotional impact of the organisational processes and activities in health care provision, especially as they affect those new to the role and the organisation whether as patients or professionals. This will then provide a framework to guide future entrants where none currently exists. Individuals are told about how to manage the negative outcome of events through such mechanisms as accident reporting and stress counselling, but managing the initial encounters is often only developed through the socialisation processes for professionals, the shadow systems for the organisations (Stacey, 1996), and complaints systems for patients, which may no longer be acceptable either morally or legally.

The principles upon which these maps can be drawn must thus first find ways of discerning the emotional values inherent within individuals and the organisation; for example, through the utilisation of techniques like synectics (Gordon, 1961) which use metaphor to gain access to feelings. The separation of basic or primary and secondary emotions may be important here, but is not the whole story. The history of the NHS and its founding principles suggest that even within the primary emotions there is a hierarchy with fear at the top, and this is frequently further reflected in the social and professional development process inherent in the organisation. Evolutionary psychology and its application in organisations may have a contribution to make here (Nicholson, 1997) especially if, as Nicholson suggests, it offers a framework for integrating the social and natural sciences, of which the NHS organisationally provides a primary example.

Mapping will involve an understanding of emotions and the barriers used at all levels as protection against them and how these are changing. Changing professional roles need to be studied in relation to the degree to which responsibility and clinical intervention are predictors of emotional distancing; for example responsibility vested in reception staff in Accident and Emergency, or through telephone advice lines, requires rapid distancing without loss of empathy if the staff are to continue in the role. Such skills are often picked up as tacit knowledge (Polanyi, 1962) from the professionals working clinically with patients, and have only recently been considered in relation to training of clinical professionals. If such skills appear at all it is under the guise of communication, and sometimes debriefing after particularly difficult events like major accidents. Such skills, of course, are also dependent on personality, experience and the context of the work, but our increasing knowledge of all these facets is already informing organisational selection and recruitment processes. However, the focus on individuals must not obscure the use that the organisation makes of emotion (Ashforth and Humphrey, 1995) to maintain control of both its providers and increasingly its users (Mark and Elliott, 1997). Understanding and agreeing the purpose within this activity will make the organisations and the people working within them more acceptable if the patient and the public are to trust the NHS of the twenty-first century.

References

Argyris, C. (1957) *Personality and Organisations* (New York: Harper & Row).

Ashforth, B.E. and Humphrey, R.H. (1995) 'Emotion in the Workplace: A Reappraisal', *Human Relations*, 48(2): 97.

Beck, U. (1992) *Risk Society: Towards a New Modernity* (London: Sage).

Bradley, F., Wiles, R., Kinmouth, A.L., Mant, D. and Gantley, M. (1995) 'Development and Evaluation of Complex Interventions in Health Services Research: Case Study of the Southampton Heart Integrated Care Project (SHIP)', *British Medical Journal*, 318(7185): 711–15.

Brewis, J. and Linstead, S. (2000) *Sex, Work and Sex Work* (London: Routledge).

Burkitt, I. (1998) 'Bodies of Knowledge: Beyond Cartersian Views of Persons Selves and Mind', *Journal for the Theory of Social Behaviour*, 28(1): 63–82.

Calhoun, C. and Soloman, R. (1984) *What is an Emotion?* (New York: Oxford University Press).

Cassell, J. (1998) 'The Woman in the Surgeons Body: Understanding Difference', *American Anthropologist*, 98(1): 41–53.

Cropper, S. (1999) 'Value Critical Analysis and Actor Network Theory: Two Perspectives on Collaboration in the Name of Health', in A.L. Mark and S. Dopson (eds), *Organisational Behaviour in Health Care – the Research Agenda* (Basingstoke: Macmillan – now Palgrave): 207–21.

Czarniawska, B. (1997) 'A Four Times Told Tale:Combining Narrative and Scientific Knowledge in Organisation Studies', *Organisation*, 4(1).

Damasio, A. (1999) *The Feeling of What Happens: Body, Emotion and the Making of Conciousness* (London: Heinemann).

Davidoff, F., Haynes, B., Sackett, D. and Smith, R. (1995) 'Evidence Based Medicine (editorial)', *British Medical Journal*, 310(6987): 1085–16.

de Vries M.K. and Miller D. (1984) *The Neurotic Organization* (San Francisco: Jossey Bass).

Dent, M. (1995) 'The new National Health Service: A Case of Postmodernism?', *Organisation Studies*, 16(5): 875–900.

Department of Health (1997) *The New NHS: Modern, Dependable*, Session 1997–8; Cm 3807 (London: The Stationery Office)

Dopson, S. and Gabbay, J. (1996) *Getting Research into Practice: Purchasing Issues and Lessons from Four Counties* (Wessex Institute of Public Health Medicine and Templeton College, Southampton and Oxford).

Downing, S.J. (1997) 'Learning the Plot: Emotional Momentum in Search of Dramatic Logic', *Management Learning*, 28(1): 27–44.

Dunning, M., Abi-Aad, G., Gilbert, D., Gillam, S. and Livett, H. (1997) *Turning Evidence into Everyday Practice* (London: King's Fund).

Ferlie, E. (1999) 'The Rise of the New Public Management', unpublished manuscript.

Fineman, S. (1993) *Emotion in Organisations* (London: Sage).

Fineman, S. (1997) 'Emotion and Management Learning', *Management Learning*, 28(1): 13–26.

Frijda, N.H. (1998) 'The Laws of Emotion', *American Psychologist*, 43(5): 349–58.

Genosko, G. (1998) *Undisciplined Theory* (London: Sage).

Gold, M. (1999) 'The Changing US Health Care System Challenges for Responsible Public Policy', *The Milbank Quarterly*, 77(1): 2–22.

Goleman, D. (1996) *Emotional Intelligence* (London: Bloomsbury).

Gordon, W.J.J. (1961) *Synectics* (New York: Harper & Row).

Gray, J.A.M. (1996) *Evidence Based Health Care* (Edinburgh: Livingstone Churchill).

Gutek, B. (1997) 'Dyadic Interactions in Organisations', in *Creating Tomorrow's Organisations: A Handbook for Future Research in Organisational Behaviour*, C. Cooper and S. Jackson (eds) (Chichester: John Wiley): 139–56.

Hammersley, M. and Atkinson, P. (1995) *Ethnography – Principles in Practice*, 2nd edn (London: Routledge).

Hassard, J. and Pym, D. (1993) *The Theory and Philosophy of Organisations* (London: Routledge, an imprint of Taylor Francis Books).

Hassard, J. (1993) *Sociology and Organisation Theory: Positivism, Paradigms and Postmodernity*, Cambridge Studies in Management (Cambridge: Cambridge University Press).

Herman, S.N. (1984) 'TRW Systems Group', in *Organisation Development: Behavioral Science Interventions for Organisation Improvement*, 3rd edn, W.L. French and C.H. Bell Jr (eds) (Prentice-Hall, Englewood Cliffs, New Jersey): 19.

Hochschild, A.R. (1983) *The Managed Heart: Commercialisation of Human Feeling* (Berkeley: University of California Press).
Holden, R.J. (1991) 'An Analysis of Caring: Attributions, Contributions and Resolutions', *Journal of Advanced Nursing*, 16: 893–898.
Huang, M.H. (1998) 'Exploring a New Typology of Advertising Appeals: Basic Versus Social, Emotional Advertising in a Global Setting', *International Journal of Advertising*, 17(2): 145–168.
Itzin, C. and Newman, J. (1995) *Gender, Culture and Organisational Change Putting Theory into Practice* (London: Routeledge).
Jones, J. and Zimmern, R.L. (1999) 'The Impact of New Technologies in Medicine-Mapping the Human Genome the Genetics Revolution', *British Medical Journal*, 319: 1282.
Kempner, T. (1987) 'How Many Emotions are There? Wedding the Social and Autonomic Components', *American Journal of Sociology*, 93(2): 263–289.
Keren, G. (1996) 'Perspectives on Behavioural Decision Making', *Organisational Behaviour and Human Decision Process*, 65(3): 169–78.
Kilduff, M. and Mehra, A. (1997) 'Postmodernism and Organisational Research', *Academy of Management Review*, 22(2): 253–281.
Lewin, K. (1951) *Field Theory in Social Science* (London: Harper & Row).
Lupton, D. (1998) *The Emotional Self* (London: Sage).
Mark, A. and Elliott, R. (1997) 'Demarketing Dysfunctional Demand in the UK NHS', *International Journal of Health Planning and Management*, 12: 297–314.
Mark, A. Pencheon, D. and Elliott, R. (2000) 'Demanding Healthcare', *International Journal of Health Planning and Management*.
Mark, A. and Scott, H. 1992 'General Management in the NHS' in *Rediscovering Public Services Management*, 1st edn, H.J. Willcocks Leslie (ed.) (London: McGraw-Hill) 197–234.
Mark, A.L. and Dopson, S. (1999) *Organisational Behaviour in Health Care – the Research Agenda*, 1st edn (Basingstoke: Macmillan – now Palgrave).
Martin, J. Knopoff, K. and Beckman, C. (1998) 'An Alternative to Bureaucratic Impersonality and Emotional Labor: Bounded Emotionality at The Body Shop', *Administrative Science Quarterly*, 43: 429–69.
Mestrovic, S.G. (1997) *Postemotional Society* (London: Sage).
Michele Issel, L. and Kahn, D. (1998) 'The Economic Value of Caring', *Healthcare Management Review*, 23(4): 43–53.
Nicholson, N. (1997) 'Evolutionary Psychology and Organisational Behaviour,' in *Creating Tomorrows Organisations*, C.L. Cooper and S.E. Jackson, (eds) (Chichester: John Wiley & Sons) 171–88.
Novack, D.H., Suchman, A.L., Clark, W., Epstein, R.M., Najberg, E. and Kaplan, C. (1997) 'Calibrating the Physician', *JAMA Journal of the American Medical Association*, 278(6): 502–9.
Pennebaker, J.W. (1995) *Emotion, Disclosure and Health* (American Psychological Washington DC., Association, 1995).
Polanyi, M. 1962 *Personal Knowledge – Towards a Post-Critical Philosophy*, Corrected Edition (Chicago: The University of Chicago Press).

Ralston, F. (1995) *Hidden Dynamics-How Emotions Affect Business Performance and How you can Harness Their Power for Postive Results* (New York: Amacom – American Management Association).

Rivett, G. (1998) *From Cradle to Grave – Fifty Years of the NHS* (London: King's Fund).

Roter, D.L., Hall, J.A., Kern, D.E., Barker, L.R., Cole, K.A. and Roca, R.P. (1995) 'Improving Physicians Interviewing Skills and Reducing Patients Emotional Distress – A Randomized Clinical Trial', *Archives of Internal Medicine*, 155: 1877–84.

Rothschild, J. and Whitt, A. (1986) *The Cooperative Workplace* (Cambridge: Cambridge University Press).

Saussure, F. (1983) and translated by R. Harris, *Course in General Linguistics* (London: Duckworth).

Seedhouse, D. (1991) *Liberating Medicine* (Chichester: John Wiley).

Stacey, R.D. (1996) *Strategic Management and Organisational Dynamics*, 2nd edn (London: Pitman).

Stewart Brown, S. (1998) 'Emotional Well-Being and Its Relation to Health', *British Medical Journal*, 317: 1608–9.

Suttie, I.D. (1988) *The Origins of Love and Hate*, first published 1935 (London: Free Association Books).

Sykes, J.B. (1982) (ed) *The Concise Oxford Dictionary*, 7th edn (London: Guild Publishing).

Weik, K. (1995) *Sensemaking in Organizations* (Thousand Oaks, Cal.: Sage).

Wilkinson, M.J. (1995) 'Love is Not a Marketable Commodity: New Public Management in the British National Health Service', *Journal of Advanced Nursing*, 21: 980–7.

Williams, S., Michie, S. and Pattani, S. (1998) *Improving the Health of the NHS Workforce: Report of the Partnership on the Health of the NHS Workforce* (London: Nuffield Trust).

Worrall, L. Campbell, F. and Cooper, C. (2000) 'Surviving Redundancy: The Perceptions of UK Managers', *Journal of Managerial Psychology*, 15(5).

12 How does Professional Culture Influence the Success or Failure of IT Implementation in Health Services?

Stephen Timmons

The implementation of IT systems in health care has not always proved to be straightforward (Audit Commission, 1995, 1992; Collins and Bicknell, 1997). Large amounts of taxpayers' money have been wasted on systems that do not work, and in some cases were never even fully implemented. Collins and Bicknell (1997) give an account of the failure of the Wessex Regional Health Authority Regional Information Support System (RISP), which was estimated to have cost as much as £35 million with no discernible benefits for patients, clinicians or managers. As they point out elsewhere in the book, other industries have experienced catastrophic computer failures, but health services seem especially vulnerable to them. While there may be many reasons for this, one which is receiving increased attention is the social environment into which these systems are implemented. This seems to be a fruitful area for research, as several other writers have pointed to the importance of sociocultural factors in determining the success or failure of IT implementations in health services (Hardiker *et al.*, 1995; Stapleton, 1994; Slaney and Hitchens, 1993). Indeed, Berg *et al.* go so far as to say that, 'It is more and more acknowledged that a sociological understanding of the complex practices in which information technology is to function is crucial' (1998: 243).

This study is based on the approach broadly subsumed under the title, 'Social Construction of Technology'. While social construction of technology is a comparatively recent innovation within the discipline of sociology, what is interesting and different about it is the way that it emphasises the flexibly-interpreted nature of technology. Central to the development of this concept is the book by Bijker, Hughes and

218

Pinch (1987), who draw on an established body of work in the sociology of scientific knowledge (SSK) to examine technology. For many writers within the sociology of scientific knowledge tradition, science is not the rational objective and modernist project that it claims to be, but can be understood in the same way as the social sciences; that is, as a socially constructed form, crucially dependent on language. Issues of power and conflict are foregrounded in SSK, while they are concealed in 'conventional' accounts of science. Examples of this kind of analysis can be found in the work of Mulkay (1979), Latour (1991) and Woolgar (1988). Sociologists in the SSK tradition, though they have their disagreements, generally believe in what Knorr-Cetina and Mulkay (1983) call 'epistemic relativism'. This is the idea that all knowledge, including science, is determined by the culture out of which it grew, and that no special claims should be made for its status. The sociology of scientific knowledge seeks to 'reveal the uncertainties, the negotiations, the dilemmas and the controversies that inform, not exceptionally, but as a matter of course, the very making of science' (Webster, 1991).

What Bijker *et al.* (1987) suggest is that technology can be analysed using the methods developed within the sociology of scientific knowledge. In everyday life it is often assumed that technology is in some way 'based' on science. Despite the difficulty of establishing exactly what counts as 'science' as a basis for technology, or why certain types of science seem to give rise to technologies, while others do not, it would seem reasonable to assume that technology can be examined sociologically in the same way that science can.

The result is a view of technology as socially-constructed. Machines have meaning, and, in fact, they can have different meanings for different groups of people. Bijker *et al.* refer to this feature as the 'interpretative flexibility' of machines. The example that they use to illustrate this is the development of the bicycle. They show how the 'Penny- Farthing' meant different things simultaneously to different groups of cyclists. To young men of means it was an exciting, fast machine which demanded a high degree of skill, and exposed the rider to a degree of risk. To women and older men, it was 'unsafe'. It was only when the 'Safety Bicycle' (the basis for most modern bicycles, originally intended for women) had 'proven' itself in racing that it became widely accepted and the 'Penny-Farthing' largely confined to museums. The flexibly-interpreted nature of technology influences its development . Bijker *et al.* also show how the development of technology is not an inexorable 'Whig' process of continuous improvement where the 'best' technology becomes dominant over a period of time, but is a result of a variety of forces acting in the social rather than the technical arena (if these two can indeed be separated). They stress that 'things could always have been otherwise'.

Perhaps the most important writer in this field in the UK, and the one whose work this study builds on directly, is Brian Bloomfield, who has applied the social construction of technology approach to these systems. Over a period of several years he has studied the implementation of computer systems to support changes in the way the NHS is managed, with reference to a particular project called the Resource Management Initiative (RMI). This project sought to involve clinicians more directly in the management of hospitals, especially the management of activity and resources. In order to enable clinicians to do this, computer systems were implemented in many UK hospitals to collect, analyse and present management information.

Bloomfield, Coombs and Owen (1994) describe how these information systems become a site where the struggles between different professional groups within the organisation are played out, showing how it is impossible to draw boundaries around the social and technical aspects of a system. What the system is and what it means becomes a contentious issue (between doctors and managers, in this case). Bloomfield, Coombs, Cooper and Rea (1992) explain how IT systems are not simply imposed on users in the NHS, but operate within a dispersed network of power/knowledge relations between actors (drawing on the work of Foucault). Doctors and nurses are not so weak that the management can impose upon them any system that suits them. The question of which or whose reality it is that computer systems seek to model is vital, bearing in mind that systems are defined by what information they include and what they exclude. At the same time, systems are explicitly implemented with the intention of reshaping reality. Systems therefore have a reflexive quality in that they are designed to reflect the reality, but also to reshape it.

This chapter takes a social construction of technology approach to the study of the use of computerised systems for the production of detailed plans for the care of hospital in-patients by nurses. Care-planning systems were introduced into UK hospitals during the 1980s and 1990s, also as part of the Resource Management Initiative (RMI). As the major cost centre within all hospitals, nursing was not excluded from this project. Care-planning systems were introduced with two main aims, to improve the quality of care for patients through more structured and detailed planning, and (therefore) delivery of care, and to provide managers with detailed information about nursing resources and how they were used. The literature on the evaluation of the Resource Management Initiative overall (Packwood *et al.*, 1991) is inconclusive.

In the light of the above, I intend to deploy a number of core ideas from the sociology of technology for my study including:

1   Technological systems are socially constructed. The care-planning system is not simply boxes, wires and software, but involves people, their beliefs and attitudes. These are fundamental, constitutive parts of the system, as much as a UNIX server or an Ethernet network.
2   There is a technological frame for care-planning systems. The staff using the system, and the managers implementing it, have ideas and 'scripts' about the system that influence how it is used, and what it becomes in the process of implementation.
3   Systems have a degree of interpretative flexibility; the meanings given to systems may not necessarily be the same. The staff may believe the systems to be something different from what the managers believe it to be. This tension will also influence what the system becomes as a 'socio-technical ensemble'.
4   Issues of power play a part in this process of construction. Power is not evenly distributed between all of the actors involved within the system, however all of the actors have some resources of power. Managers have the power to 'implement' the system, the power to make things happen, to make the staff use the computer. However, staff have power to resist the implementation of the systems, and to continue to resist it even when it has been 'successfully' installed and is 'working'.
5   The actions of all those involved are also susceptible to flexible interpretation. One actor's 'resistance' is another's 'putting patients first'. 'Subversion' may also be 'working around a badly designed system'.

THE HOSPITALS AND THE SYSTEMS

Three UK hospitals were selected for this study. All of them were District General Hospitals (DGH), providing a wide range of emergency and elective medical and surgical care, including General Medicine, General Surgery, Trauma & Orthopaedics, Gynaecology,

222   *The Influence of Professional Culture*

Obstetrics, Intensive Care, Accident & Emergency and Paediatrics. They are broadly representative of the majority of hospitals in the UK. However, they were selected largely for reasons of geographical convenience. The systems had been implemented at the three hospitals selected for this study over a period of two or three years. At one of the hospitals being studied, the system being implemented was the second-generation nursing system, replacing an older system. Though all the hospitals used care-planning systems from different manufacturers, they were broadly similar in their functionality, interface and usage.

Nursing care-planning systems are predicated on certain concepts about how nursing work should be done. These are the nursing process, a method of organising nursing work introduced into UK practice in the 1980s, and a nursing model, a conceptual framework against which patients can be assessed and their care planned and evaluated. All of the systems under investigation used the model of nursing devised by Roper, Logan and Tierney (1980), which considers psychological, social and spiritual needs, as well as physical needs. These physical needs are subdivided into 12 activities of daily living (including eating, breathing, elimination and so on.) Patients can be assessed according to these 12 activities, and their care planned appropriately.

On admission to a ward, a nurse will assess the patient, using the computer, and plan their care. Typically, she selects one of the activities of daily living from the nursing model. This is linked in the computer's library to a set of potential problems, of which one or more will be selected as appropriate. The computer then provides links to goals appropriate to the resolution of each problem, and each goal is further linked to the appropriate nursing interventions. The nurse thus builds up a detailed care plan by picking from the lists provided by the computer at each stage. In addition to this 'bespoke' method of producing care plans, the systems also support the production and use of 'off-the-peg' care plans, referred to as core care plans. These tend to be used in specialities like orthopaedic surgery, where certain groups of patients exhibit a high degree of homogeneity.

Once a care plan has been produced, it is supposed to be regularly updated during the patient's stay, whenever any event of any significance in that patient's care occurs. The whole of the care given to that patient is also supposed to be evaluated when the patient is discharged.

Methods

Semi-structured interviews of about 30 minutes were conducted with qualified nursing staff in a variety of wards in three UK hospitals. More prolonged interviews (about 90 minutes) were undertaken with the project managers who had implemented the systems in each of the three hospitals in the study, who were also all trained and qualified nurses. A qualitative approach was chosen in order to investigate how their perceptions about the systems, and the use they made of them, were grounded in the beliefs and values of the nurses interviewed about, for instance, what nursing work was. Individual interviewees were not selected in advance. Particular wards were identified within each hospital in order to give some variety in terms of speciality, and also to investigate whether there was any relationship between whether the ward was a high or low-tech area, and resistance to the system.

Resistance, if it occurs, is typically a diffuse and often covert activity. Interviews provide a way of asking actors about their actions in a way that gives them a degree of control over their responses. Thus they can feel 'safe' about discussing certain issues (such as, for instance, unprofessional actions) because they can control what is revealed and concealed. The interviewees in this study did sometimes talk about instances of unprofessional behaviour, but in such a way that they were clearly distanced from it. Interviews are also useful in a study such as this one, where the rhetorical strategies and justifications that are offered by the interviewees, as well as the way in which certain courses of action are described, are of central importance to the whole study.

Once the wards had been selected, the sister or charge nurse was approached to nominate an interviewee. No special thought seemed to go into this process. The person selected was usually whoever was free at the time the interviewer called. Most sisters said, 'Just come along at hand-over. I'm sure we'll find someone to talk to you.' (Hand-over refers to the time in the day when the early and late shifts overlap. It usually occurs between 1 and 2 p.m.) The use of interviews is part of the methodological mainstream when studying computer systems in health care. Brown (1995) used semi-structured interviews to study the implementation of a Hospital Information Support System in the UK NHS, in terms of the political processes. Schneider and Wagner (1993) studied a nursing information system in a French hospital using interviews as their main method. McLaughlin and Webster (1998) used observation and interviews in their study of the implementation of a computer system into a hospital pathology laboratory.

All of the interviews conducted were transcribed and an analysis undertaken, supported by QSR NUD*IST software. NUD*IST was chosen because of the flexibility that it offers in terms of how the coding structure can be constructed and then rearranged. Once all of the data had been entered, the codes were refined. This was in order to reduce their numbers, eliminate duplication, and to permit the development of more sophisticated analytical categories. As this process continued, new links between codes became apparent. Another feature of the software which was used at this stage was the ability to write memos (*aide-mémoires*) which could be included within the overall structure of the data. The most important way in which the software was used to support the analysis was through it's reporting features. This enabled all of the sections of transcript which related to a particular code or codes to be retrieved in one block, enabling the drawing out of similarities and differences. Reports were also generated based on searches for particular words or phrases in the data, as well as being based on more complex Boolean queries.

On rereading the account of this process, it might seem that the researcher has fallen into the trap of what Pinch and Collins (see Bijker *et al.*, 1987, and Collins *et al.*, 1997) would call experimenter's regress, that is, making a process that was in reality messy, vague, full of accidents and false starts seem like a smooth and inexorable progress towards a predefined goal. It was, of course, characterised far more by the former set of adjectives than the latter.

FINDINGS

Central to the whole study is the idea of resistance. Was the implementation of computerised care planning resisted by nurses? What forms did this resistance take? Why were they resisted? The findings that have emerged suggest that systems are, on the whole, resisted, but not directly. It was rare to find someone who just refused point blank to use the systems, though this did occur. Interesting in this regard was the manager (ward sister) of one ward who had refused (successfully) to have the system on her ward at all. She had been able to do this by deploying a professional rhetoric. Her ward was explicitly multidisciplinary, and thus did not use the theoretical concepts that underpinned the system, like nursing models and the nursing process. She therefore argued that the system was based on inappropriate ideas for use on her ward. It should be pointed out that this individual is a particularly strong and articulate woman (even by the high standards of ward sisters). This was an exceptional case. More commonly reported in the interviews was the situation where there was one member of staff who refused to use the system, and the rest of the staff just tolerated it. Interestingly, no interviewee claimed to be that member of staff; it was always 'someone else'.

Largely, resistance emerged in other ways. Some nurses tried to minimise their use of the systems. Others tried to find what the project managers described as 'excuses' not to use it. These 'excuses' are quite significant, as they are flexibly constructed depending on the standpoint of the speaker, and show that the users were sometimes prepared to go to some lengths to avoid using the system. For instance, one of the security features of the system was that if an individual password was not used for a certain period of time, it expired and would no longer allow access to the system. The ward staff appeared to be well-aware of this, and so those who did not want to use the system would allow their passwords to expire, and thus be able to say, 'I can't use the system; it won't let me in'. Only if the project manager happened to ask why a particular person had not used the system would this become apparent and a new password issued.

An analogous phenomenon, reported by the project managers, was the non-reporting of technical faults. For instance, a monitor would be broken, but the fault would not be reported for several days, during which time the system was not used. What both of these have in common is a strategy whereby the system can be blamed for the users not using it. The project managers felt that as soon as one reason for not using the system had been dealt with, another one would be found, even if it was, apparently, contradictory. This idea that the system is always to blame, not the users, recurs later in more sophisticated criticism of the system, as we shall see.

The majority used the systems, grudgingly, 'but moaned about it' (to quote one interviewee). Their opinions of the systems were largely negative. When asked to sum it up, one nurse memorably described it as 'a dinosaur'. They were able to give long lists of the problems that it caused for them, including things as simple as a lack of keyboard skills, to quite complex ideas like, for instance, the perception on the part of patients and relatives that use of the system was 'not real work', and that the nurses were thus available to be asked questions when they were using it. Despite this, they all spent a substantial part of their time working on the system. Two main reasons were given for using the system, neither of which was directly related to improving the quality of patient care.

The first motive was the periodic audits of the system's usage that were undertaken by the management of the hospital. The data in the system was checked, and if a ward had not met its targets in terms of the number of care plans completed in the requisite time, ward sisters/ charge nurses would get 'a hard time about it'. In one of the hospitals being studied, league tables of wards' performance were produced and circulated. This monitoring process did not seem to have a strong effect on the behaviour of the staff. Typical were the remarks of one interviewee, 'The charts [of performance in using the system] are sent round . . . Oh, we've done worst again.'

The reasons for this are quite revealing. Firstly, both the ward staff and the project managers knew that no really major sanctions could be brought to bear against an individual member of staff for not using the system. As mentioned earlier, everybody seemed to know somebody who didn't use the system and got away with it. Secondly, the interviews with the project managers showed that they were, at one level, quite sympathetic to how busy the ward nurses were, and to the idea that this made it difficult for them to use the system. As all of the project managers were ex-ward nurses themselves perhaps this is not surprising.

The second motive for using the systems was much more power- ful. This was the threat of litigation. Annandale (1996) has written about the climate of risk within which nurses and other health care professionals work, and the effect that this has on their behaviour, notably in terms of record-keeping. Porter confirms this with specific reference to hand-written care plans, 'Indeed the only reason that nurses bothered with care plans at all was to "cover their asses" . . . They realised that . . . care plans were legal documents that could be called upon in cases of litigation or disciplinary action' (Porter, 1998: 79).

This fear of litigation, leading to meticulous completion of records, both on the computer and in writing, was confirmed by almost all the interviewees. 'You realise you've got to document every time you sneeze over a patient, it's the whole legal thing.' 'It's to do with complaints from relatives, covering your back.' This led to a regrettable degree of duplication of hand-written and computer records.

'Working Round'

That the systems had to be used, although not altogether enthusiastic-ally, meant that the nurses developed a variety of strategies for work-ing round the systems. Mentioned by many interviewees was 'doing the minimum'. Knowing that their performance would be monitored against certain criteria (like the creation of a care plan for a patient within a specified time limit after admission) and not others (like whether the care had been evaluated), the nurses tended to do the things that had to be done, and not do the others. Other interviewees reported 'leaving' the computerised care plans for the next shift or the night staff to do. They reported that this process did sometimes lead to patients not having care plans written for them before they were discharged.

Conversely, some interviewees were positive and enthusiastic about the computers. They thought that the standardisation and comprehen-sive nature of the computerised care plans were beneficial to the hospital as a whole. The benefits were seen more managerial, rather than being expressed in terms of patient care. Among the benefits of the systems were also considered to be protection against the threat of litigation, as mentioned earlier.

The reasons given for resistance to the systems seem to be grounded in the informal culture of nursing. The most common reason given being that it was time-consuming to use, and that it thus took time away from direct patient care. Others (Melia, 1984, 1987) have reported on the centrality of 'hands-on' care to nursing culture, and the low status ascribed to tasks like 'paperwork' or 'admin'. The systems were also criticised for being too restrictive. Perhaps, as Harris (1990) suggests, the nurses thought that they were an attempt by the management to more closely monitor and control their work. How-ever, the interviews tended to suggest that the nurses were relatively unconcerned about the potential for the system to monitor their work. A more telling criticism is that the system did not accurately reflect what they did and how they did it. This was, presumably, not the intention of the system's designers. These problems centred on the concepts (the nursing process and nursing models) around which the system was designed, discussed earlier.

While the nurses were supportive of the ideas of the nursing process and nursing models when asked, their replies to other questions sug-gested a more ambivalent position. They said things like 'I plan care up here (pointing to head) rather than on paper'. 'The system records only about 20 per cent of what we do'. This was confirmed by one of the project managers who said, 'I'm not implementing a computer system, I'm implementing the nursing process. That should have happened ten years ago.' This mismatch between what should be done, what is supposed to happen, and what actually happens in practice, is a much observed and discussed phenomenon in nursing, usually being referred to as the theory–practice gap. Some of the nurses interviewed were obviously aware that this issue was problematic, but the strategy that they used to resolve this problem, in the course of the interview, is perhaps quite revealing. What they did was to say that while they were in favour of nursing models and the nursing process, they had not been correctly implemented in the system, again blaming the system for their unwillingness to use it.

Similar findings to this study's were reported by Porter and Ryan (1996). The nurses in their study, when asked, were in favour of using the nursing process. When their practice was observed (using paper-based, rather than computerised systems) Porter and Ryan found that the nurses did not, on the whole, use the nursing process as it was intended, if at all.

This issue shows how useful the insights of the sociology of technology can be. As Latour (1991) once remarked, 'Technology is society made durable', that is, machines embody certain ideas about the world and how it should be organised. These systems are a case in point. They embody the 'official' 'correct' view of how nursing should be done, that which is taught in Schools of Nursing and written about in the *Journal of Advanced Nursing*. When groups of people sit down in an 'official' setting to design a system, it is, naturally, this view of nursing work which prevails. Most people would be very unwilling to say, in public, that they don't do their work in the way that is generally accepted to be right. However, the reality of daily life and work in the real world is much more complex, and people working under pressure have been known to cut corners. Thus a system can be designed that does not actually reflect the way in which work is done in the real world.

These findings are confirmed by Berg *et al.* (1998) and Berg (1999) who points out, in his recommendations for systems design (based on a long term study of a computerised patient record in an intensive-care unit in the Netherlands), that ideas about how nursing (and medical work) are organised should be derived from real-world observations of practice, rather than what he calls the 'generalised and rationalised textbook-abstractions about the structure of "nursing" or "medical" work' (1998: 249).

The informal structure of daily life and work on the ward played an important part in how the systems were used. It was rare to find an interviewee who reported that the systems were used at the times that were originally intended. Instead, the systems was seen as something to be 'caught up on' on quiet afternoons, nights or weekends, rather than being in constant use through the working day, as the designers intended. Clinical work, hands-on dealing with patients always took priority, again confirming the findings of Melia (1984, 1987).

One of the main factors which was cited by the interviewees as a reason for not using the system at the time that they were supposed to was one of access. Most wards had only two terminals (for reasons of cost and space), and there could be as many as eight admissions taking place within a short period of time. In addition, updates to care plans were supposed to be done for, typically, 30 patients at some point during the day. These problems of access were compounded by the fact that the same terminals were used for the pathology results reporting system, which meant that the doctors were also in competition for the available terminals. Unsurprisingly, several interviewees reported being unable to complete care plans because they were 'thrown off' the terminals by doctors who wanted to get pathology results. This practice was generally accepted, showing, perhaps, that the inequalities of power between the medical and nursing professions are in some ways as prevalent as they ever were.

The factors identified at the beginning of the study as potentially important (use of technology, and the specialism of the ward) did not appear to have any direct relationship with whether interviewees were more or less-resistive. One of the nurses most vehemently opposed to the system worked in Intensive Care (a high-tech area), one of those most enthusiastic about it, in care of the elderly (more low-tech). In fact, the discussion that took place with interviewees about the technology (other than the system) that was in daily use on the wards tended to suggest that the distinction between high and low-tech is somewhat misleading. The nature of health care in hospital in the 1990s is such that while there may be variations in the amount and complexity of the technology in use, no area could really be described as low-tech. It is also possible that to categorise nurses as being enthusiastic or resistive to technology in general is something of an oversimplification.

These factors seem to have transformed the systems from what they were intended to be, a system for the planning and evaluation of care, to what they became, a system for recording the care given. Other authors have reported analogous findings (McLaughlin and Webster,

1998). Far from transforming the organisation, as writers like Zuboff (1988), and Hammer and Champney (1993) have suggested, in the hospitals examined by this study the computer system has been transformed by the organisation, and specifically by the informal culture and practices of the people who used it. This has substantial implications for any manager or systems designer who is seeking to use IT to change how a health care organisation works. What this study suggests is that any attempt to design computerised systems should start with a frank, detailed look at the reality of everyday life and practice in the areas where the system is to be implemented, even if this process results in some uncomfortable findings.

Bijker *et al.* (1987) have shown how technology can literally embody ideas that are part of the social world. The systems under discussion in this paper embody certain ideas about how nursing should be done; ideas not necessarily shared by the people who use the systems. Hence the systems are resisted.

References

Annandale, E. (1996) 'Working on the Front Line; Risk Culture and Nursing in the New NHS', *The Sociological Review*.

Audit Commission (1992) *Caring Systems: A Handbook for the Managers of Nursing and Project Managers* (London: HMSO).

Audit Commission (1995) *For Your Information: A Study of Information Management and Systems in the Acute Hospital* (London: HMSO).

Berg, M. (1999) 'Patient Care Information Systems and Health Care Work: A Sociotechnical Approach', *International Journal of Medical Informatics*, 55: 87–101.

Berg, M., Langenberg, C., van der Berg, I. and Kwakkernaat, J. (1998) 'Considerations for Sociotechnical Design: Experiences with an Electronic Patient Record in a Clinical Context', *International Journal of Medical Informatics*, 52: 243–51.

Bijker, W., Hughes, T. and Pinch, T. (eds) (1987) *The Social Construction of Technological Systems: New Directions in the Sociology and History of Technology* (London: MIT Press).

Bloomfield, B., Coombs, R. and Owen, J. (1994) 'A Social Science Perspective on Information Systems in the NHS', in J. Keen (ed.), *Information Management in Health Services* (Buckingham: Open University Press).

Bloomfield, B., Coombs, R., Cooper, D. and Rea, D. (1992) 'Machines and Manoeuvres: Responsibility, Accounting and the Construction of Hospital Information Systems', *Accounting Management and Information Technology*, 2(4): 197–219.

Brown, A. (1995) 'Managing Understandings: Politics, Symbolism, Niche Marketing and the Quest for Legitimacy in IT Implementation', *Organisation Studies*, 16(6): 951–69.

Collins, T. and Bicknell, D. *Crash* (1997): *Ten Easy Ways to Avoid a Computer Disaster* (London: Simon & Schuster).

Hammer, M. and Champney, J. (1993) *Reengineering the Corporation: A Manifesto for a Business Revolution* (New York: Harper Business).

Hardiker, N., Heathfield, H. and J. Kirby (1995) 'Introducing Information Systems to Nursing Practice: The Professional and Cultural Barriers', in B. Richards (ed.), *Current Perspectives in Healthcare Computing* (Weybridge: BJHC Limited).

Harris, B. (1990) 'Becoming Deprofessionalised: One Aspect of the Staff Nurse's Perspective on Computer-Mediated Nursing Care Plans', *Advances in Nursing Science*, 13(2): 63–74.

Knorr-Cetina, K. and Mulkay, M. (1983) *Science Observed* (London: Sage).

Latour, B. (1987) *Science in Action* (Cambridge, Mass.: Harvard University Press).

Latour, B. (1991) 'Technology is Society made Durable', in J. Law (ed.), *A Sociology of Monsters: Essays on Power, Technology and Domination* (London: Routledge).

Melia, K. (1984) Student nurses' Construction of Occupational Socialisation. in *Sociology of Health and Illness*, 6(2).

Melia, K. (1987) *Learning and Working* (London: Tavistock).

McLaughlin, J. and Webster, A. (1998) 'Rationalising Knowledge: IT systems, Professional Identities and Power', *Sociological Review*, 46(4).

Mulkay, M. (1979) *Science and the Sociology of Knowledge* (London: George Allen & Unwin).

Packwood, T., Keen, J., Buxton, M. (1991) *Hospitals in Transition: The Resource Management Experiment* (Buckingham: Open University Press).

Porter, S. (1998) *Social Theory and Nursing Practice* (London: Macmillan – now Palgrave).

Porter, S. and Ryan, S. (1996) 'Breaking the Boundaries Between Nursing and Sociology: a Critical Realist Ethnography of the Theory Practice Gap', *Journal of Advanced Nursing*, 24, 413–420.

Roper, N., Logan, W. and Tierney, A. (1980) *The Elements of Nursing* (Edinburgh: Churchill Livingstone).

Schneider, K. and Wagner, I. (1993) 'Constructing the "Dossier Representatif"': Computer Based Information Sharing in French Hospitals', *Computer Supported Co-operative Work*, 1: 229–253.

Slaney, G. and Hitchens, K. (1993) 'Achieving Acceptance', *Nursing Times*, 89(40) (6 October): 62–3.

Stapleton, P. (1994) 'Nurses' Attitudes to Computer Systems', in B. Richards, (ed.), *Current Perspectives in Healthcare Computing* (Weybridge: BJHC Limited).

Webster, A. *Science, Technology and Society: New Directions* (Basingstoke: Macmillan – now Palgrave).

Woolgar, S. (1988) *Science: The Very Idea* (London: Tavistock Press).

Zuboff, S. (1988) *In the Age of the Smart Machine: The Future of Work and Power* (Oxford: Heinemann).

13 Developing Whole-Systems Learning: A Linked Approach

*Lynda Jessopp and Sean Boyle**

INTRODUCTION

Provision of effective health care requires contributions from different services. Each of these services is part of an overall care system but operates within its own separate organisation (Harrison, 1997). With the current emphasis on multidisciplinary collaboration within health care provision, health service managers have come to appreciate the benefits of different approaches, and the skills they imply, to developing coherence across services. Thus, there is an important role to be played by research as manifested in the growth of evidence-based medicine, planning and policy. Equally, there is growing recognition of the benefits of applying new methods of computer modelling to complex systems. Similarly, the opportunities for applying a range of organisational development methods are being taken up within managerial thinking in the health service.

In practice, however, although these different approaches may be used simultaneously, they are most often viewed in isolation and their impact felt at different levels of the health system. This chapter argues that, to improve the operation of health systems through a better understanding of the whole system, there is a need to link all three: research, organisational development and modelling.

The ideas we put forward are based on experience of working with the system of urgent care services in one health authority. We discuss briefly the nature of health systems and, specifically, the urgent-care system. We describe the three theoretical approaches on which we drew with reference to the work we did in Lambeth, Southwark and Lewisham Health Authority (LSL). This is followed by reflections on our

* We would like to acknowledge the contribution to this project of Jane Bryan-Jones, Anothony Harrison, Lorna Hipkins, and Jeff Tansley.

232

experience and presentation of how we see the methodology developing in the future as a system learning tool. This learning tool links health-services research and analysis, organisational development and real-time computer simulation modelling.

COMPLEX SYSTEMS IN HEALTH CARE

Any study that attempts to examine the outcome of the behaviour of individual decision-makers is by its nature engaging with a complex system (Stacey, 1996b). Where there are complex sets of relationships between large numbers of organisations and/or individuals in a system, understanding the interactions between the various parts of the system is central to the ability to manage well. This is relevant to all systems where it is necessary to cope with understanding complex social and economic interactions so as to be able to influence outcomes in a directed way. Recent examples of using a systems framework have focused on the interactions of individual decision-makers to better understand areas as diverse as financial markets, control of the housing market, the preservation of the environment and transport flows (Bernard, 1999; Farmer and Lo, 1999; Geisendorf 1999).

The health care system comprises many sub-systems. These are most often analysed and managed separately: for example, the acute hospital, primary care, mental health services, medical education and medical research (Harrison, 1997). Within each of these, further subdivision is possible. But the typical analytic and managerial framework for dealing with issues concentrates on the individual parts rather than seeing the parts in relation to each other. Whatever the focus of interest – cancer care, hip- fracture, urgent care – it is inevitably part of a wider system. These 'virtual care systems' comprise contributions from different organisations. Rarely does one organisation provide all aspects of care and each organisation will be part of many systems; and it is unusual for any one person or organisation to have overall sight or control of the whole system (Boyle *et al.*, 1998). The relationships across organisations tend to develop in *ad hoc* ways in response to a clear need for joint working. These relationships are then based on informal alliance or partnership.

Systems can be described at almost any level of abstraction. One systems approach becoming more familiar within health care is based on the notional stages of care of an individual patient with a given condition – the care pathway. The complete care pathway for patients with a hip-fracture 'episode' can involve at least 13 different professions (Scottish Office, 1993). There is considerable interaction between the outputs and inputs of different people involved in the care pathway and considerable potential for things to go wrong. Setting a consistent national system for caring for patients with hip-fracture is no easy task; guidelines and protocols must be multidisciplinary and cross traditional boundaries.

In addition, the care-pathway approach rarely allows for independent decision-making by the individual patient to have an effect on the care or its outcome. In other words, the focus is on the interaction of the professionals involved in the care pathway: the patient is treated almost like a non-sentient input to this process.[1]

In determining 'urgent care' as our area of study we were consciously trying to break out of this restricting definition of care and its pathway. If we define our system boundaries appropriately, it becomes clear that the individual's decisions may have as much impact as those of the professionals.

DEFINING THE SYSTEM OF URGENT CARE

Our interest is in a system that cuts across client groups and conditions but is identifiable as the collection of services and/or organisations meeting needs which are manifested in demands for emergency or urgent care. In what sense can we say that this collection of emergency and out-of-hours services do form a system?

The key features in traditional systems thinking applied to organisations defines a system as having a boundary, purpose and information feedback, and as containing inputs, transforming processes and outputs. This model gives rise to a concept of the system, such as the care-pathway approach described above, in which the input is 'passive'. This does not fit with the urgent-care system and our approach is informed by the concept of organisational systems as developed from complexity theory (Stacey, 1996a). Stacey (1996b) defines a system as a network of people operating within group and individual rules. The features which concern us are:

- human systems are characterised by non-linear feedback;
- complex systems are characterised by a multitude of non- linear feedback relationships which are unpredictable and may be counter-intuitive;

- feedback relationships are separated in space and time;
- systems are self-organising; and,
- whole systems contain both a formal 'legitimate system', which defines the formal rules and behaviours of the system, and an informal 'shadow system' in which agents may either support or subvert the legitimate system.

Urgent care is rarely conceptualised as a system but it is possible to recognise these characteristics. Urgent care differs from other health systems in that it does not necessarily[2] consist of a series of services through which patients progress but, rather, represents a group of services from which a given population may *choose* to access care. Central to defining the system then is the inclusion of the population of individuals whose choices form the input. This population includes patients and *potential* patients who may or may not access the formal health care system in response to a given 'urgent event'.

Some components of the system are fixed by national requirements (there must be a 24–hour Accident and Emergency (A&E) department, GPs have 24–hour responsibility, out-of- hours services are for urgent care) but modified according to local needs. The 'real' system which emerges is visibly self-organising at the systemwide level (some systems include MIUs (Minor Injuries Units), some have primary-care practitioners in A&E); and sub-system level (one hospital has a separate children's A&E, good relationships exist between mental-health professionals and GPs in one part of the system but not another). The urgent-care system also has to respond to the changing external environment – rising demand, government initiatives, reconfiguration of the supra-system of acute health care and so on.

The separate parts of the system provide a range of services, from major trauma, minor injury, minor illness treatment, to transport, advice and reassurance in response to different needs. Each service interprets those needs differently; the common element is the unplanned nature of the demand on services which arises from the perception of individuals that they have an urgent need to consult the formal health system. Taken as a whole, these services should provide a full response to the urgent needs likely to arise in a given population. Individual patients may only access one part of the system, for example A&E, for their 'episode of care' to be complete. So at the individual level the whole system may not be visible.

However, at the population level the system effect is evident. For the individual patient, the experience of a very long wait in A&E

may mean that they change their behaviour when a subsequent urgent event occurs, and ring their GP rather than go to A&E. For a given part of the system, responses to patients with urgent events will influence activity in other parts of the system. For example, as waiting times build up for out-of-hours GPs, they are likely to lower the threshold for referral to A&E. Theoretically the feedback mechanisms at work in the system are easy to abstract and for the whole system of urgent care we can hypothesise chains of events (see Box 13.1).

However, at the level of 'actuality' – what happens in the real system – it is much less easy to see if this is indeed how such feedback mechanisms operate since:

- there are very few checks in the system – positive feedback continues until the extreme measure of closure to 999 ambulances, or the epidemic (fuel) burns itself out;
- each bit of the system apparently copes by working harder/faster;
- proactive system management only comes into effect in the event of major incidents/disasters – even then only partially;
- the feedback is widely spaced over space and time; and,
- nobody is actually looking for feedback mechanisms at a system level.

Box 13.1   Feedback mechanisms

Positive feedback
A health scare → increased demand on in-hours general practice → more demand on out-of-hours general practice → long waits → more people go instead to A&E → adverse publicity that GPs not coping in face of 'epidemic' → even greater demand on A&E.

Negative feedback
Difficulty in accessing GP → more people go to A&E → long waits in A&E → self-selection out of system or demand exceeding capacity → closure to 999 → demand reduced within this system (i.e. moved to another system).

We have no real 'hard' evidence about what happens because we do not take a whole-systems approach to monitoring activity: the complexity of the system seems to make the whole impossible to grasp. The different components form the whole but are not dependent on each other (as they might be in a care pathway); however, they do affect each other. Stacey (1996b), quoting Weick, describes this as 'loose coupling' and suggests that such systems are safer in the face of uncertainty but that the relationships within them are more difficult to discern than in 'closely-coupled' systems.

At the level of individual practitioners (clinicians/health care providers) and even at organisational level, parts of the system may come into view but the whole is obscured. Thus, there may be good individual and organisational working relationships between GPs and A&E, but knowledge of the demands and capacity in other parts of the system is extremely limited. For example, the out-of-hours GPs do not routinely know waiting times in A&E departments, and similarly A&E may only have anecdotal awareness of the demands on GPs from flu epidemics.

Finally, many of the subtleties and self-organising characteristics of the emergent system – the good personal relationships, the local agreements, the research studies – are hidden from view once the size of the system within the gaze is too large. In this sense, much of the operational detail, which fundamentally affects the whole, exists within the shadow system.

For the purposes of our project, the basic input for our system was the population pool of Lambeth, Southwark and Lewisham Health Authority who may access the health care services provided for that population. Figure 13.1 illustrates the system as we defined it. The major health care providers are included, but the system could have been extended to bring in, for example, social services emergency teams, voluntary-sector helplines and so on. The working definition is dependent on local circumstances and the key drivers for the work. In our case, the arrival of a completely new service to the health care scene was posing significant questions about the potential effects on demand and workload. NHS Direct, the 24-hour nurse helpline, has been set up as a new access point explicitly to direct people to 'appropriate' services (redirect demand in the system) and encourage self-care (reduce demand on the formal system). However, it clearly also has the potential to bring new patients into the system from the pool of potential patients (increase demand).

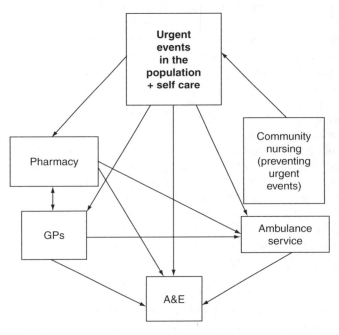

Figure 13.1   Urgent care system

Our definition of the system was therefore based on the LSL environment: a defined population base and local system. It was designed to address the specific issue of the introduction of NHS Direct and excluded those elements on which NHS Direct would have little impact. If we had been interested in emergency admission, the system might have included the Rapid Response scheme (reducing admissions) and the Supported Discharge scheme (reducing re-admissions). Finally, it was also pragmatically based around a unique systemwide set of activity data that had been collected as part of a different project (Out of Hours Project, 1997). We were able to use this data to encapsulate the whole system. The aims of our project in LSL were to increase the visibility of the whole system to those commissioning and working within it, and to examine the consequences of changes to the system.

THE METHODOLOGY

Our approach draws on three distinct disciplines: we set out to work with the 'real' system using methods which are well- accepted within each discipline but not generally brought together. We believe that the synthesis of these perspectives is the key to enabling learning which, crucially, can be sustained and built on over time. Our own process in developing the methodology has involved a huge learning exercise in working with our different theoretical perspectives, linking them together and reflecting on our experiments. However, the process has also been emergent in the sense that as we have worked with emerging systems, we have found new ways of thinking about the methodology as a result of the way individuals reacted to and interacted with the combination of these radically different approaches.

Our aims were to:

- increase understanding of the system of service provision in LSL among key players within it; and,
- increase appreciation of taking a whole-systems perspective on changes and improvements to the system.

We worked from three premises:

- the whole system is complex and difficult to understand;
- knowledge of the system is held by the agents within it; and,
- health-services research only provides partial information (and reflects the legitimate system rather than the shadow system).[3]

Our intention was to 'kick-start' a process which could lead in many directions. Although a central issue for the 'real system' became to understand the effects of introducing NHS Direct, we did not have a 'problem' as such to solve at this stage of the process. Rather, we saw this work as laying the foundations for an approach to future problem- solving. We now consider the three strands of our approach in turn.

Organisational Development

Organisational development is a process of change in an organisation's culture and is therefore concerned with the individual and collective norms, values and assumptions about how the world works. It therefore emphasises how things get done as well as what gets done and, from a systemic perspective, is concerned with ensuring the congruence of structure, strategy, culture and processes (French and Bell, 1995). From an organisational development standpoint, therefore, it should not be expected that changes in service delivery will be successful without addressing the cultural factors influencing the agents in the system. The traditional top-down approach to change, whether in clinical services or implementing research findings (French and Bell, 1995; Baker and Kirk, 1998), is limited.

For our work, the key insight from organisational development is the focus on the values, beliefs and behaviours of the agents within the system, as it is their behaviours (managerially and clinically) which create the 'actuality'; that is, the 'on-the-ground' system. It is these behaviours (alongside the behaviours of the public) which we have attempted to simulate. The second key insight which focused our work was the important distinction between 'espoused' theory – that is the way people say they behave – and 'theory in use' – the world-view which actually drives behaviour (Argyris and Schon, 1978). Clearly, if we were to model behaviours as they occur in the real world we would have to begin to reveal actual practice based on theories in use. Finally, we were interested in applying the distinction between an organisation's legitimate and shadow systems to our 'whole system' of urgent care. The legitimate system is taken to be the formal intentions, structures and rules of an organisation whereas the shadow system is the collection of informal networks which offer a mechanism for negotiating ambiguity in the legitimate system (Stacey, 1996a). A key property of shadow systems is that, by definition, they are self-organising.

As our system is not synonymous with an 'organisation' in the conventional sense, the legitimate system is minimal – there is, at present, no systemwide strategic vision nor formal structure, and the 'rules' which exist are the products of the 'legitimate systems' of the constituent organisations. In this situation, the shadow system becomes extremely important in its potential both to support and subvert the whole system. Lack of awareness by managers and planners of actual 'on-the-ground' practice hampers understanding and decision-making. Lack of system awareness among service providers can also lead to local developments which have a positive effect in one part of the system but may be detrimental to the whole. For our purposes, therefore, we needed to work with the 'shadow' system in order to bring informal ways of working to light.

The Intervention

With this background thinking, our interventions were designed to encourage whole-system learning through addressing the 'mental models' of participants, developing shared vision and promoting systems thinking (Senge, 1992). The interventions took place on two whole days separated by two months, and included representatives from the key system players. As far as possible we tried to involve both management and front-line staff. The local population was represented by community organisations.

On the first day, we used small-group exercises to develop systems thinking, to map our system (Figure 13.2), to generate visions of the 'ideal' system, to recognise the influence of one part of the system on others and to consider how we could know how well the 'whole system worked'. We used a variety of creative methods such as drawing, messaging between groups, to encourage new ways of thinking (Boyle *et al.*, 1999). We also presented the computer simulation of the LSL system and ran two potential scenarios of local change. One modelled the effects of introducing NHS Direct, and the second the impact of severe increases in winter demand.

The second day was designed to address specific issues arising from the first and included further work on NHS Direct, next steps with the simulation, understanding need and demand and defining whole-system objectives. Our intention was to bring the resources of the simulation and research expertise (external to LSL) to bear on these issues.

Our approach was therefore one of assisting the system to define and change itself by working with the individuals in the system, by encouraging them to interact with each other and encounter and challenge each other's perspectives. We conceptualised the role of simulation as a tool for developing appreciation of the actual system and testing alternative systems.

Communicating Agent Simulation Modelling

The use of computer modelling seems, at first sight, completely at odds with a people-based organisational development approach. Computer models are usually evidence-based (hard facts), predictive and experimental. They are designed within a paradigm which regards cause and effect as linear in one direction and sees organisations as machines. They give 'an answer' and the impression of order and control, and are often devised in isolation by economists or planners and given, as a finished product, to managers.

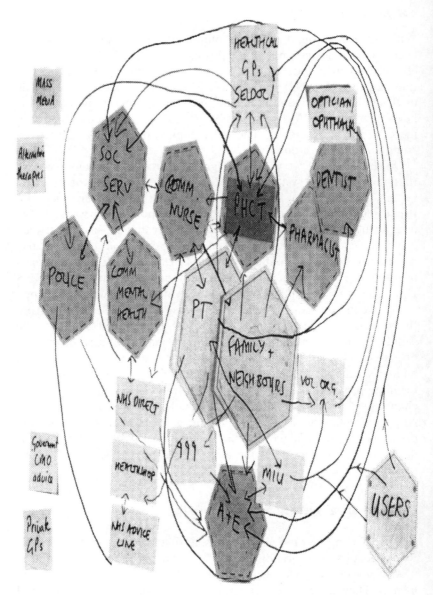

Figure 13.2　One group's map of the whole system

While this may be an oversimplification, we see two problems which are inherent in this type of approach. The 'evidence' is, in reality, only sketchy, and therefore assumptions are made but they are hidden. Secondly, they are based on the legitimate system – they simulate the system as it 'should' work rather than as it does in practice.

The modelling approach we adopted was to build a model of the 'actual' system using Communicating Agent Simulation (CAS) technology.[4] This method makes it possible to build the simulation based on the behaviour or choices of agents. Each individual in the LSL population and each service involved in the system of urgent care is modelled as a separate process or agent, with a set of scripts to represent its structure and decision-making processes. In the simulation, these become dynamic communicating agents. This is very different from techniques applied in most applications of modelling to health services which tend to be attempts to fit mathematical models to aggregate historic data. The Communication Agent Simulation runs in real time. It does not offer certainties and solutions but a range of *potentialities* – 'pictures' of the possibilities. The system model is based on *evidence and explicit assumptions* about behaviours; it can assess the effect of using different assumptions as well as observed changes in the system. The crucial point is that the simulation models the behaviours of people within the system with all the inherent uncertainty and unpredictability. The building blocks of the simulation are:

- the individual decisions made by citizens experiencing an urgent event on whether to access the formal system; and,
- the individual decisions made by service providers/clinicians/managers reacting to these demands for access.

Decisions made by citizens are based on their own perception of the urgency of their condition and their knowledge of the appropriateness and availability of health services. So an individual citizen, for example, may decide to call an ambulance, make their own way to A&E, phone their GP for an appointment, or consult the local pharmacist. Each of these services may be able to deal with the problem or they may re-route to another part of the system. It is the interaction of these individual processes which the simulation models.

The results of the simulation were calibrated against the existing evidence on flows of people through the LSL system (mainly relying on the data-set referred to earlier). It was possible to examine potential effects of the introduction of external factors such as a flu epidemic or a new service, or changes in behaviour of citizens of service providers. However, the results were only ever as good as the system's own understanding of how it worked (as encapsulated in the model). As we discuss in the next section, this was not often apparent to the members of the 'actual' system.

Health-Services Research

The use of health-services research and policy analysis in working on individual service issues is well-established. However, its application within a whole-system framework is not. Nevertheless, we were able to draw on existing research sources.

Research often refers to the testing of propositions through a range of analytic techniques involving the gathering of new data and intelligence, and/or the establishment of new theoretic frameworks. But in relation to the LSL project, we use the term primarily in the sense of the systematic and appropriate use of existing research evidence. This contrasts with the more anecdotal use of research evidence which may occur in development projects where the research element is not very 'visible'. We anticipated that although our methodology would throw up research questions that could be tested through local studies, time would not allow this extra research 'loop' to occur.

A key source of 'hard' data and facts about the system that we were simulating was the unique system data resulting from a previous research project (Out of Hours Project, 1997), though this was limited. Other local data and intelligence were used where available, and this was supplemented by other sources of data and research concerning how parts of the system might operate; for example, surveys of self-care.

A key feature of local data was that it was largely based on system outputs. It could tell us nothing about the existing structures and decision rules that determine the way in which interactions take place within the LSL system. This 'soft' data required the experience of local agents in the system. These aspects of the shadow system are rarely subject to formal research; the knowledge held within it tends not to be accorded the status of research data.

REFLECTING ON OUR PROCESS

The initial approach, which we developed and used in LSL, had essentially three strands. First, we were working with the 'human whole-system' group to increase understanding of the system and stimulate a vision of joint working. Second, we developed a computer simulation of the LSL system using existing data and building in the key assumptions. We relied heavily on the third aspect of our approach, the research element, in order to build the model and also give a focus to the work with the human whole-system group.

Difficulties

- *Developing whole system understanding*
  We started out by working with a small number of people who were involved in the management of the system – though it would be wrong to use the term 'system-managers' as this implies a purposefulness which did not exist. This group was intended to act as a test-ground for building the initial computer model, providing significant input and reaction before taking the process out to the bigger whole-system group. However, we underestimated the effort and time necessary to take even such a small group through a process of whole-system understanding. The small group did not wholly engage with the task.
- *Combining people-based experiential development processes with 'harder' simulation modelling*
  There were two issues, which came into focus on the first-day event. First, several people were 'turned off' and possibly intimidated by the use of complex computer software and were not able to engage with it. Second, for many, the simulation appeared as an add-on or even a diversion from the interactive processes we were trying to foster. We underestimated the need to introduce simulation itself and explain our model – the concept of simulation is difficult and particularly for a group whose expectation is for a conventional predictive linear approach providing short-term answers.
- *Applying 'research data'*
  We underestimated the resistance to using the knowledge in the group and making assumptions in the absence of 'hard' data. Our group were used to looking for evidence and facts and were very uncomfortable with building the simulation using assumptions. There was considerable concern that the model would not be 'right' – that is, not a 'true' reflection of reality. They felt the simulation was not complex enough and could never be complete or accurate enough to give 'reliable' answers and did not see it as a heuristic device.

Successes

● *Participants' personal learning*
The event as a whole was valued highly by participants (Boyle *et al.*, 1999) who felt they gained:

  – an appreciation of the issues and perspectives of other service providers;
  – information about other services;
  – greater understanding of the interrelationships between services; and,
  – an ability to see the whole system and all the parts.

● *Group learning*
The discussion of future directions demonstrated that there were many common aspirations across the group and they generated images, such as choirs singing in harmony and one-button access to services, with a very real sense of the whole being greater than the parts (Boyle *et al.*, 1999). The simulation also engaged the interest of some people who could see the value of generating a range of scenarios based on different assumptions, and a small group began to generate ideas about using the simulation in their own settings and adapting it around specific issues.
It was also evident to the project team that playing through the future scenarios with the simulation did kindle a new appreciation of the links between the formal care services and the informal 'self-care' which happens within the population. Demonstrating the effects of NHS Direct potentially drawing more demand into formal care brought this into sharp relief.

● *Team learning*
The hostility to simulation has, although negative on the day, been an interesting and useful result of the work. The simulation model reflects a detailed account of how the system works in real time on an hour-by-hour basis. However, participants felt that this account was not good enough even though none could see how it was possible to provide a better account. But, if we see this as the group questioning their own understanding of the system, to come up with their own perspectives on reality, then their questioning has a positive aspect.
Overcoming this deep-rooted belief in the ability of the past to predict the future is part of the task which we were addressing but

on which we had relatively little impact. However, observing the impact that it did have confirms our view that it is a valuable tool.

LESSONS FOR FUTURE DEVELOPMENT

The key lesson from the work in LSL is the need to make the links between the three elements of our process more explicit to the 'real' system with which we are working. This requires a fundamental shift in the system's thinking about each element so that each is seen not as a separate activity, but as an integral part of a unified methodology. To achieve this, we would now turn our process around so that, rather than presenting the simulation, we would work with the people in the system to create the simulation model, drawing on their own understandings and making use of available research. The three elements of the process and the 'actual system' are shown in Figure 13.3.

Within a whole-system group, it would be possible to work on the development of a simulation by presenting the decision or choice points in the system and working with the group to agree what assumptions should go into the model.[5] Using both 'evidence' from research but, most importantly, their own experience it would be possible to agree reasonable possibilities of what behaviours might be. In this way, the implicit behaviours of the self-organising system are brought to light.

Once the model is agreed and developed it could be used to assess the effects of changes in behaviour (or test different assumptions), to identify crucial gaps in research knowledge and to generate research questions. In this way, working with a group over a sustained period of time it would be possible to involve the four elements of our approach, as shown in Figure 13.3, in an integrated way. Currently most people would recognise these four elements as different aspects of work which

System development	Researching
(increasing agents' knowledge and understanding	(Providing evidence of system behaviour)
Actuality	**Modelling**
(agents working in and changing the system in the here and now)	(simulating agents' choices)

Figure 13.3 The elements in the methodology

are carried out in many health-service projects. However, we argue that there is rarely any linking between the individual elements, and, where there is, it is rarely sustained. Taking NHS Direct as an example:

- System development – we are not aware of any systemwide work on the effects of NHS Direct, although some may have occurred within single organisations. However, organisational development techniques for whole-systems working are becoming more widespread and new work has recently been published (Pratt *et al.*, 1999).
- Researching – the national evaluation of NHS Direct (Munro *et al.*, 1998) and the local LSL evaluation are attempting to look at the impact on both users and other urgent services.
- Modelling – there has been some computer modelling of, for example, the potential demand for NHS Direct over the Millennium.
- Actuality – NHS Direct sites are developing operationally in the light of local circumstances.

We are aware of no effort to link these activities. In Figure 13.4 we suggest there should be an explicit linkage so that system development becomes interactive – making use of research and modelling – which are informed by system experience – which feeds into the actuality. The process is one of continual interaction and hence results in a loop of learning through each approach.

This interaction has several properties:

- each element has a validity in its own right;
- it is continuous and cumulative;
- there is no necessary order;

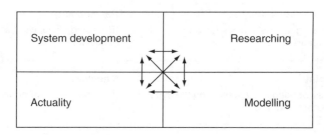

Figure 13.4   Linked thinking

- each element contributes to change in the whole and is changed by it in a reciprocal process; and,
- simulation has the additional dimension that the learning is captured.

We argue that following our methodology can result in an integrated and continuous process. Taking each element in turn.

System Development

The process by which the agents in the system increase their understanding of the way the system works both as separate components and as a whole. This is a 'whole-system' process centred on a 'task' for the participants, which is not to problem-solve, but to create a simulation of the system.[6] In order to do this, they must begin to conceptualise the system and uncover the implicit assumptions in their mental maps and make them explicit. The behaviours which follow also need to become explicit – they need to move from the shadow. At any decision point in the model, they would have to consider the likely behaviours of agents. They would have to consider the 'evidence' and accept the level of uncertainty that exists and make best guesses.

There is at present little published literature on promoting learning across whole systems made up of several organisations, and therefore our approach draws on methods used within single organisations. However, we believe it would be possible to design a project over a relatively long period to develop a usable model of any such system. From our experience, the steps might be:

- introducing the concepts of system and the specific system in question;
- introducing the concept of simulation – possibly, first simulating a completely different system such as shopping behaviour;
- setting up basic parameters for the model – such as population size, key services;
- identify key decision points for small group work (for example, in urgent care this could be concerned with the consulting behaviour of parents of small children, or the responses of GPs to particular clinical occurrences);
- taking the results of the work into the model; and,
- playing back the model and experimenting with changes to the assumptions.

The work could be conducted alternately with small groups and the larger group to focus on different components of the model step by step. We believe that by engaging with the process several things will happen. The participants will enhance understanding of their own mental maps and behaviours and those of others. This increased understanding will affect their behaviour in the 'actuality' and the system will self-organise on a more informed basis; these developments can then be played into the simulation. The participants will also understand that the 'products' of the simulation element of the approach are contingent on those guesses and are only a small selection of possible scenarios.

Research

The research strand involves both conceptual and analytic reasoning in establishing the conceptual framework of interest, developing a rigorous review of what is known about key topic areas. This includes 'hard' facts and a consideration of the potential impact of national policy. We are interested not just in data that might give an insight into what happened in the past – though this can be useful – but information about how decisions arise, how they are made and by whom, who they affect and how these people react. While the apparent results of such decisions may be interesting we want to understand the way that things change as a result.

We also question the distinction often drawn between research evidence and the evidence of the experience of (people within) the system. The evidence most suitable in our context may not fit the conventional definitions of 'research', but to exclude it for that reason may be a grave error.

The research element often consists entirely of using evidence from past research, but it is possible that new research work might be developed simultaneously to answer specific questions that arise in the course of the project.[7] This is more likely to happen where the links between development, research, modelling and actuality are strong. Further, developing the understanding of the system is itself a form of research. The key research question that our project was addressing was: Is it possible to integrate research, development and modelling in a way which results in improved understanding of how the actuality operates? When we know this we can begin to contemplate improvements.

Finally, the application of this approach to whole complex systems will almost certainly suggest new areas of future research. We argue there is a need for programmes of research into the nature and working of health systems. There should be a clear interaction between the development of systems understanding as outlined in this chapter and health-services research, both in applying research findings in practice, and in turn in generating areas for research by identifying gaps in knowledge.

Modelling

If used in the way described, the type of modelling process we used has two functions. First, it serves as the focus for the system learning about itself and, second, the model once established can be used to test changes and assumptions.

The computer provides a means by which learning is captured, can be reviewed as well as written about and disseminated further to increase the spread of the learning. The combination of development for the people in the system and development of the simulation of the system has value over and above the value of each component by:

- providing a structure and focus for the group to open up their implicit understandings and consequent behaviours;
- highlighting how much is unknown and uncertain and therefore unpredictable;
- indicating areas where we need to know more and could gather evidence; and,
- holding the complexity of the system and taking the learning beyond the group involved in the learning process.

Actuality

The process of learning will affect the actuality of how the system operates on the ground – changes will occur in the shadow system. Changes may also be made to the legitimate system. These changes can be played back into the process in terms of deepening the system's understanding of itself. The aim of our methodology is to create a learning process which is a continual interaction between the elements as shown in Box 13.2. In this way, the participants in the system are learning, the system is learning and is changing itself.

Box 13.2   Interactive learning process

...the actual self-organising system... → the simulation of that
system... ... → the research feeding into the simulation... → the
experience of working on the simulation and the 'pictures' produced
by it... ... → feeding back into the real system... → which change
the behaviours in the actual system... → which are fed back into
the simulation... → and so on.

CONCLUSION

We began this chapter by referring to the resources available to managers operating in complex health systems. Many would argue that in
their efforts to manage the resources they have at hand, they use
each of the elements described here, both in terms of day-to-day tactics
and at a strategic level. But we claim that these are most commonly
seen as separate processes and certainly operate separately. By using
a truly linked approach where research, development, modelling
and actuality are seen as integral to the one process, managers
would be able to enhance the real system's ability to formulate a
model of its own whole system framework, and to develop this so as
to react to increasing knowledge and a changing external environment.
In other words the system will manage better (or self-organise better).

The methodology that we have described has the following characteristics:

- learning is participative and owned;
- values the knowledge of people in the system;
- involves large numbers of people;
- is not a top-down implementation of research findings; and,
- is based on bottom-up derivation of the aggregate behaviour of
  system variables resulting from the interaction of the decisions
  of individual agents.

However, it is not a simple process. It takes time and resources. It
requires significant shifts in thinking – it is all too easy to think and

use terminology 'as if' events are ultimately predictable and controllable. But we observe an increasingly complex health care environment where the health decisions of individuals and the health system that they encounter cannot be assumed to give good outcomes by chance. We suggest that there are considerable benefits to be realised by attempting to enhance a whole system's understanding of itself.

Notes

1. Care pathways – as the term is most often used in the literature – can thus be seen as a form of industrial process where getting the parts of that process right is the objective, but the 'widget' that emerges plays no part in this. If we take cancer care as an example, then a sufficiently holistic definition of the pathway, to include key decisions of the individual – even throughout their life – may give most insight into how the 'formal' care system should best be arranged.
2. An individual patient may move between services, say from GP to A&E department, but usually not as part of a care pathway. This is most often an example of a routing decision between two services.
3. Research tends to focus on what the theoretical structure of the system suggests is happening (the legitimate system) rather than on what actually happens – that is the actuality of the system in real life (the shadow system). The system may function as it does because of hidden relationships and practices. In some cases these make the system work, in others they have a negative effect.
4. The model and its simulation uses communicating agent technology based on Milner's calculus of communicating processes (Milner, 1989). This is incorporated into a software package to simulate human behaviour (Rivett *et al.*, 1998). The software includes a strongly-typed functional language that is specifically designed for large, fast simulations while being able to provide near-natural language protocol descriptions.
5. We recognise, however, that there is still the problem of where to start from; the very act of constructing some modelling framework implies a set of assumptions about what is or is not important in the system under study. If we then enter some historic data we must be wary of straying into the realm of providing an answer rather than posing the questions. But our approach retains the notion of individual decision-making even if we then present some of the implications at an aggregate level. This is in contrast to a System-Dynamics approach to modelling complex systems which tends to assume the individual complexity out of the problem.
6. It is possible to use particular problems or issues as a way of working with, and building, mental maps of the system, but the danger is that the

solutions to these become seen as the outcomes in themselves. This is as true of any of the methodological elements that we are describing.
7. Once again an important constraint is the time period over which the work occurs.

References

Argyris, C. and Schon, D.A. (1978) *Organizational Learning II. Theory, Method and Practice* (Reading, Mass.: Addison-Wesley): 10.

Baker, M. and Kirk, S. (1998) *Research and Development for the NHS: Evidence, Evaluation and Effectiveness*, 2nd edn (Oxford Radcliffe Medical Press): 10.

Bernard, R. (1999) *Using Adaptive Agent-based Simulation Models to Assist Planners in Policy Development: The Case of Rent Control*, 99–07–052, Santa Fe Institute, www.santafe.edu/sfi/publications.

Boyle, S. Harrison, A. and Jessopp, L. (1999) *Urgent/Emergency Care in Lambeth, Southwark and Lewisham: Developing a Systems Approach*, Lambeth, Southwark and Lewisham Immediate Access Project, April.

Boyle, S., Harrison, A., Bryan-Jones, J. Tansley, J. (1998) *Packaging Systems for Health Managers to Use*, Paper presented at EHMA (European Health Management Association) Conference, Dublin.

Farmer, J.D. and Lo, A.W. (1999) 'Frontiers of Finance: Evolution and Efficient Markets', Proceedings of the National Academy of Science, 96 (Washington, DC: NAS): 9991–2.

French, W.L. and Bell, C.H. (1995) *Organization Development: Behavioral Science Interventions for Organization Improvement*, 5th edn (Englewood Cliffs, NJ: Prentice-Hall International).

Geisendorf, S. (1999) *Genetic Algorithms in Resource Economic Models: A Way to Bounded Rationality in Resource Exploitation*, 99–08–058, Santa Fe Institute, www.santafe.edu/sfi/publications.

Harrison, A. (1997) *The London Health Care System* (London: King's Fund).

Milner, R. (1989) *Communication and Concurrency* (London: Prentice-Hall).

Munro, J., Nicholl, J., O'Cathain, A. and Knowles, E. (1998) *Evaluation of NHS Direct First Wave Sites. First Interim Report to the Department of Health* (University of Sheffield: Medical Care Research Unit).

Out of Hours Project (1997) *A 'Snapshot' of Out of Hours and Emergency Services in Lambeth, Southwark and Lewisham Health Authority* (London: Department of General Practice and Primary Care, Guy's King's and St. Thomas' School of Medicine).

Pratt, J., Gordon, and P. Plamping, D. (1999) *Working Whole Systems* (London: King's Fund).

Rivett, R., Tansley, J., Bryan-Jones, J. and Turner, D. (1998) *Human Behaviour Simulations using EpiScript Solutions* (Edinburgh: An Teallach Ltd).

Scottish Office Home and Health Department (1993) *Clinical Resource and Audit Group Clinical Guidelines: Report of a Working Group*, Edinburgh.

Senge, P.M. (1992) *The Fifth Discipline. The Art and Practice of the Learning Organisation* (London: Century Business).

Stacey, R.D. (1996a) *Complexity and Creativity in Organisations* (London: Berrett-Koehler).

Stacey, R.D. (1996b) *Strategic Management and Organisational Dynamics*, 2nd edn (London: Financial Times Pitman Publishing).

14 Learning, Unlearning and Relearning: Facilitation in Community Nursing for Delivering the New Primary Care Agenda

Mansour Jumaa and Jo Alleyne

INTRODUCTION

> Most leaders instigating change are like gardeners standing over their plants imploring them: 'Grow! Try harder! You can do it!' But if a seedling has no room to grow, no soil, and no water, it will never become a tree. Similarly, if organisations don't foresee the obstacles that arise naturally whenever growth and learning take place, their change initiatives will fail. All effective organisations take part in this 'dance of Change', a balance between growth and the limits to growth, whose impact can be anticipated and mastered. (Senge, 1999)

These statements, by Peter Senge, captured the content, context and processes involved when a research-interventionist approach was used to assist 46 District Nursing Team Leaders (DNTLs) from the largest NHS Community Care Trust in the UK.

Developments within the United Kingdom National Health Service, as well as other European countries, have led to the need to focus emphasis on funding health care through public sources, and that reform efforts should target, particularly, the processes involved in the delivery of care. In addition, new policy initiatives that are surfacing reflect the urgent need for evidence-based primary care, public health and other alternatives to hospital-based care (DoH, 1998).

The growing need for evidence-based health care practice has not come as a surprise to staff in the NHS. Sackett (1996) defined evidence-based practice as:

256

The conscientious, explicit and judicious use of current best evidence in making decisions about the care of individual patients. The practice of evidence based medicine means integrating individual clinical expertise with the best available external evidence from systematic research.

In this chapter, evidence-based clinical nursing leadership (EBCNL) is defined as a

> process whereby clinical nurses critically appraise, and incorporate tried and tested management and leadership frameworks and concepts into clinical practice, and decision-making, in order to improve the quality of patient care. (Jumaa and Alleyne, 1998b)

This chapter presents the focus of this research, background literature, rationale for the research intervention, research aims and objectives, and the investigation process (overall research design, sample details, data-collection approaches and tools, data analysis, ethical issues and discussion). Emphasis, however, is on a systematic reflection of the *processes of learning, unlearning and relearning*, through the use of facilitation skills to create, 'actionable knowledge' (Argyris, 1993). Actionable knowledge is the knowledge that people use to create the world. It focuses on two domains of actions – actions around difficult problems, which are likely to be embarrassing or threatening, and secondly its production by researchers so that it represents a valid test of the theory of action that informed the production of the knowledge. Action knowledge, must, therefore, be produced in the form of *if–then* propositions that can be stored in and retrieved from the actor's mind under conditions of everyday life (Argyris, 1993: 2–3).

RESEARCH FOCUS

Initially, this project was going to be only a management and leadership development consultancy assignment. The commissioner for the project was persuaded to allow the project to be implemented, doubly, as a research process. The main rationale supporting this request was that, as a research project, the investigation of the clinical leadership effectiveness of the DNTLs would be systematically investigated, not only to discover and produce new evidence-based ideas, but also to produce knowledge that the DNTLs could access and use, as evidence, in their everyday clinical practice. Consequently, not only would the process benefit the participants and their patients, but also advance our knowledge of the process of evidence-based effective clinical leadership. In addition, the leading position, amongst community care NHS Trusts, of the Camden & Islington Community Health Services (NHS) Trust would also be strengthened.

RESEARCH AIMS AND OBJECTIVES

The specific aim of this project was to promote the professional, management, leadership and personal development of District Nursing Team Leaders (DNTLs), given the changing contexts of nursing (Jumaa, 1999). The project was required to:

• Explore the concept of Clinical Team Leadership.
• Recognise what Attitudes, Skills and Knowledge (ASK) are required to perform the role of DNTL effectively.
• Commence the process to develop the DNTLs in the identified areas of ASK above.
• Develop Action Plans in these areas for the DNLTs' Professional and Personal development.

The following definitions of *strategic*; *strategy*; *strategic learning*; *strategic clinical leadership*; *learning, unlearning, relearning*; and *facilitation* are central to the overall design of this project. Strategic is defined in this study as 'that of a strategy', which in turn is defined as:

A pattern in the decisions and behaviour of an organisation, team or individual in creating or responding to change.   (Grundy, 1994)

Strategic clinical nursing leadership is defined as:

An open process of nursing decision-making which seeks to persuade and influence the client, user, and the customer to agree to the chosen direction in relation to social and health services provision. This process is premised on a reflection of both the internal and the external factors impacting on the social and health services.

(Jumaa and Alleyne, 1998a)

The definition for strategic learning in nursing is adopted from the work of Grundy (1994), who defined it as

An open process of exploring complex and ambiguous issues affecting organisations, teams, and individuals. This process involves reflecting and debating on the linkages, tensions and conflicts between issues and seeing these in the wider context.

The processes of *learning, unlearning, and relearning* is used here to refer to the type of systematic changes in behaviours as a result of changing personal and group relations (Sherif, 1966); a process that Lewin would refer to as 'unfreezing, change and refreezing' (Lewin, 1951). Facilitation is defined as

the practitioner (that is, the researcher-facilitator) being motivated by a real concern for the interests of the client (the DNTLs).
(Heron, 1990)

LITERATURE REVIEW

There is no specific literature on evidence-based clinical nursing leadership (EBCNL).This study is the first that specifically set out to develop evidence-based clinical leadership amongst District Nurses in the UK. Hewison and Weale (1996) described an approach to encourage evidence-based practice, with emphasis on staff working in individual wards and departments. The approach described had the potential to be a systematic study, but unfortunately the presentation was anecdotal and was not located within a research process. Hunt (1984) confirmed the longstanding problems that nurses and the nursing profession have in relation to the application of research findings into clinical practice. Kendrick and Luker (1996) claimed that the problem persisted because of lack of interest and resistance to research and development by managerial factors.

Griffiths and Luker's study was based on the premise that, 'there is scant evidence of teams actually existing in any multidisciplinary sense. It is, therefore, difficult to judge whether teamworking is in the patient's best interest or not' (Griffiths and Luker, 1993: 1039). They concluded that organisational rules binding these 'teams' are not obviously in the patient's best interest, rather, they appear to serve the needs of the individuals and the organisation. They suggest care management as an alternative approach, and advocate a strong need to make district nursing more visible within the Primary Health Care Team (PHCT). Poulton and West's (1994) study sought to answer these questions: 'What are the teamworking effects that are wanted? Who wants them? How could their achievements be assessed, measured and/or compared?' They then set out to discover whether it is possible to judge effectiveness in a PHCT by the extent to which the team satisfies the criteria of all its main stakeholders. They conclude that the outcome of the study would allow PHCTs to be in a position to decide for themselves, as a group, which outcomes they wanted to achieve, if they could.

West and Pillinget (1996) set out to describe and evaluate team-building methods used in primary health care settings. They conclude that team-building approaches should be task and service-centred, and focus on developing clear, agreed long-term objectives, strategies and processes for addressing the health needs of the local population. They also suggest the use of coaching teams in the process of continual review and reflection, and in process skills such as communication, decision-making, service planning and managing meetings.

None of these studies made reference to the use of facilitation to help develop the skills-gap, they discovered. Significantly, none of the studies produced actionable knowledge. Hunt (1984) did not make explicit how to resolve the problems identified. What skills would be required and how to develop them to implement a care-management approach as well as to make district nursing more visible within a primary-care team were missing from Griffiths and Luker's (1994) study. All these studies were about applicable knowledge and not actionable knowledge. Applicable knowledge does not concern itself with providing the district nurses (or the study participants) with the appropriate behavioural specifications as well as assisting with having the skills to produce them; actionable knowledge does (Argyris, 1993).

There is, however, a significant literature in the UK and the USA which concentrates on the 'understanding of the concept of leadership as applied to nursing' (Girvin, 1996). A comprehensive literature review by Girvin (1996) provides an adequate background and critical review for research studies in leadership and nursing. The review confirmed that a lot of nursing literature relating to leadership is opinion-led and anecdotal. Some discussed training and preparation for leadership roles, although the studies on teambuilding and teamworking have relevance for the study of clinical leadership.

Nevertheless, there is a significant gap in the systematic study of developing evidence-based clinical nursing leadership in primary health care.

CONCEPTUAL FRAMEWORK

The research process focused closely on Argyris' (1993) method of developing actionable knowledge, and the facilitation process was based on Heron's (1989, 1990) approach. Other pragmatic and creative management tools, techniques, concepts and frameworks (Henry and Walker, 1995) were used as appropriate. This study was based on Grundy's (1994) software for strategic learning, which showed how it is possible to make management tools work for nurses by integrating them with a learning process. The study was committed to the views of management as put forward by Mintzberg (1973, 1991), Ranade (1994), Eccles and Nohria (1992) and Handy (1989).

The most powerful management tools were carefully selected, which were then brought together and applied to practical clinical issues through an orchestrated learning process. The management and leadership concepts, theories and frameworks chosen for this research process were based on their comprehensiveness, consistency and congruity when applied to the clinical/nursing/care/education environment. This learning process is called '*strategic learning*', hence emphasising how learning may help devise and implement strategy at corporate, business and individual levels. According to Grundy (1994), 'Strategic learning embraces a variety of frameworks and tools. It is the glue that holds them together'. Strategic learning is a holistic approach to individual and organisational development (Cunningham, 1994).

SAMPLE DETAILS AND ETHICAL ISSUES

Participants in the project were requested to attend the management and leadership development programme; however, participation in the research process was left to their discretion. There were 46 DNTLs from over 12 health centres across North London, of which 44 took part in the research-intervention process. Appropriate ethical, moral and political processes relating to the project were addressed as they arose. Participation in the project was entirely voluntary, and names used (if at all) in the project were changed for purposes of confidentiality.

DATA COLLECTION APPROACHES AND TOOLS

The following assumptions underlie the rationale and choice of the methodology for this project:

- that researchers are themselves active participants in the situation researched and that the researcher–situation relationship deserves to be studied;
- that the framework and variables of studies themselves change in the course of study; and
- that an important way of testing the validity and significance of social knowledge is to feed data back into the setting researched, studying how this feedback influences further action (Torbert, 1981a).

To this end, the following were used as and when appropriate: questionnaires; open-ended interviews; one-to-one consultations; discussion and focus groups; literature review; individual and group case-study reports; feedback groups; and letting others know (for example through presentations at conferences, but national and international).

The method of data collection in this project, multi- method through triangulation, is necessary for this type of research so that the choice of methodology is responsive to the research 'situation' (Schon,1991). The need for this type of approach is re-emphasised by Campbell and Fiske (1959: p.82), that:

> when a hypothesis (or the identified situational problem) can survive the confrontation of a series of complementary methods of testing, it contains a degree of validity unattainable by one tested within a more restricted framework of a simple method. Findings from this latter approach must always be subject to the suspicion that they are method-bound: will the comparison totter when exposed to an equally prudent but different testing method?

Hence, multiple triangulation, for the purpose of completeness, was used and included investigator, data source, method, unit of analysis and theory triangulation (see Table 14.1). This responsive methodology,

Table 14.1 A summary of the project methodology: multiple triangulation methodology

Type of triangulation	Approach	Purpose
Method	Questionnaire Open-ended interview One-to-one sessions	Approach to strategic management; identification of significant indicators, and Assessment of strategic leadership qualities
Data source	Time Personal Location	Making sense of quality strategic learning, leadership and contextual influences
Investigator	One main researcher, one co-facilitator, 46 collaborators and 2 clinical service managers	Collaborative inquiry combines theoretical and methodological expertise
Unit of analysis	Individuals Line manager Significant events	A holistic and political understanding of the context of strategic leadership and learning
Theory	Review Application Development	Understanding, analysis and evaluation of strategic leadership and learning

(1) Questionnaire given to each member of the four DNTLs' groups to complete as a diagnostic process.
(2) Open-ended interview conducted based on the questionnaire responses.
(3) One-to-one sessions arranged with volunteers.
(4) Line managers interviewed at the end of all the data-collection processes.
(5) Work book given to each participant to assist with everyday clinical nursing decisions and problem-solving leadership activities. Work book contains true, tried and tested, *nursing-friendly* and *relevant* strategic management principles (tools, models, concepts, frameworks).
(6) Decision-making and problem-solving activities were encouraged and evaluated through the use of a double-loop, learning and action-strategic process, and via working in learning sets.

through triangulation, is also used to reduce some of the criticisms against this research methodology concerning issues around internal and external validity. This research situation is not an environment that could be studied effectively using an 'experimental design' or a similar approach.

DATA ANALYSIS

The type of research project discussed here relates to the actual work activities and situations as described by the nurse professionals taking part in the research-intervention project. The overall assumption of this type of *collaborative inquiry* is that, as distinguishable as research is from action analytically, both are bound together and intertwined in real practice. Knowledge is always gained through action and for action (Polanyi, 1958). It seems, therefore, that if we are to question the validity of knowledge from the workplace (social knowledge) we need, as Torbert (1981b) indicated, to question not how to develop a *reflective* science *about* action, but how to develop genuinely well-informed action. Valid social knowledge, he contends, depends first and foremost on the development and *agreement* among persons of a new politics based on a shared wish to research their everyday lives together. After all, 'The most incomprehensible thing about the world is that it is comprehensible' (Albert Einstein). Therefore, the role of feedback is essential to the analysis and the interpretation of data collected.

Data was fed back to the participants during the workshops and the focus groups in order to elicit their views and perceptions as to what the data is actually telling us, and so that they could use their new knowledge and skills to improve the quality of their clinical practice. The interpretation of the quality and meaning of the data were based, explicitly and implicitly, on a management science perspective, a psychological viewpoint , and with reference to nursing actions.

PROJECT ACTIVITY

Throughout the workshops and focus groups the goal of each activity was to create a climate where all tasks were 'questioned', so that an atmosphere of always wanting to know 'how?' 'when?', 'why?', 'what?', 'where?', 'with whom?' and 'how to use at work' the concepts presented prevailed. Evidence-based clinical nursing leadership (EBCNL) will become noticeable within the UK NHS when district nurses (indeed all nurses) are able not only to demonstrate that they know what they are doing, as they would be expected to know, but also why now?, why there? and why them? and how?

Clinical Goals

Within each DNTLs' group, Learning Sets were created. At the beginning of the workshops, both the feedback from the questionnaires and the initial verbal responses from the DNTLs confirmed that the DNTLs were not, then, 'building any' NHS. This was reflected in statements such as: *'if we do not understand what is happening to District Nursing, how can we help team members to understand their roles?'* Initially, the DNTLs demonstrated a lack of awareness and understanding of the strategic goals and objectives of their NHS Trust, and in most cases the operational objectives of their clinical service managers (CSMs) and the general practitioners they worked with. This inevitably led to conflict situations between district nurses, their managers and GPs within and across the primary health care teams. Questions raised during the workshops, were, for example:

• Do team members, for example the GPs, understand and accept the team's primary tasks?
• What are the district nursing team's priority objectives?
• what are my manager's objectives?

The first of the five strategic questions was posed here, *'Where do we want to go in our nursing service?'* Participants were then introduced to the 'Five Rules' of setting goals and objectives – SMART (Lewis, 1995: 158–60) – and the matrix (OUBS, 1998) shown in Figure 14.1 in order to tease out how to order clinical practice priorities. The DNTLs then worked within their learning sets, using the work book they were given, sharing their knowledge and professional experience, while the researchers-facilitators maintained an arm's-length supervision stance.

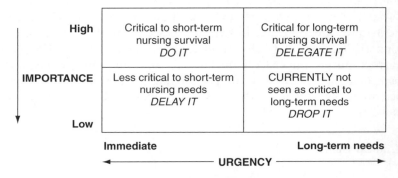

Figure 14.1   Effective clinical-resources management

Clinical Roles

Time constraints were prominent in the list of 'complaints' by the DNTLs. Recent health policies in the UK (DoH, 2000, 1998, 1997, 1993) have placed the GP at the centre of all primary-care services. This not only increased the power and control that doctors have over other health professionals, but also power and control over the actual activities others perform, especially the district nurses. Workshop participants asked questions such as:

● Within the primary-care teams, what are the degrees of freedom for district nurses?
● What are the expectations of district nurses within the PHCT?
● What are the expectations of GPs of district nurses?

These questions made explicit the lack of clarity which exists in relation to roles within the PHCT. The second strategic question was then posed, '*Where are we now in our nursing service?*' The DNTLs were introduced to Mintzberg's (1973) ten roles of a manager, which suggested that as managers they have 'formal' authority and status in their jobs, and that from this position came their *interpersonal roles*. These interpersonal roles should enable them as managers to perform the *informational roles* and the *decisional roles* explicit and implicit within their roles *as DNTLs*. Once they were comfortable with the ten roles they were 'exposed' to Mansour's Matrix (Alleyne and Jumaa, 1998); This is a synthesis of Mintzberg's ten managerial roles on the vertical axis which are plotted against Reed's

(1976) organisational roles analysis (ORA) on the horizontal axis. This matrix, used in small groups followed by plenary discussions, helped to 'surface' role conflicts and contradictions, as well as to raise the DNTLs' sensitivities to stakeholder analysis and management.

Mansour's Matrix with the 'Ten' roles were found to be useful tools, especially in clarifying issues such as professional responsibility and autonomy, understanding the 'political map' of their Trust, as well as those issues which led the DNTLs to perceive themselves to be '*torn*' between the expectations of their clinical service managers and general practitioners.

Clinical Processes

Analysis of the pre-workshop questionnaires gave an early indication of the extent to which there appeared to be a lack of coherent approach in managing change within the district nurse teams. Discussions within the workshops further confirmed this analysis. There were three broad areas of 'process' problems, identified as:

- problems with decision-making processes;
- problems with communication processes; and
- problem with leadership and management styles processes

The source of most of the problems with decision-making and communication processes revolved around the lack of clarity as to 'who' really is managing the DNTLs – GPs? or their line managers? They were then asked to explore the third and fourth strategic clinical questions, '*How can we get to our clinical service goal?*' and '*Which route must we take to get to our service goal?*' Working in small groups, problems with leadership and management styles were explored using Blanchard *et al*'s (1987) situational-leadership style and developmental-levels approach. The members of each small group applied this to themselves in order to determine not only their developmental levels, but also the leadership style they frequently used at work.

Some groups chose this approach to apply to their team members back at the workplace, thus demonstrating that theory that is actionable can be tested by practitioners in the field, as they implement it in everyday clinical practice. Significantly, this means that theory is no longer limited to empirical testing only by 'scholars'.

A significant discovery by most of the DNTLs was that, to be an effective clinical leader, both the developmental levels and the leadership styles (Blanchard *et al.*, 1987) must be dynamic and flexible.

Clinical Relationships

Relationships are complex and 'messy'. One of the assumptions of this project is that if problems with goals, roles and processes are effectively managed within the hierarchy of team issues, problems with relationships will not assume a high profile, if they exist at all.

The fifth and final strategic question was posed, '*What must we do on our journey, as well as checking our clinical progress to ensure that we get to our clinical practice goals?*' To manage relationship issues, the DNTLs were introduced to OPEN relationships behaviour (BP, 1991) (Table 14.2).

Table 14.2   The OPEN relationships behaviours

Open thinking	We expect all district nurses, at every level, to approach clinical problems in a fresh way. To rethink negative traditional nursing approaches, challenge and modify the way things are currently done (if negative). Open thinking promotes bottom-up' participation
Professional and personal impact	We expect all district nurses to influence others, through professional behaviour, personal example and recognition of people's individual needs and aspirations
Empowering all levels of district nursing staff	We expect all levels of staff to be assisted to improve their skills and capabilities and build commitment through clear job roles and objectives; clarifying and respecting individuals' contributions
Networking to increase personal satisfaction and improve district nursing service	We expect all staff, especially those who have access to more information, to share this information, to aid the achievement of the unit/team's objectives, and to celebrate the team's success

Managing and dealing with problems with clinical *goals*, clinical *roles*, clinical *processes* and clinical *relationships* were the focus of the learning, unlearning and relearning processes addressed by the research project activities.

RESEARCH FINDINGS

The study achieved its aim and objectives. The study was about the process of developing actionable knowledge (Argyris, 1993), knowledge that promotes the evidence-base for clinical district- nursing leadership. A major emphasis about the outcome of this study was the nature of EBCNL in primary health care. Issues of *process* therefore assume great importance. Processes have been described by Hammer and Stanton (1995: 4) as *'groups of related tasks that together create value for the customer'*. If we are comfortable to refer to the DNTLs as 'customers', then this study has been very successful on process outcomes.

This project was about working with the district nurses, cited above, to resolve their work-based problems. But, 'In order for organisations to learn, however, individual learning may be a necessary precondition, but by itself it is insufficient' (Poell, 1997). Both the work and the learning systems must be conducive to, and promote the employees' contribution to organisational learning (Senge, 1996). It is not possible to comment on the extent to which organisational factors continue to facilitate or hinder the professional and personal development of participants of this programme. There is evidence, however, that prior to this research-intervention experience, most of the DNTLs were not active in their professional and personal development. Currently, most are attending professional development short courses, and some have enrolled on work-based professional and personal development-related undergraduate programmes.

The attitudes, skills and knowledge required by the DNTLs for effective performance of their roles were elicited from the processes of this project which led to the development of the CLINLAP model (see Figure 14.2). These qualities are embedded in the concepts shown in Box 14.1.

On a more general basis this study confirmed previous assumptions of how to manage and lead teams effectively as well as problems relating to 'hierarchy of team issues'. (Moxan 1993) Evidence from this research-intervention process confirmed that frameworks like

270

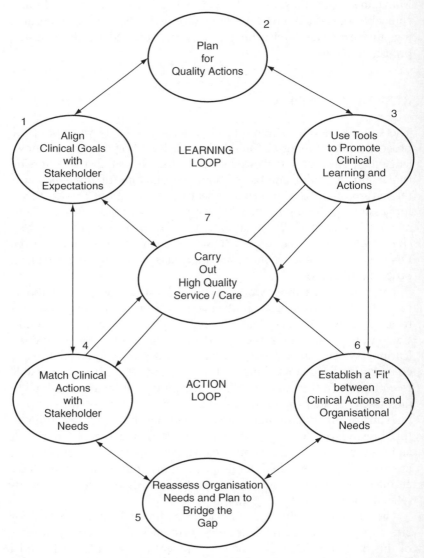

Figure 14.2   CLINLAP: implementing clinical governance in the National Health Service
Source: CLINLAP: Clinical Nursing Leadership Learning & Action Process © M.O. Jumaa (1997). A strategic clinical learning framework developed by M.O. Jumaa (1997) 'Strategic Clinical Team Learning through Leadership', unpublished MA research project (London: Middlesex University), adapted from T. Grundy (1994) *Strategic Learning in Action* (London: McGraw-Hill).

Box 14.1   Attitudes, skills and knowledge required for effective clinical leadership

Specific Clinical Goals via

- Stating the purpose of the clinical team, based on an
- understanding of stakeholder issues, analysis and management, leading to
- deciding and agreeing on SMART goals and objectives.

Explicit Roles via

- An awareness of the impact of forces in the external environment.
- The effect on community care due to changes within the health care industry and the NHS.
- Identification of the required resources and clinical capabilities for the team's viability and success.

Clear Processes via

- SWOT analysis to determine the clinical team's relative strengths and opportunities.
- Knowing the team's Key Success Factors.
- Identifying the difference between needs and wants and the cost implications.
- A working knowledge of the new NHS clinical governance quality framework.
- Ability to analyse cause and effect of clinical activities

Box 14.1   *cont. overleaf*

Box 14.1 *cont.*	
Open Relationship via	• An understanding of power issues and effect on what gets done. • Management of resistance. • Having the capacity to manage constant change. • ability to work with/change the dominant cultural paradigm.

CLINLAP, used effectively, as demonstrated in this study, could assist the district nurse team leaders (indeed any clinician) to become more effective as clinical leaders by ensuring in their practice and teams that:

• Clinical goals are specific and agreed;
• Clinical roles are made explicit to all concerned;
• Clinical processes are clear so that all concerned know what is expected of them; and that
• Clinical relationships are open.

DISCUSSIONS AND IMPLICATIONS

An acid test about the validity of this research approach would be to subject this study to the same evidence-credibility criteria put forward at the beginning of this chapter – a form of 'meta-evidence' (that is, evidence about evidence). The key questions, therefore, would be: To what extent is this approach's contribution to developing actionable knowledge for evidence-based clinical nursing leadership, valid, authentic, current, transparent and sufficient? Argyris (1993) suggests, that the ultimate test of validity when creating actionable knowledge is the extent to which research outcomes can support change intervention in an on-line capacity. Heron's definition of validity states that, 'In a subjective–objective reality, the agreement sought between inquirers is not total unanimity but the illumination of a common area of inquiry by differing individual perspectives' (1989: 44). We have evidence throughout this chapter, especially the sections on Project Activities and Findings, to conclude that the approach put forward in this study was valid and has led to actionable knowledge.

On the issue of authenticity, the essence of focus should be the extent to which the 'tools', 'concepts', 'techniques', 'theories' and 'frameworks' introduced reflect that they are 'tried', 'true' and 'tested'. Are these widely referred to in the management and leadership literature? Do they provide a true and accurate picture to support the claims put forward about their uses? Using Mansour's Matrix, for example, it was clear that a thorough attempt to make explicit the difficulties of moving towards actionable knowledge was present. The matrix, when filled-in with the information needed by a DNTL, or a group of them, demonstrated the possible sources of role conflict. Specific actions as to what to do were discussed within small working groups during the workshops.

The concept of currency refers to the recency of the management and leadership concepts put forward for this study. Of course, the concept of recency itself alerts us to at least two key questions:

- How recent are 'recent' management and leadership concepts?
- Are concepts dating back thirty years or more acceptable as recent concepts?

The answers to these questions were partly determined by the researcher on the basis of expert and 'differential' knowledge when compared to the project participants. The participants, on the other hand, also determined the relevance and the appropriateness of these concepts through their comments, reactions and usage of the concepts, especially as these concepts were acceptable because they supported clinical activities in an on-line capacity. Concepts introduced and mentioned have included the works of:

- Mannheim (1936) which was used to illustrate how our perception of the world and ways of thinking are mediated by the social milieu (Jumaa and Alleyne, 1998a).
- Tuckman (1965) which was used to illustrate how as clinical leaders, and to be effective, it is essential to have a thorough understanding of the characteristic behaviours that groups show as they grow and develop, and the sequential corresponding behaviour required of the leader, if s/he is to be effective.
- Mintzberg (1973) which was used, most of the time, to emphasise that managerial roles are not as straightforward as Fayol's (1949) managerial functional approach suggested.

How current the concepts introduced were was evident in the findings reported in this study. The question of how 'old' the concept was, was not 'really' the issue.

A transparent approach to developing actionable knowledge for EBCNL, in this chapter, refers to the consistency of outcomes whenever the management and leadership concepts introduced in the study were used. What this means, therefore, was that different DNTLs using such actionable knowledge to add value to their clinical leadership activities would always arrive at comparable outcomes. It does tell it as it really is. Even when these concepts were used on different occasions over time, by the same DNTL or by a different DNTL, s/he would still arrive at similar comparable clinical outcomes. This is a significant breakthrough and is precisely what the present Labour government wants and demands from clinicians in the 'new' NHS. 'We need consistent action locally to ensure that national standards and guidance are reflected in the delivery of service' (DoH, 1998, section 3.1). The approach used in this study was transparent, which is evident from the findings of the study. Furthermore, this work has led to the development of CLINLAP, a holistic normative framework that will always promote *transparency, validity, authenticity, currency* and *sufficiency*, wherever, by whoever and whenever it is used.

CONCLUSIONS

This chapter has presented a detailed research-intervention project exploring the development of evidence-based clinical nursing leadership (EBCNL), with a focus on the effective clinical leadership development via effective facilitation skills of 46 district nursing team leaders. The project found that a focus on the 'hierarchy of team issues' (goals, roles, processes and relationships) could assist, in a more practical way, to promote effective clinical leadership. The study confirmed that effective clinical nursing leadership could be achieved through an explicit attempt to move forward actionable knowledge. This was achieved, in this project, when clinical team leaders were beginning to explore and ensure that, in their clinical teams, clinical goals were specific and agreed; that clinical roles were made explicit to all who need to know what is expected of them; that clinical processes were clear; that all concerned know how to do what is expected of them; and that clinical relationships were open, to encourage professional and personal development and discourage a 'blame and punish culture'.

One of the most significant outcomes of this study was ensuring evidence-credibility criteria continuously throughout the project. This was achieved as already discussed, as well as by observing the usability of the ensuring frameworks in everyday clinical leadership activities. This 15-month case-study research-intervention approach appeared to have had a profound positive effect on many of the DNTLs still working in the Trust. This was evident in the percentage of the DNTLs who, after the project, enrolled on either a one-year post-experience Certificate or Diploma in Management (Health care Services), while others enrolled on post-registration professional under-graduate nursing models and courses.

The latest positive effect of this project has been the establishment of the 'OPEN CARE' project. This is a research project and part of a doctoral studies programme in Professional Studies. One study is using CLINLAP within a facilitator-led group clinical supervision. The project is seeking to improve, through actionable knowledge, the skills required for evidence-based practice, to improve the quality of clinical decision-making by community nurses. The written request to start this project came, unsolicited, from past participants of the project reported in this chapter.

The government needs to encourage this approach to research just as they have done for other research methodology. This is not about the competition of research methodologies, but about securing what works for the patient/user/client/customer in the NHS. The final words of this chapter come from the contemporary 'father' of actionable knowledge:

The underlying assumption in my view is that seeking truth in the service of improvability is a valuable purpose for science and for practice. Seeking truth is an ongoing activity – never fully achieved, always approximated. It has always been regarded as the ultimate purpose of research. I should like to emphasise combining the activities of seeking truth with seeking improvability. Why? Because the universe that we are studying is created by humans. It is a virtual world constructed by the players, who then live within its requirements. The likelihood that the worlds we create are perfect or near perfect is low. They are more likely to be imperfect, with gaps that we slowly fill by living in our worlds and trying to make them more effective.   (Argyris, 1993: 284)

References

Alleyne, J. and Jumaa, M.O. (1998) 'Using Work-Based Learning Methodology to Resolve Role Conflict at Work: Introducing "Mansour's Matrix"', paper presented at the 6th International Conference on Experiential Learning, *Experiential Learning in the Context of Lifelong Education*, University of Tampere, Finland, 2–5 July.

Argyris, C. (1993) *Knowledge for Action* (San Francisco: Jossey-Bass).

Blanchard, K., Zigarmi, P and Zigarmi, D. (1987) *Leadership and the One Minute Manager* (Glasgow: Fontana Collins).

Campbell, D.T. and Fiske, D.W. (1959) Convergent and Discriminant Validation by the Multitrait-Multimethod Matrix, *Psychological Bulletin* 56 p81–105 cited in H.W. Smith (1975) *Strategies of Social Research* (London: Prentice-Hall International).

Cunningham, I. (1994) *The Wisdom of Strategic Learning: The Self-Managed Learning Solution* (London: McGraw-Hill).

Department of Health (1993) *The Challenge for Nursing Midwifery in the 21st Century* (London: DoH).

Department of Health (1997) *The New NHS: Modern, Dependable*, Session 1997–8; Cm 3807 (London: The Stationery Office)

Department of Health (1998) *Our Healthier Nation*, a government Green Paper (London: DoH).

Department of Health (1998) *A First Class Service: Quality in the New NHS* (London: DoH).

Department of Health (1998) *Partnership in Action: New Opportunities for Joint Working between Health and Social Services* (London: DoH).

Department of Health (1999) *Making a Difference: Strengthening the Nursing, Midwifery and Health Visiting Contribution to Health and Health Care* (London: DoH).

Eccles, R.G., and Nohria, N. (1992) *Beyond the Hype: Rediscovering the essence of Management* (Boston MA.: Havard Business School Press).

Fayol, H. (1949) 'General Industrial Management', ch 4: 19–42, in D.S. Pugh (1987) (ed.) *Organization Theory: Selected Readings* (London: Penguin).

Girvin, J. (1996) Leadership and Nursing (pt 4) *Motivation, Nursing Management* (3) no 5. September: 16–18.

Griffiths, J.M. and Luker K.A. (1993) 'Effective Multidisciplinary Teamwork in Primary Health Care', *Journal of Advanced Nursing*, 18: 918–925.

Grundy, T. (1994) *Strategic Learning in Action: How to Accelerate and Sustain Business Change* (London: McGraw-Hill).

Hammer, M. and Stanton, S. (1995) *The Re-engineering Revolution: A Handbook* (New York, Harper & Row).

Handy, C. (1989) *The Age of Unreason* (London: Business Books).

Henry, J. and Walker, D. (1995) *Managing Innovation* (London: Sage Publications in association with Open University).

Heron, J. (1989) *The Facilitator's Handbook* (London: Kogan Page).

Heron, J. (1990) *Helping the Client* (London: Sage).

Hewison G and Weale S. (1996) 'Evidence of Local Care', *Nursing Management*, 3(6): 8–9

Hunt, J. (1984) 'Why don't we use these findings?', *Nursing Mirror*, 22, Feb 158(8): 29.

Jumaa, M.O. (1997) 'Strategic Clinical Team Learning Through Leadership' unpublished research project report, MA-WBLS (Strategic Nursing Leadership and Management) (London, Middlesex University).

Jumaa, M.O. (1999) 'Nursing Beyond the Year 2000: Towards Strategic Leadership and Learning in Nursing', invited guest paper presented at a CAPITA initiative conference on *The Changing Role of Nurses and GPs: Clinical Governance and New Partnerships in the New NHS*, April (London)

Jumaa, M.O. and Alleyne, J. (1998a) 'Clinical Nursing Leadership Learning and Action Process (CLINLAP)', paper presented at the 6th Biennial International Conference on Experiential Learning *Experiential Learning in the Context of Lifelong Education*, University of Tampere, Finland, 2–5 July.

Jumaa, M.O. and Alleyne, J. (1998b) 'Developing Evidence Based Clinical Nursing Leadership in Primary Health Care', paper presented at the 16th Annual International Conference of the Association of Management, Fairmont Hotel, Chicago, USA, 5–8 August.

Kendrick, H. and Luker, K.A. (1996) 'An Examination of the Influence of Managerial Factors on Research Utilization in District Nursing Practice', *Journal of Advanced Nursing*, 23: 697–704.

Lewin, K. (1951) 'Field Theory in Social Science cited in J.B. Quinn., H. Mintzberg, and R.M. James, (1988)', *The Strategy Process: Concepts Contexts and Cases*, London: Prentice-Hall International, 539.

Lewis, D. (1995) *10-Minute Time and Stress Management: How to Gain an 'Extra' 10 Hours a Week* (London: Book Club Associates).

Mannheim, K. (1936) 'Ideology and Utopia', cited in J. Henry (ed.) 1995 *Creative Management* (London: Sage Publications in association with the Open University).

Mintzberg, H. (1973) *The Nature of Managerial Work* (New York: Harper & Row).

Moxon, P. (1993) *Building a Better Team* (Aldershot: Gower).

Open Up BP (1991) *BP Human Resources Strategy* (London: BP).

Poell, R. (1997) 'Learning Projects in Organisations', paper presented at the EGRIS Conference, *Lifelong Learning in Europe*, Dresden, Germany, 28–30 November 1996, cited in R. R. Poell *et al.*, 'Can Learning Projects Help to Develop a Learning Organisation?', *Lifelong Learning in Europe*, II(2): 67–75.

Polanyi, M. (1958) *Personal Knowledge: Towards a Postcritical Philosophy* (London: Routledge & Keegan Paul).

Poulton, B.C., and West, M.A. (1993) 'Effective Multidisciplinary Teamwork in Primary Health Care', *Journal of Advanced Nursing*, 18: 918–925

Poulton, B.C., and West, M.A. (1994) 'Primary Health Care Team Effectiveness: developing a constituency approach', *Health and Social Care*, 2: 77–88

Ranade, S. (1994) *The New NHS* (London: Longman).

Reed, B. (1976) 'Organisational Role Analysis', in C.L. Cooper (ed.), *Developing Social Skills in Managers: Advances in Group Training* (London: Macmillan – now Palgrave).

Sackett, D.L., Richardson, W.S. and Rosenberg. W. (1996) 'Guidance-based Medicine: what it is and what it isn't', *British Medical Journal*, 312: 71–2.

Schon, D. (1991) *The Reflective Practitioner: How Professionals Think in Action* (London: Avery Press).

Senge, P. (1996) *The Fifth Discipline: The Art and Practice of the Learning Organisation* (New York: Century Business).

Senge, P. (1999) Quotation accessed 10 December 1999: at http://www.field book.com/main.html: 1.

Sherif, M. (1966) *Group Conflict and Co-operation: Their Social Psychology* (London: Routledge & Kegan Paul).

The Open University Business School (OUBS) (1998) *Personal and Team Effectiveness (701-PTE)* (Milton Keynes: Open University): 26.

Torbert, W.R. (1981a) 'Why Educational Research has been so Uneducational: The Case for a New Model of Social Science Based on Collaborative Inquiry', in P. Reason and J. Rowan (eds), *op. cit.*: 145–51.

Torbert, W.R. (1981b) 'Empirical, Behavioural, Theoretical, and Attention Skills Necessary for Collaborative Inquiry', in P. Reason and J. Rowan (eds), *Human Inquiry: A Sourcebook of New Paradigm Research* (Chichester: John Wiley & Sons): 437–46.

Tuckman, B.W. (1965) 'Development Sequence in Small Groups', *Psychological Bulletin*, cited in C. Handy (1999) (4th edn) *Understanding Organizations* (London: Penguin): 150–179.

West, M.A. and Pillinget, I. (1996) *An Evaluation of Team Building in Primary Care*, A Report for the Health Education Authority, Oxford HEA (Health Education Authority).

15 Methodological Innovations and the Implications for Research: Reflections on the Future of Organisational Behaviour and Organisation Studies in Health

Lynn Ashburner

INTRODUCTION

The quality or validity of any research output is determined by a number of factors. The simple equation that '...the data produced by research is a function of the problems posed and the methods used' (Frankenberg, 1984:88) now requires that the assumptions behind the choices of problem and methods be made explicit. This means exploring the epistemological basis of the underpinning theories in use, and the values inherent in them. This chapter takes the theme of the Conference, 'Reflections on the Future', as an opportunity for reflexive analysis of the use of methodologies within health studies. Just as we, as researchers, analyse the beliefs and motives of others to understand organisations and the work processes within them, so we should apply similar analyses to ourselves and our work. The concept of reflexivity has formed a thread through sociological and psychological methodologies for several decades, but there is still a need to make such reflections more explicit. (There are several levels to which the process of reflexivity can be applied, from the simple one above to those which address the paradigm debate and facilitate the process of transdisciplinarity; see Holland, 1999.)

This chapter takes an overview and is critically reflexive about the current 'state of play' of research methodologies within the health sector. Different strands of theoretical and methodological thought will be explored that can be brought together to suggest additional and alternative approaches to research. The context for research in health is ever-changing and there are new tensions and pressures upon us as academic researchers, which need to be addressed. These include the need to remain responsive to the problem-focused nature of many of the funders' calls for bids.

Transdisciplinarity is a strength rather than a weakness in health studies. This, and the emergence of 'new' paradigm research, from which has developed several action-research approaches, offers the health researcher greater methodological scope to increase understanding and give voice to the multiple perspectives within any research area, whilst retaining a focus on rigour and validity. A purist to a particular methodological approach will be tied to one particular epistemology, and will see the use of the word 'alternative' as literal. This is a personal choice rather than a methodological necessity. Individual research methods can be seen as a means to an end, and it is the research design as a whole that represents the researchers' values and theoretical perspective. When grounded in a particular paradigm, this becomes the basis for judging the validity and quality of the research, rather than a call for exclusivity. Parts of 'mainstream' academia are slow to acknowledge that any paradigm other than that based upon the pursuit of 'scientific' knowledge has legitimacy. It will be a less rich world of knowledge and learning if certain forms of research and knowledge are seen as of lesser 'value' than others.

In comparing approaches from a positivist or traditional perspective, with those based upon an alternative established epistemology, I am not suggesting that the two are interchangeable, but that both have legitimacy. After many years of qualitative research, with its usual limited dissemination and impact, the author chose to explore alternative methodologies which, whilst retaining rigour, enabled 'respondents' to become 'participants' in the research. An outcome of the research process is that the learning involved is far wider than in conventional research both for the participants and the 'researcher'. Having experienced academic life in both arenas, I am aware that many adherents to each 'paradigm' place a low priority on engaging with the other. My ambition is therefore to encourage researchers to be more critically reflexive and to understand why they work within a particular paradigm, and to consider the efficacy of their methods to achieve the research objectives.

That research seeks to have an impact is not solely an issue of dissemination but is about the nature and relevance of research and its methodologies, and the 'knowledge' that research purports to uncover; whose knowledge this is and to what use it is being put. Specific research 'outputs' invariably focus on findings which emphasise substantive areas identified in the research, and these do not necessarily relate to the how and why of implementation. Neither may they meet the needs or the intentions of those commissioning the research, of the subjects of the research, and, even, of the researchers themselves. Whether it is acknowledged or not, the researcher is as much a part of the research as the participants, and the values and experience they bring to the process need to be recognised. Similar to Schratz and Walker (1995), I feel that it is important to 'write about *doing* research in ways that go beyond describing different methods that can be used to collect data and the uses that can be made of them in different settings, and to recognise the essentially social and personal nature of research' (1995:1).

This has many implications and I will explore just some of the issues raised by my search for more appropriate, responsive and ethical methodologies. As an overview chapter, rather than one grounded in 'empirical' data, it makes reference to both my past research and to numerous other papers and articles which carry forward the arguments presented here in a much more thorough and persuasive way. This chapter thus represents an ongoing process of thought, which may illuminate the prospect of new possibilities for the future of organisational behaviour (OB) and organisational research within health care.

IDENTIFYING THE ISSUES

There has been a wealth of 'social' research on and within the health service that needs to be acknowledged and appreciated in a way that both allows knowledge to develop but also avoids being prescriptive about what is to be called 'research'. Following the first OB in health care conference in Middlesex in 1997, Mark and Dopson wrote:

> organisational behaviour as a discipline, has few shared templates or standards, but the assumption that it should build *only* on past

perceptions of the purpose of research. In future, it may be that such templates are not meant to exist, but rather that methodologies must be found to capture meaning which continually changes; combining the interaction of feedback from researchers (action research) and feedback from implementation in the management domain (action learning) into actionable knowledge (Argyris, 1997), which enables the knowledge gained to be used to create (but not replicate) intended actions elsewhere.

(Mark and Dopson, 1999: 257, my emphasis)

This quote goes part way towards recognising that building on past perceptions or previous research is not necessarily the only way forward.

One key issue relates to the nature of 'knowledge'. I suggest that, as academics, our perception of 'knowledge' tends to be very proprietorial, in that we define it in the language of the scientific method, with the implied enhancement of status. This brings the disciplinary structure of knowledge into the spotlight. If, as Stewart suggests, a body of knowledge is that which 'starts from early research that is recognised as the foundation of later work and from which new developments can be traced.' (1999: ix), then this puts the focus on knowledge within the realm of academia which, of necessity, will be to a greater or lesser extent partial (depending on what research funds are gained), selective (depending upon the researchers' personal theoretical interests) and driven largely by academic agendas. This not only removes from the 'body of knowledge' (by definition) all knowledge thus excluded, but other forms of knowledge embedded within the research field and its participants. It is not necessary to reject the concept of 'building on the shoulders of giants' just because we disagree with their methodological premises, but we do need to have more than one type of 'giant', and sources other than 'giants'. To address this we need to question our narrow perception of what constitutes 'knowledge', and allow ourselves a broader base upon which to build. Such a base would necessarily be multidisciplinary and would acknowledge the validity of an alternative epistemological stance.

Another issue raised by the concept of building on previous research is that some 'knowledge' becomes so entrenched that we cease to question it or to look beyond it for the assumptions upon which it was based. A central requirement of any form of methodology should be its ability to be reflexive, and to put its own assumptions under scrutiny. We reify the past in the form of tradition, in what is taken for granted. Giddens (1999) in his recent Reith lectures counselled against the blind following of tradition, in that it was seldom worthy of the symbolic importance it had taken on. What was dangerous, he said, was that by following tradition there was no need to ask about alternatives, as it closes our minds.

As researchers we promote the idea of asking questions. For me, the problem is that these questions can stop when we are called upon to address the fundamentals of our own perceptions of what our task as researchers is, and processes of theory formulation and choice of methodologies. We need to start with the recognition that perceptions of the development of knowledge within our discipline-based academic world are deeply rooted in a single epistemology, positivism, which has influenced the development of all subsequent theorising. This need not be inevitable, as there are other equally robust epistemologies. I suggest that one way forward rests on recognising the limitations of traditional forms of academic research and developing alternative ways of creating knowledge and seeing the world that have different but equally valid philosophical roots.

The health sector has enabled different rich and varied forms of research to flourish, which include various types of what has been called 'action research' which are increasingly being used by practitioners. It is important to recognise that the term 'action research' is itself a delimiting one since current practices have moved a long way since its inception in the earlier part of this century, from Revans' (1988) concept of 'action learning' and Lewin's (1952) concept of 'action research'. Since then there have been developments within several disciplines. In social and organisational studies, the Tavistock Institute was one focus for the action approach with its emphasis on socio-technical systems thinking, and its subsequent work aimed at linking research and action. Rooted as this approach has been in organisations and practice rather than academia, it has sometimes remained on the margins of social and management theory and there has been insufficient recognition of its implications for methodology by mainstream academics. We need to further explore the possibilities for the development of methodology and theory in order to develop deeper levels of understanding and not just focus on the current requirement for 'evidence'. (Although, as with 'knowledge', what actually counts as 'evidence' and why, remains a key issue.) To be able to assess reliability and validity in research findings, there is a need to know the research methodology used.

Beyond Positivism

The growth of universities and discipline-based study has occurred under the dominance of positivism. This has created a strong history, tradition and context which remains difficult to challenge, as so much is taken for granted, despite a series of developments from postmodernism to the current development of Critical Theory across a range of disciplines. Within management the development of 'critical management' is symptomatic of a growing recognition of the problems in current theory, to respond appropriately to the needs of organisations and managers in the face of growing levels of complexity and change within organisations. The search for 'solutions', however, tends to remain within the dominant epistemology and resists the prospect of making the quantum leap into alternative forms. Can it really be the case that to question positivist foundations would be to risk undermining the whole basis of the university structures, discipline-based knowledge, peer-reviewed routes to academic success, and the RAE (Research Assessment Exercise)? Schon (1995) challenges the epistemology of the modern research universities in the USA, which have striking similarities with those in the UK, and talks of the need for an alternative epistemology. He shows how the positivist epistemology controls what counts as legitimate knowledge, but that such a view need not be consciously espoused by individuals as it is built into the institutional structures and practices. The foundations of earlier knowledge and how it is built upon are controlled by the curriculum, the examination systems and the bases for promotion of academic staff. He adds that if we are to take new forms of scholarship seriously then knowledge must be produced that is testably valid, according to criteria of appropriate rigour, and the claims to knowledge must lend themselves to intellectual debate within communities of inquiry.

   Positivism grew out of the desire for certainty and the search for 'truth' (often a single truth) upon which all the sciences could be based. Specifically, this truth relates to linear causal relationships. The incalculable impact of this and its undoubted value, as part of an ongoing process of thought, can blind us to its shortcomings. Yet the metaphysical base from which positivism emerged included the recognition of unobservable entities, deep causes and non-observable mechanisms; however, these were dismissed by positivists as merely idle speculation. In an illuminating paper, Chia (1997) explores the relationship between the different epistemological bases of knowledge and suggests that ontological and epistemological commitments are shifting within both the natural and the social sciences, back, away from positivist developments. He describes as a fundamental ontological error of positivism the ascribing of concrete status to socially-constructed objects of knowledge in the building-up of a body of knowledge. We construct the boundaries of disciplines and the categories within them; which we then accumulate 'knowledge' around and thus ascribe to them a reality which is limited by their socially-based construction. As he notes, stars exist, but the idea of constellations is a human construct. Such boundaries are a necessary convenience but should remain flexible and potentially disposable.

The methodological implications of positivism are that it resists transdisciplinarity, and the focus is put onto conceptions about what qualifies as data; the search for causality, the search for 'truth', or evidence, and the way data is collected. The way that data is *organised*, based in structural concepts, can restrict the development of other forms of methodology that might allow research to capture the dynamics of real life. The creation of disciplinary boundaries around different areas of knowledge is necessarily artificial; they are not random but neither are they absolute. What needs to be explored is the extent to which these constrain future development. The lack of integration across these and the categories that have been imposed within them, whilst necessary to help us order a complex reality, are often grounded in a narrow perception of a socially-constructed world. The concepts we use, as academics, to understand what happens in the social world, are all socially constructed and come from a narrow perspective perceived as being that of the 'expert'. One consequence is that we risk paying insufficient attention to the dynamics of the real world.

Chia also believes, as do I, that there is a need to reconceptualise organisation analysis in a way that acknowledges the dynamic nature of social life. In the social world, non-linear, systemic relationships predominate over those of linear cause and effect. It is the nature of the 'knowledge' accumulated that has led to our perceptions of organisations in terms of stability and endurance which have downplayed the dynamic and precarious nature of reality. As an alternative, Chia suggests a process-based ontology which generates a radically different set of theoretical priorities. The emphasis is on processes of becoming, transforming and perishing, with a focus on interaction and relatedness. Thus the essence of nature is change and not stability. He shows how this different set of priorities are epistemologically robust in helping us develop a more insightful understanding of the modern organised world. This reinforces the need for action-based methodologies within research.

The essence of OB and organisation studies are their 'real-world' context. Such 'immediacy' may impact less directly on other disciplines in their methodologies and theoretical considerations. As noted earlier, the origins of OB are multidisciplinary, which is a strength that needs to become more overt, as it offers an appropriate forum for cross-fertilisation of concepts and theories from a range of disciplines. There is little purpose to theoretical exclusivity beyond the retention of boundaries. The range of disciplines represented across the health sector encourages multidisciplinary working, and has meant that both funders and researchers have increasingly focused on multidisciplinary studies. It is questionable as to whether this has led to any real integration of ideas and theories, or whether it just means having individuals representing different disciplines working alongside one another. There is a need to recognise the increasing complexity of the issues we seek to study and of the organisations within which we work. The complexity issue forms the context both practically and academically that spurs us on to seek more meaningful forms of research. In this we need to be sure of the epistemological basis of the research we seek to build on, but must engage in a debate about methodologies and research designs.

The Academic and Funding Context in Health

Despite a sense that the main demand from the health sector is for research design which pays homage to the randomised control trial, a far richer diversity of methods are possible. There is variety in the approaches taken within the health service, across regions, disciplines and individuals. Thus the research context is a complex set of relationships between the multiple funding sources, the extensive range of potential researchers, and the infinite number of possible research sites and participants. There is, within many regional directorates and at other levels in the service, a growing willingness to fund research which is not only recognised as 'qualitative' but can involve relatively new approaches such as participative action research.

The need for research to be responsive to funders, whilst retaining rigour, relates to all social research. The debate about the relevance of much academic research and the need for new approaches which address real problems, was central to a recent ALSISS conference (Association of Learned Societies in the Social Sciences, 1999).

Without this, does university research risk losing relevance? The Director of the Rowntree Trust said their aim when commissioning research was, 'not the development of knowledge for its own sake but for the capacity to change policy.' She was very critical of universities where, she believed, the influence of the RAE had led to discipline- based lone scholarship aimed at peer-reviewed academic journals, where researchers did not have the skills necessary to listen to and work with people. She noted an 'underlying arrogance amongst academics in relation to their "we know best" attitudes'. Rather than having to choose between relevance and scholarship, she was seeking an interactive form of social research so that she could have both, beginning with relevance, and adding that dissemination should be the core of the research and not an optional 'add-on'. In the concluding session, the research director of the Economic and Social Research Council (ESRC) reiterated the view that universities should not be so complacent and needed to make their work more relevant, and transferable to others, adding that without it the commercialisation of the research process was a possibility.

There are many conflicting pressures on researchers. Between the requirements of the RAE and those of funders, as well as career considerations, researchers also have their own values and perceptions of the type of research they wish to pursue. They attempt a balancing act that inevitably creates tensions: between the value systems of the university, the funder and themselves, for example; and between report writing and journal writing, or in many other ways that impact upon the choices made, both academically and personally. It is the struggle to surface and understand these tensions that is at the heart of this chapter.

EXPLORING METHODOLOGICAL POSSIBILITIES

This section explores the opportunities for pushing the boundaries of research further by developing forms of methodology which create a more grounded approach to data collection; for example, by utilising co-inquiry, and through acknowledging the subjective nature of the processes involved. The purpose is not to limit, categorise or oversimplify the richness and complexity of the data, but to work with it in order to create new forms of knowledge and understanding. Such understandings then facilitate the process of change and enhance the capacity of organisations, through a process of research which includes organisational and individual learning.

Nowhere is this tension more explicit than in the area of health-studies research. It is inevitable that the sector in which the research is carried out has an influence on the research methods used. As noted earlier, the perception of what the subject and methodology of research should be can be extremely narrow, but this is not the case across the sector as a whole, so we should be wary of allowing this to confine our thinking. The term 'evidence-based' is widespread and is, in one sense, incontestable, but with a socially complex and ever-changing context what counts as 'evidence' is not self-evident. It has to be verified, it needs to be contextualised and the rigour of the methodology used to elicit it needs to be shown. If 'evidence' is seen only in the narrow sense of that unearthed by positivist methodologies, then the richness and value of 'evidence' from other perspectives is lost.

What then is the role of OB and organisation studies in the debate about health-research methodologies? What has occurred to date is predominantly a refinement of qualitative methodologies within an already overstretched positivist framework. A new terminology is emerging around critical theory and new paradigm research, which reflects dissatisfaction with the state of current theory and methods. Related to this, new areas of study are emerging, for example, in complexity and chaos theory and the use of narrative and metaphors in organisations. If the essence of organisational life is constant change (Chia, 1997), then what is required is a process-based methodology which can capture the dynamics of real life. This would enable activity and movement to take precedence over substance and entities. Instead of thinking in terms of discrete individualities, the emphasis is on the primacy of process, interaction and relatedness. Similarly, instead of thinking in terms of outcomes and end-states, primacy is accorded to the process (of becoming). Apparently discrete phenomena such as the 'organisation' and its supposed attributes, are a result of freezing a moment in time in what is essentially a dynamic and transforming complexity of interactions. Within such a process we are more likely to become aware of what has previously been rendered invisible. We can use conceptualisation to 'slow' the process of change down, but the concepts are contextually constrained by both time and the environment, and therefore need to be constantly revised: 'to capture meaning which continually changes' (Mark and Dopson, 1999: 257).

Every action of a researcher is an intervention, therefore researchers cannot remain 'outside' what is being researched. There are many misconceptions about what has been called action research, which relate in part to the way the process has been (mis)used in the past.

There is a need to distinguish between different approaches, not all of which would qualify as 'research'. Dash (1999) has produced an excellent paper on the current debates in action research which outlines its long history and identifies the main issues remaining to be addressed. There are numerous researchers such as Flood and Romm (1996), Marshall (1995), Midgely *et al.* (1996) and Reason (1996) who, via their research, are in different ways pushing the boundaries of current knowledge to develop new action research or collaborative inquiry-type methodologies. A number of strands of theory are emerging, making for useful debates and exchanges each of which has a different origin – for example from within sociology, psychology, education, community studies, health, feminist studies, systems thinking or organisation studies.

An 'action' researcher is not actively involved in directing or choosing the direction of the change, but in carrying out research within the change process. The type of collaborative or participative action-research methodologies which are now emerging are based upon collaborative research between researcher and researched, who become co-inquirers. It is the quality of the researchers' interaction that facilitates or hinders the dialogue between the parties. The purpose and process of the research is the outcome of a dialogue between the different groups or individuals involved. There are frequently issues of power and politics that can make problematic a completely free exchange and a process of listening. What is required is a recognition of the different interests of each group or individual, and the need to find a space for agreement on a topic or area that is of mutual interest or mutual recognition of the need for change.

Who is to say which groups' perceptions of reality constitute our knowledge of that reality? There are many 'knowledges'. What any single organisational factor may 'mean' for any group or individual will vary depending on a wide range of individual and contextual factors. It is from the process of dialogue, with all parties agreeing to be present as co-inquirers, that new concrete relationships can be formed where others' meanings become clearer, and where there is an opportunity to develop shared meanings. Each group or community will have its own language, perceptions and concepts and these can interfere with open dialogue, so it is up to the researcher to facilitate in reading the languages of others. While language carries meaning, it is also a barrier. This interpretative process enables shared understandings to emerge, and where this exists it can be referred to as a 'community of practice' (Wenger, 1999). It is also a process of learning, which comes directly from the practice and actions of those involved in the research.

This type of research calls upon a different range of skills for the researcher, as it can be more time-consuming. The researcher remains a peripheral participant in such a community or group of communities; a third party or facilitator, who has a role in identifying and mediating the relationship between them. The issue of power remains central, because in discourse the powerful will invariably gain control over the definition of the issues and relationships and can control the negotiation of the terms for collaboration. The process of facilitation needs to identify this process and by the use of reflection enable others to recognise for themselves the nature of their own behaviour. It does require effort on the part of all participants to stay in an open listening, reflective mode. Meaning emerges not as an output but as part of the process and the outcome may be a redefinition of the issues.

One argument for this type of research is the opportunity for knowledge generation and learning. It focuses on the recognition and incorporation of a range of 'knowledge' within the research site and enables the process of change. Dissemination after the 'completion' of the research process has repeatedly been shown to be limited in its impact. I refer to my own research looking at the different professional roles in primary care (Ashburner *et al.*, 1998; Ashburner, 1999) and it included time and resources for dissemination. I produced the report, and I went round many regional meetings presenting and discussing its findings. But I remain to be convinced that anything at all has actually changed as a result of the research. As a consequence, my ongoing research within primary care seeks to utilise the principles of participative research as outlined above. This is an enormous challenge as the extent of the control I previously had within my research role becomes clearer, and how letting go of this requires new and more complex conceptual frameworks.

How else can the capacity for dissemination or change in organisations which are so tightly constrained be introduced? The alternative is research which reports the views of one or more of the different groups whilst leaving all of them without a real understanding of others. Such research replicates or even exacerbates the fixated images different groups may have of one another. It is this essentially conflictual context which prevents the development of new forms of organising and is invariably based upon existing power hierarchies. To create a true dialogue and the opportunity for learning, there needs to be an interruption to the current mode of interaction. Even a report that tries to explain all perspectives and which may be seen as a useful vehicle for broadening understanding between groups, is unlikely to create change or even to be read by the people that it needs to reach. This is my continual frustration as a researcher. If we are interested in the dissemination of our findings, we are interested in creating a context for change without being prescriptive about its substance. If this is actually recognised and acknowledged in the research methodology it enables it to become part of the process.

It is clear that most researchers in OB and organisation studies have moved a fair distance from the concept of the distant scientist doing experiments. There is a wide literature based in health research, predominantly within nursing research, in education and community studies which traces the development of a range of approaches within the broad action-research frame of reference. The following examples of health-sector research are given as an illustration of what is possible within the sector, across a range of professions and all areas. Cornwall and Jewkes (1995) review the use of participatory research within health services, with a focus on power and the issue of control over the research process. Cooke (1997) looks at development practice with implications for practitioner training; Soltis-Jarrett (1997) considers the role of the researcher as facilitator; and in Lindsey *et al.* (1999) the focus in on creating effective partnerships. One traditional area for participative research is patient and community involvement, particularly involving doctors (Macaulay *et al.*, 1999). Josefson (1996), in Sweden, describes the use of reflexive dialogue with three groups of doctors. More commonly, participative and action research has been developed within the nursing profession with increasingly refined and reflexive approaches. Hart and Bond (1996) have developed a typology of forms of action research; Manley (1997) has used the approach to study the development of new nursing roles; Fraser (1999) has focused on curriculum development; and Waterman (1998) has explored issues of validity.

A key tension which needs to be challenged is that academic rigour is compromised in tackling real-world issues. There is a growing body of work which seeks a more interactive approach, to explore new forms of knowledge and learning and to establish an intellectual rigour in relating new methodologies to theory. As Lather (1991) warns, 'Lack of concern for data credibility within praxis-oriented research programmes will only decrease the legitimacy of the knowledge generated therein' (1991: 68). (Praxis-oriented research is that which seeks to develop 'theory both relevant to the world and nurtured by actions in it', *ibid.*:11.)

The potential for new forms of research for organisational and OB researchers within health care remain relatively unexplored. This opens up new possibilities not just for the development of theory that is more contextually sensitive, and for the process of dissemination, but for the strengthening of a wide area of research that has struggled to retain a clear identity in the face of the dominant positivist/medical model.

CONCLUDING THOUGHTS

There are a number of general observations picking up on points raised in this chapter:

• The social and organisational worlds we inhabit are riddled with contradictions and complexity and it is difficult to hold objectivity as the ideal. To deny the subjective meaning and context does not offer a route to real understanding.

• There is a need for different levels of reflexivity to question our assumptions and 'taken-for-granted' knowledge.

• There are implications for teaching and making the process and materials relevant for the lives of those who come to 'learn'.

• We need to be critically aware of the implications of the approaches, values, beliefs and behaviours that are sanctioned within the academic world.

• Research that is action/praxis-based still requires validity and rigour in its methodology.

• The role of the academic is to increase knowledge and understanding, but not in an uncritical way. They must constantly ask, 'on whose terms?' and 'to what end?'

There is another question, so far not addressed. What is the relationship between different methodologies, whatever their epistemological basis? There cannot be an easy answer to this, and there will be scope for much theorising. This issue, for example, touches on earlier debates about paradigmatic closure in organisational research (Hassard and Pym, 1990) which, as Holland (1999) observes, are themselves 'humanly' constructed. If the boundaries between paradigms are thus arbitrary, then they reveal the ideological content of human-science theories and undermine arguments for paradigm autonomy. From an earlier work (Burrell and Morgan, 1979) Morgan (1986) has proposed ways of traversing the paradigm map. In relation to developing wider cultures of inquiry and research, Hall describes 'the choices between the routes of science and interpretation, history and theory, objectivism and relativism' as 'more illusory than real' (1999: 1). He looks for the common forms of discourse across methodologies and suggests that there are four different kinds – value discourse, narrative, social theory and explanation/interpretation, and it is the balance between these within any particular inquiry that distinguishes the different approaches or paradigms. Whichever argument is taken, the one thing that is increasingly clear is that no form of methodology needs to be autonomous from any other.

References

Argyris, C. (1997) 'Actionability and Design Causality' in C.L. Cooper and S.E. Jackson (eds), *Creating Tomorrow's Organisations – a Handbook for Future Research in Organisational Behaviour* (Chichester: John Wiley).
Ashburner, I. Latimer, J. and Quy, S. (1998) *Primary Care Professional Education Development: Project Report* (November) W. Midlands Region NHS Executive).
Ashburner, L. (1999) 'Nursing Education – Continuing Developments: The Challenge of Primary Care Nursing Development', *West Midlands Journal of Primary Care* (NHSE).
Burrell, G. and Morgan, G. (1979) *Sociological Paradigms and Organisational Analysis* (London: Heinemann).
Chia, R. (1997) 'Essai: Thirty Years On: From Organisational Structures to the Organisation of Thought', *Organisation Studies*, 18(4): 685–707.
Cooke, B. (1997) 'From Process Consultation to a Clinical Model of Development Practice', *Public Administration and Development*, 17(3): 325–40.
Cornwall, A. and Jewkes, R. (1995) 'What is Participatory Research?', *Social Science and Medicine*, 41(12): 1667–76.
Dash, D.P. (1999) 'Current Debates in Action Research', *Systemic Practice and Action Research*, 12(5): 457–92.
Flood, R.L. and Romm, N. (1996) *Critical Systems Thinking: Current Research and Practice* (New York: Plenum).
Frankenberg, R. (1984) 'Incidence or Incidents: Politics and Methodological Underpinnings of a Health Research Process in a Small Italian Town', in C. Bell and H. Roberts (eds), *Social Researching: Politics, Problems, Practice* (London: Routledge & Kegan Paul).

Fraser, D.M. (1999) 'Delphi Technique: One Cycle of an Action Research Project to Improve the Pre-registration Midwifery Curriculum', *Nurse Education Today*, 19(6): 495–501.

Giddens, A. (1999) *The Reith Lectures* (BBC).

Hall, J.R. (1999) *Cultures of Inquiry: from Epistemology to Discourse in Socio-historical Research* (Cambridge: Cambridge University Press).

Hart, E. Bond, M. (1996) 'Making Sense of Action Research Through the Use of Typology', *Journal of Advanced Nursing*, 23(1): 152–9.

Hassard, J. and Pym, D. (1990) (eds) *The Theory and Philosophy of Organisations: Critical Issues and New Perspectives* (London: Routledge).

Holland, R. (1999) Reflexivity, *Human Relations*, 52(4): 463–84.

Josefson, I. (1996) 'Articulating Practices: Methods and Experiences – Practical Traditions of Knowledge Among Physicians', *Concepts and Transformation*, 1:2/3 249–56.

Lather, P. (1991) *Getting Smart: Feminist Research and Pedagogy with/in the Postmodern* (London: Routledge).

Lewin, K. (1952) *Field Theory in Social Science*, Selected Theoretical Papers edited by D. Cartwright (London: Tavistock Publications).

Lewis, J. (1999) Speaking at the ALSISS Conference, Social Science – *The Production and Consumption of Social Interactive Science Research*, Brighton, January.

Lindsey, E. Shields, L. Stajduhar, K. (1999) 'Creating Effective Nursing Partnerships: Relating Community Development to Participatory Action Research', *Journal of Advanced Nursing*, 29(5): 1238–45.

Macaulay, A. Commanda, L. Freeman, W. Gibson, N. McCabe, M. Robbins, C. Twohig, P. (1999) 'Participatory Research Maximises Community and Lay Involvement', *British Medical Journal*, 319(7212): 774.

Manley, K. (1997) 'A Conceptual Framework for Advanced Practice: An Action Research Project Operationalising an Advanced Practitioner/Consultant Nurse Role', *Journal of Clinical Nursing*, 6(3): 179–90.

Mark, A. and Dopson, S. (eds) (1999) *Organisational Behaviour in Health Care: The Research Agenda* (Basingstoke: Macmillan – now Palgrave).

Marshall, J. (1995) *Women Managers Moving On: Exploring Career and Life Choices* (London: Routledge).

Midgely, G. Kadiri, Y. Vahl, M. (1996) 'Managing Stories About Quality', *International Journal of Technology Management*, 11: 140–50.

Morgan, G. (1989) *Images of Organisations* (London: Sage).

Reason, P. (1996) 'Reflections on the Purposes of Human Inquiry', *Qualitative Inquiry*, 2(1): 15–28.

Revans, R.W. (1988) *The Golden Jubilee of Action Learning* (Manchester: Manchester Action Learning Exchange, University of Manchester).

Schon, D.A. (1995) 'The New Scholarship Requires a New Epistemology', *Change* (Nov/Dec): 27–34.

Schratz, M. and Walker, R. (1995) *Research as Social Change* (London: Routledge).

Soltis-Jarrett, V. (1997) 'The Facilitator in Participatory Action Research: Les Raisons d'etre'. *Advances in Nursing Science*, 20(2): 45–54.

Stewart, R. (1999) Foreword, in A. Mark and S. Dopson (eds), *Organisational Behaviour in Healthcare* (Basingstoke: Macmillan – now Palgrave).

Waterman, H. (1998) 'Embracing Ambiguities and Valuing Ourselves: Issues of Validity in Action Research', *Journal of Advanced Nursing*, 28(1): 101–05.

Wenger, E. (1999) *Communities of Practice: Learning, Meaning and Identity* (Cambridge: Cambridge University Press).

16 Discussion

Lynn Ashburner

This chapter draws together the themes of the book illustrating possible ways forward for organisational behaviour (OB) and organisational studies in health. The contributors have reflected the main areas of, and approaches to, current research in health services in the range of topics and methodologies covered in this volume. As it shows, this can produce a very rich picture of the health sector at a particular moment in time and lay out a number of new possibilities for the future.

NEW WAYS OF SEEING

'Futures' research shows how by studying potential futures we can influence the present. Dargie and Dawson note several important assumptions, generally made, about the future organisation of health services which they feel may be challenged. A key concern, the future sustainability of the NHS workforce, has been a contentious issue for some time, and is one which has been acknowledged in the current policy emphasis on recruitment from overseas. However, in this case the research by Brooks and MacDonald may serve to question how this policy is implemented. Another example is the assumption that the doctor is in face-to-face contact with the patient. The study by Schofield on how IT is bringing 'virtual' care to reality shows that this is increasingly not the case. What also concerns Dargie and Dawson is that IT, which underpins so many of the NHS changes, is largely absent from the NHS Plan. This may indicate one area where planned change underestimates what is required in practice. It is also important to understand why resistance to IT is still prevalent, as shown by Timmons, despite its now being present almost universally across the NHS.

It would be interesting to consider the growth of 'virtual caring', as presented by Schofield, and the distance this places between clinician and patient and to try to understand how this impacts upon the emotional health of the individuals and the organisation, as explored by Mark. The introduction of an intermediary may serve to remove essential 'human' elements from the encounter between clinician and patient. Many aspects of personal health care can touch on sensitive and personal issues; how will the impersonality of a video screen affect this? The expanding use of IT also raises issues about the potential for greater control of staff with monitoring possibilities. How this will affect staff who are already immersed in emotional work needs to be understood.

It is important that we are constantly reminded about the extent to which our lives, concepts, analytical categories and even our work organisations and the technology within them are socially constructed. The myth of objectivity blinds us to asking enough questions about why certain things have become accepted as the norm and all the assumptions that are based thereon.

NEW WAYS OF WORKING

Several of the chapters are concerned with issues of reorganisation, but each with new forms of collaboration as their essence. As cooperation across organisational boundaries increases, and networks and 'virtual' organisations become more commonplace, it is necessary to question the extent to which hierarchy as it currently exists in most organisational forms is still necessary. Jessopp and Boyle show how effective health care increasingly requires contributions from different organisations, but when combined there is rarely any single person in control of the whole system. This they have called the 'virtual care system'. Sheaff, in his study of PCGs, shows how all organisations have elements of different organisational types, which include elements of networks and hierarchies, and for new organisation forms such as PCG's it is not possible to predict at what stage of development any particular form will become established, or whether this is predominantly as networks or more traditional hierarchies. This begs the question of whether we continue to assume that the process of development necessarily moves from networks to more hierarchical forms? Is movement the other way also possible, as new forms of integration and cooperation emerge in more established parts of the NHS, making likely the development of new organisational forms?

This is a major theme of the chapter by Cropper who showed how conflicting institutional pressures could be handled in the search for an effective organisational form, but also that there was a need for a level of formality, relating to rules and procedures, to ensure the survival of the collaborative form. This relates to the process of standardisation and legitimacy, rather than any inference of increase in hierarchy. Sheaff's study focuses on the formal side of the organisational development of PCGs and was concerned with the process of organisational formation and change rather than on organisational effectiveness, but it still raises interesting questions about the relationship between the two. These are issues which have concerned OB and organisational theorists from the outset. In terms of the origins and developments of networks, where, as Cropper shows, informality is a key characteristic, the interplay between formal and informal organisational processes and structures may be critical.

This need to study *all* aspects of organisations, not just the formal or the 'measurable' is made apparent in the chapter by King *et al.* which addressed the issue of whether structural reorganisation was sufficient by itself to promote integration and cooperation between services. They look at formal organisation structures and informal relationships, and their research shows the significance of the latter as being in fact *more* important than the former. As Jessopp and Boyle observe there is a need for a greater understanding of whole systems.

Current policy places greater importance on the involvement of the user or patient than has been the case in the past, but as Berrow and Humphrey show, 'user involvement' as a concept is very problematic to implement. What qualifies anyone to be a 'representative' of users? What mandate do they have? Can they ever be effective in terms of the level of information they have access to and the fact that they are not formally part of any governance structures? This is an issue that has become more prominent policy-wise, but has never been seriously addressed in application. Given the lack of power of the user and the huge problems in giving them a voice, let alone an impact, it is hardly surprising that this is one area where it appears to be in the interests of very few to make this more than just rhetoric. As Berrow and Humphrey show, much of what has been done has been developed as an 'add-on' rather than as part of the process, especially as regards monitoring. This is an issue which again cannot be reduced to the level of the individual, by, for example, suggesting a process of training, so much as the need for organisational systems to be designed, where appropriate, with user representatives as an integral part.

Another potentially controversial element of current policy is the reliance that health services will need to place on the recruitment of doctors and nurses from overseas, especially in the short term. Brooks and MacDonald present a complex picture of what such workers actually experience when they arrive in Britain, which raises several issues. This suggests that there needs to be an analysis of the cost-effectiveness of bringing nurses from abroad, for short periods of time, many of whom are working at lower levels than their training would allow in their own countries. The differences in treatment of doctors and nurses is very significant in aspects as varied as the type of accommodation offered and opportunities for career enhancement, and this raises issues about how professional and gender differentials are being reinforced. For example, the recruitment of doctors was dealt with by a higher level of the organisation than for nurses, and there were more opportunities for doctors to remain in the UK longer-term. The way that current policy is being implemented seems unlikely as a strategy to make a significant impact upon nursing staff shortages, in the short or long term.

Clinical governance represents a major policy change and an attempt by government to exert a more direct influence on the behaviour of the medical profession. For the first time, accountability for medical outcomes has become a management responsibility. Thorne uses a specific form of method, discourse analysis, to shed new light on the complex relationship between government, doctors and managers in relation to the introduction and development of clinical governance. Medical power is again a significant influence on the outcomes that will emerge as the processes become organisationally established. As Thorne explains, the tensions between management and the medical profession may be exacerbated by these developments, in which doctors attempt to control the clinical governance process while managers struggle with the implementation of the policy.

What is evident from all these studies is the insight offered on the development of policy and the subsequent changes that are occurring. Taking three studies which are different in their approach but covering similar areas, such as those of Cropper, Sheaff and King *et al.*, an interesting question is raised as to what would emerge if each chose to study the same part of the health service and their different conclusions and outcomes were compared. This form of triangulation would enable a deeper understanding to emerge that could inform practitioners, theory and our understanding of the differences that our methodologies make.

NEW APPROACHES TO METHODOLOGY

The variety of methodologies utilised by the studies in this book show that it is possible for a wide range of methods to coexist in a field and for academic rigour to be maintained. What is essential is that this variety survives and is broadened. Øvretveit stresses the need to not let the thinking behind 'evidence-based medicine' take over how 'good' research is defined. The term 'evidence-based' may seem incontestable, but it all depends upon what is counted as evidence. In medical terms, where the concept is based, this is usually limited to evidence that emerges from randomised control trials (RCTs) or other experimental, controlled studies. It is now commonly accepted that in the areas of OB and organisational studies, which reflect the more complicated world of social and organisational life, research based on the premise of experimental design is problematic.

Øvretveit, Ferlie *et al.*, Ashburner, and Mark and Dopson all argue the need for greater use of subjectivist methodologies. It is the chapters by Jumaa and Alleyne, and Jessopp and Boyle that have moved the nearest to this form. Jessopp and Boyle take an interesting step in combining three different paradigms, of research, organisation development and computer-simulation modelling to highlight their desire to develop more whole-systems approaches to the study of organisations and their processes. They show that when studying complex and adapting systems it is also important that the methodology is emergent, contextually-specific and capable of adaptation. As a way of working and as a way of understanding implicit assumptions, this type of methodology can challenge prevailing attitudes about work, as well as the research methods used. They, like Jumaa and Alleyne, are also interested in integrating the concept of learning within the methodological approach. Jumaa and Alleyne's study focused on the need to create 'actionable knowledge' as they explored issues of effective leadership; learning and dissemination formed part of the research process itself. The development of new forms of collaborative and action research that are occurring within other disciplines are not yet apparent within OB or organisational health research, although, as Ashburner notes, this is less true for nursing research.

CONCLUSION

There is increasing complexity in all aspects of the work of both researchers and practitioners: in organisational processes, forms, ways of working, ways of seeing and ways of studying. Contributors have expressed the requirements of research in this field, from the pressures to respond to funders' and users' needs to the pressure to contribute to the development of theory. It is important, as Øvretveit warns, that OB is not only responsive to the needs of managers. The managerial perspective represents only one of many; what should be the value of research, as opposed to various forms of consultancy interventions, is that it does not take a single perspective but attempts to include the multiple perspectives that are part of the 'reality' of what is being studied. Research in the OB and organisational studies fields is not just the domain of a clearly defined group of academic practitioners, it is open to anyone, including practitioners. Although resisted in some quarters, there could be greater sharing across the boundaries between academics based in business departments with others placed in a range of different locations such as public health or nursing.

What this means is that there is a need for research *and* development. In the past there has been a greater focus on the research side while the development, application and exploration of the practical implications of the research has largely been left to chance. An increasing focus on dissemination again does not go far enough. It is clear that merely knowing about certain research findings is not the same as understanding how they apply to specific cases or being able to implement changes. There is a need to have a far greater level of understanding of the various contexts if the potential for application is to be properly assessed. So while the academic contribution is essential to provide the framework and rigour to the research, the involvement of the practitioner is also essential to enable context, complexity and application to become more integral to the research from the outset.

As Øvretveit concludes, the aim of research in health should be to contribute to the practical problems in health organisations and to scientific knowledge; but few studies achieve both. He believes that OB has the potential to become a discipline in its own right. 'Evidence-based management, or OB', he feels, is unlikely, but management decisions and education do need to be more informed by research. To help in this, OB researchers need to be clear who are the users of the research, ensure that the research is accessible, and to work with the users to explicate the practical implications of the research. Øvretveit feels that action research and action evaluation still have not found a place within OB, but they could make a contribution in the future if a more flexible attitude was taken towards methods and if action researchers described their methods more clearly and related their work to previous research and theories.

The question of how health-services research contributes to theory remains. It is up to researchers to utilise theory in the planning of research and in the analysis of findings. This is just as feasible with research focused on practical problems as well as that designed specifically to test a theory. Many of the studies in this volume were designed around established theories. There is a need to be more explicit about how research findings modify existing theories or create new theory. Schofield, for example, suggests areas of theory for which research on virtuality and its impact on organisations might be relevant. This is something that could become a part of all studies just as an exposition of the methodology used should be. As Ferlie *et al.* show that it is problematic to generalise across several major studies to begin to elicit findings that show strong enough patterns to enable a significant contribution to theory.

Several contributors call for research which is relevant and useable. If both are to be satisfied there is a need for theories which are 'actionable'. So we need not just 'actionable knowledge', but 'actionable theory'. Whatever methods are used there is a need for more large-scale studies if data are to be amassed to be able to make a significant contribution to theory. Given the nature of funding and the lack of opportunities for large-scale or long-term studies, then one way might be the use of the community of researchers to collaborate more closely across studies at their inception. Collaboration between researchers may be developing, but currently this is mainly within academic areas and less often does it traverse disciplines. It is important that arenas of debate remain inclusive not exclusive, and are open to the opportunities to have the work questioned.

There is no either/or when it comes to deciding if research should be practical or theoretical. The question posed by Ferlie *et al.*, 'What is good quality research?', could be the starting point for such a discussion. However, the necessary accompanying question should be, 'From whose perspective?' This would encourage us to question our own motives and assumptions more closely and to begin to identify new ways forward.

Index